"In their commentary on *Dialectic of Enlightenment*, Hammer and Rush achieve the almost impossible: they explain its intellectual context and the individual sources from which it draws in such an unmistakably clear manner that the line of argument and the historical-philosophical substance of the individual chapters become almost completely comprehensible for the first time. For anyone who wants to grasp the dark timelessness of this book today, this commentary is essential reading."

Axel Honneth, *Columbia University, USA*

"Presents the background and main steps of Horkheimer's and Adorno's seminal work masterfully, succinctly exposing and evaluating its controversial features. Precisely because these highly controversial considerations of the *Dialectic of Enlightenment* account for its undiminished topicality, this *Guidebook* is the ideal aid for anyone who exposes themselves to its claims and attempts to think with it."

Christoph Menke, *Goethe Universität Frankfurt am Main, Germany*

"In this impressive work of patient reconstruction Hammer and Rush – two of the field's leading scholars – have made a remarkable contribution to elucidating *Dialectic of Enlightenment*'s key ideas whilst, at the same time, insightfully drawing attention to a range of philosophical, political, and contextual ideas previously neglected in the literature."

Brian O'Connor, *University College Dublin, Ireland*

"Hammer and Rush have produced an exceptionally clear and accessible guide to the most important text of the Frankfurt School critical theory tradition. It not only situates the *Dialectic of Enlightenment* in its intellectual and historical context, guiding readers through each of its chapters and core concepts, but also equips them to grasp the enduring significance of its central thesis: that what we take to be progress, guided by reason, contains regressive, barbaric, and even self-destructive tendencies."

Kyla Bruff, *Carleton University, Canada*

"Students are often keen to study *Dialectic of Enlightenment*, but find it tough-going. This book is an excellent aid in unriddling the context, structure, and goals of the *Dialectic*. Scholars will find it is equally well suited for the purpose of getting acquainted with the deeper features of the *Dialectic*, and as a teaching aid in discussing it with others."

Owen Hulatt, *University of York, UK*

The Routledge Guidebook to Horkheimer and Adorno's *Dialectic of Enlightenment*

Composed whilst in exile in the United States during the Second World War, Max Horkheimer and Theodor W. Adorno's *Dialectic of Enlightenment* is the most famous and influential text of the Frankfurt School. A theoretical exploration of history, modernity, and culture, its core warning of crisis and regression remains highly relevant today. However, it is also a notoriously complex work of philosophy.

The Routledge Guidebook to Horkheimer and Adorno's Dialectic of Enlightenment is the first fully contextualized introduction to this foundational text in philosophy and social theory, addressing its central themes, reception, and influence. This Guidebook examines:

- The conceptual and intellectual background to *Dialectic of Enlightenment*.
- The ideas, themes, and arguments of the text.
- The reception and legacy of *Dialectic of Enlightenment*.

A comprehensive and clearly written guide to this important text, *The Routledge Guidebook to Horkheimer and Adorno's Dialectic of Enlightenment* will be invaluable to students coming to the work for the first time, as well as more advanced students and researchers in philosophy, politics, sociology, and the history of ideas.

Espen Hammer is Professor of Philosophy at Temple University, USA. He is the author of *Stanley Cavell: Skepticism, Subjectivity, and the Ordinary* (2002), *Adorno and the Political* (Routledge, 2006), *Philosophy and Temporality from Kant to Critical Theory* (2011), *Adorno's Modernism: Art, Experience, and Catastrophe* (2015), and *After the Death of God: Secularization as a*

Philosophical Challenge from Kant to Nietzsche (2025). He edited *German Idealism* (Routledge, 2007), *Theodor W. Adorno II* (Routledge, 2015), and *Kafka's The Trial* (2019), and co-edited *The Routledge Companion to the Frankfurt School* (2019) and *A Companion to Adorno* (2020).

Fred Rush is Professor of Philosophy at the University of Notre Dame, USA. He is the author of *On Architecture* (Routledge, 2009) and *Irony and Idealism* (2016). He edited *The Cambridge Companion to Critical Theory* (2004) and co-edited *Philosophy of Sculpture: Historical Problems, Contemporary Approaches* (Routledge, 2020).

THE ROUTLEDGE GUIDES TO THE GREAT BOOKS

The Routledge Guides to the Great Books provide ideal introductions to the texts which have shaped Western Civilization. The Guidebooks explore the arguments and ideas contained in the most influential works from some of the most brilliant thinkers who have ever lived, from Aristotle to Marx and Newton to Wollstonecraft. Each Guidebook opens with a short introduction to the author of the great book and the context within which they were working and concludes with an examination of the lasting significance of the book. *The Routledge Guides to the Great Books* will therefore provide students everywhere with complete introductions to the most significant books of all time.

Berkeley's Three Dialogues
Stefan Storrie

Smith's Wealth of Nations
Maria Pia Paganelli

Paine's Rights of Man
Frances A. Chiu

Moore's Principia Ethica
Susana Nuccetelli

Nietzsche's Thus Spoke Zarathustra
Matthew Meyer

Hume's A Treatise of Human Nature
P. J. E. Kail

Horkheimer and Adorno's Dialectic of Enlightenment
Espen Hammer and Fred Rush

For more information about this series, please visit:
https://www.routledge.com/The-Routledge-Guides-to-the-Great-Books/book-series/RGGB

The Routledge Guidebook to Horkheimer and Adorno's *Dialectic of Enlightenment*

Espen
Hammer

and

Fred
Rush

Routledge
Taylor & Francis Group

LONDON AND NEW YORK

First published 2026
by Routledge
4 Park Square, Milton Park, Abingdon, Oxon OX14 4RN

and by Routledge
605 Third Avenue, New York, NY 10158

Routledge is an imprint of the Taylor & Francis Group, an informa business

© 2026 Espen Hammer and Fred Rush

The right of Espen Hammer and Fred Rush to be identified as authors of this work has been asserted by them in accordance with sections 77 and 78 of the Copyright, Designs and Patents Act 1988.

All rights reserved. No part of this book may be reprinted or reproduced or utilised in any form or by any electronic, mechanical, or other means, now known or hereafter invented, including photocopying and recording, or in any information storage or retrieval system, without permission in writing from the publishers.

Trademark notice: Product or corporate names may be trademarks or registered trademarks, and are used only for identification and explanation without intent to infringe.

British Library Cataloguing-in-Publication Data
A catalogue record for this book is available from the British Library

ISBN: 978-1-032-04892-5 (hbk)
ISBN: 978-1-032-04890-1 (pbk)
ISBN: 978-1-003-19504-7 (ebk)

DOI: 10.4324/9781003195047

Typeset in Times New Roman
by codeMantra

Contents

	Acknowledgments	x
	Introduction	1
1.	The Historical Background	11
2.	The Dialectic of Enlightenment	44
3.	Odysseus between Myth and Enlightenment	77
4.	From Kant to Sade	104
5.	Culture and Commodification	130
6.	Conjectures on Antisemitism	164
7.	The Reception of *Dialectic of Enlightenment*	198
	Concluding Remarks	226
	Bibliography	231
	Index	243

Acknowledgments

Our thanks to Iain Macdonald and Brian O'Connor for reading the manuscript in draft and providing very helpful suggestions for improvement. J. M. Bernstein, Raymond Geuss, Peter E. Gordon, Axel Honneth, and Martin Shuster will know how important they have been for this project. It has been a delight to work with Tony Bruce and everyone at Routledge in bringing this book to press. Thanks also to our indexer, Eli Israel.

INTRODUCTION

Co-written in their American exile during the Second World War, Max Horkheimer and Theodor Adorno's *Dialectic of Enlightenment* (1944/7) (=*DE*) is the most famous and philosophically influential of all the texts associated with the classical phase of the Frankfurt School. Whereas the Institute for Social Research, to which the authors belonged, had initially been engaged in an interdisciplinary program combining empirical sociological research with philosophical reflection in order to throw light on both regressive and progressive social tendencies in a time of crisis, *DE* represents a decisive turn to pure theory. In the tradition of Hegel, Nietzsche, Weber, and Freud, it provides an interpretation not of emancipatory struggles in the then-present but a philosophical and social-theoretical account of human history from its Neolithic origins through the advent of modernity and up to the calamities of the twentieth century.

It is a dark book. The despair it expresses about the state of Western civilization during the darkest years of the Second World War and its pessimism about modern conceptions of reason and the potential for human liberation these conceptions were supposed to promise eventually made *DE* a bible of leftwing disenchantment with politics, culture, and philosophy. The image of a *Flaschenpost*, a message in a bottle, which Adorno used to describe his own work, evokes shipwreck and stranding, a sense of emergency and isolation in which all that is left to one is to send a report that may never reach anyone and almost certainly will never receive a response. Today, as the world faces the consequences of its mode of rationalization in many forms, including the environmental crisis, the nuclear arms race, and neoliberal restructuring of state and society, *DE*'s crucial idea, namely that what we take to be progress may harbor regressive, even self-destructive, elements, seems just as relevant as when the book was first composed. While always controversial and contested, even within the Frankfurt School, few works of twentieth-century social thought have turned out to be as eerily prescient.

DE is, then, not only the culmination but also the radicalization and dramatization of much of what the early Frankfurt School stood for. It is also a text that documents its authors' loss of faith in Marxist narratives of inevitable progressive transformation, which had all but defined both the early Institute's social scientific brief and large swaths of the European Left. Existing readings of *DE* typically acknowledge its abiding dependence on select, key features of Marx's social ontology, such as the idea of commodity fetishism. Interpreters have pointed as well to parallels with more conservative thinkers such as Nietzsche, Spengler, and Heidegger, for whom modernity breeds widespread individual and social disintegration, not the promise of increasing human fulfillment. On Jürgen Habermas's influential account, the vast critical scope of Horkheimer and Adorno's work slots into this more conservative line of thought and stands in danger of jeopardizing the critical impulse itself. If reason, as Habermas takes *DE* to argue, is necessarily lawlike, instrumental, and, thereby, incapable of staking out intrinsically meaningful rational ends, then critique itself becomes impossible. Social change is cast as a blind process, more akin to natural causation than to intentional agency. Much of the debate surrounding *DE* turns on whether it undermines the very possibility of rational social criticism. While Habermas worries that its authors are on the verge of lapsing into irrationalism, recent reception has been more open to the possibility that Horkheimer and Adorno aim less to conduct a wholesale critique and eventual rejection of reason than to diagnose and correct select, though central, excesses of rationality by expanding the idea of reason itself. Even in a book this pessimistic, there remains a utopian dimension.

* * *

The *Routledge Guidebook to Horkheimer and Adorno's Dialectic of Enlightenment* takes the reader through the whole of the book, section by section, argument by argument. We begin by introducing the philosophical, sociological, and psychoanalytic prerequisites for understanding the text, culled from the nineteenth and early twentieth centuries. We then turn to the various chapters, offering in-depth expository readings of each. While visited in various contexts, we do not devote a separate chapter to the notes and sketches that follow the more extended text of *DE*. Contemporary German editions and the English translation we use here include all of those found in Horkheimer's *Nachlaß*; Horkheimer and Adorno included some but not all of them in the first distribution of the manuscript. These are in the style of Adorno's and Horkheimer's more "personal" works of this period (*Minima Moralia*, parts of *Dämmerung*), and a chapter devoted to them alone would have to shift radically in exegetical method and tone. We have decided, therefore, to include them where we think illuminating in the general discussion of the chapters and excursuses. We conclude by singling out and critically assessing the reception of ideas from *DE* that appear in the work of subsequent thinkers.

DE was written in Los Angeles during the Second World War, where some members of the Frankfurt School, as well as many other prominent German intellectuals, were in exile. While the two authors discussed preparation of every chapter in detail and co-edited drafts, there is evidence both stylistically and in terms of the selection of topics and treatment of ideas on the basis of which one can assign each chapter a main author. Horkheimer seems to have penned the drafts of the chapters on the concept of enlightenment and Sade/Kant; Adorno was the main author of those dealing with the *Odyssey* and the culture industry. The chapter on antisemitism was co-written.

Two principal challenges confront writing a guidebook to *DE*. First, the relevant intellectual context for it is vast and intricate, ranging as it does from classics of German philosophy to studies of archaic Greece, from then-contemporary popular culture to theories of antisemitism, from the philosophy of science to Weber's interpretation of modernity, from theories of technology to anthropological accounts of myth and the genesis of human subjectivity, and from modern conceptions of hedonism to psychoanalytic metapsychology. In order not to drown the reader in this material, we have had to be selective: There are synopses of the relevant features of Kant, Hegel, Marx, Nietzsche, Freud, and Weber, as well as discussions of the central concepts in Georg Lukács and Walter Benjamin. Second, the very structure of *DE* as a book presents exegetical difficulties. It is not entirely unified, at least not if one's idea of the unity of a philosophical treatise is Kant's *Critique of Pure Reason* or Spinoza's *Ethics*. Indeed, Horkheimer and Adorno intended it not to take the shape of a "traditional theory," which they considered too allied to the kind of reductive thinking that they sought to reject. They initially called the manuscript simply *Philosophical Fragments*, emphasizing not only its open-endedness but also the fact that it presents itself more like a collection of self-sufficient essays on discrepant topics than as a typical philosophical monograph. Even the division of chapters is unusual. Following a Preface, an Introduction, and the first chapter, there are two extended "Excursuses," and then two more chapters followed by a long section entitled "Notes and Drafts." The Introduction and the first and second chapters are often regarded as containing the heart of the argument. However, in recent years the subtlety and sophistication of other sections of this book have also become evident as new scholars have sought to overturn many of the old biases against *DE*, especially that its sole purpose is to lament the regressive effects of instrumentalization.

The way we tackle these challenges is to make sure that the emphasis throughout lies with themes that weave through the entire work: the nature of reason and of progress, the mechanisms that account for the integration of contemporary society, and the emancipatory potential inhering in our mimetic capacities and relations to nature. Because *DE*'s legacy by now spans two or three generations of social theory and philosophy, the Guidebook contains a consideration of select important moments of this reception.

We hope that the reader will be left with the view that *DE*, despite some of its extravagances, is still a fascinating, provocative, and compelling account of the nature and fate of human subjectivity and rationality in modernity. As in the other Routledge Guides, following each chapter there is a list of recommended further readings.

* * *

Much has been written about the two authors' lives.[1] Both Adorno (1903–69) and Horkheimer (1895–1973) grew up in prosperous, high-bourgeois circumstances. While only Adorno's father, the wine merchant Oskar Wiesengrund, was Jewish – meaning Adorno was for purposes of Jewish law a gentile – Horkheimer grew up with two Jewish parents in what may be characterized as a conservative household.[2] Intellectually, their early interests intersected: Kant and German Idealism, Marx and Marxism, psychoanalysis, modern literature, and, especially important for Adorno, music. They both studied and wrote doctoral dissertations with the liberal, neo-Kantian Hans Cornelius at the University of Frankfurt. They also shared a keen interest in politics and contemporary social affairs, viewing the First World War, the struggles and disappointments of the working class, and the abiding conservatism and militarism of German culture with considerable concern, inclining toward a pessimistic view not only of politics but, influenced by Schopenhauer, of the human condition in general. Although Horkheimer wrote short stories in his youth and considered, in opposition to his father's wish for him to eventually take over the family's company, the possibility of becoming a writer, Adorno was by far the more artistically inclined. His earliest work was as a music critic, and he studied composition for a time with Alban Berg, a key figure in the Second Viennese School.

Toward the end of the 1920s, while regularly meeting in Frankfurt, their orientations may seem to have diverged considerably. Influenced especially by his friends and mentors, Siegfried Kracauer and Walter Benjamin, Adorno started developing the "micrological" and "constellational" thinking that later informed his signature work: *Minima Moralia* (1951), *Negative Dialectics* (1966), and *Aesthetic Theory* (1970). With this as his lodestar, in 1929 Adorno completed his *Habilitation* (the postdoctoral dissertation that used to be prerequisite for the *venia legendi*, the right to teach in a German university) on Kierkegaard and, in 1931, held his inaugural lecture as *Privatdozent* (unpaid junior lecturer) at the University of Frankfurt. On the other hand, Horkheimer, whom Cornelius had been hoping would succeed him in his professorial chair (in the end, Max Scheler obtained that position), became gradually more interested in Marxist theory and questions of social justice and in 1930 was offered the position of Director of the recently founded Institute for Social Research in Frankfurt. A year afterward he gave his inaugural lecture as Chair of Social Philosophy at the University of Frankfurt.

Apart from some articles on music, Adorno did not contribute much to the Institute's research until later in the 1930s when he also formally became a member. But Horkheimer quickly established the Institute for Social Research as a dynamic center for investigation into modern history, culture, economics, psychoanalysis, and Marxist theory. Joined by the psychoanalyst and social psychologist Erich Fromm, the political economist Friedrich Pollock, the cultural historian Leo Löwenthal, the philosopher of law Franz Neumann, the political scientist Otto Kirchheimer, and the philosopher Herbert Marcuse, Horkheimer envisioned a collaboration between sociology and philosophy (sometimes referred to as "interdisciplinary materialism") and for a form of theory that, opposed to positivism, would be mindful of the constitution of social facts within systems of power and domination and keenly observant of the distinction between progressive and regressive social tendencies. Having as its ultimate goal to help society move beyond the purportedly unjust and ideologically opaque nature of capitalism, especially in its organized, monopoly form, Critical Theory was intended to be both explanatory and anticipatory.[3] It would critically explain social life as it is while anticipating, even if just negatively, a better, more fulfilling and just form of life to come.

Since its founding in 1923, the associates of the Institute had looked at the failed attempts in Germany after the First World War to establish socialism, as well as the rapid rise of fascism throughout the later Weimar years, as very likely to combine to catastrophic effect. Much of its research focused on how this was even so much as possible. Why would the forces of regression rather than the forces of progress prevail? This catastrophe affected the researchers personally and professionally. When Hitler seized power and quickly transformed the nation into a dictatorship, the Institute was forced to relocate – first to Geneva and then to New York, where Columbia University offered to house and financially support it. After a stint in Oxford, where he worked toward a D. Phil. under the philosopher Gilbert Ryle, Adorno joined Horkheimer and the other members of the relocated Institute in 1938.

Responsive to, and to some extent pressured by, the prerogatives of then-current American social scientific research, the Institute embarked on a number of empirical projects, most famously the *Studies on Authority and Family* (1936) and the *Studies in Prejudice* series of monographs (1949–50), which examined the nature and formation of authoritarian attitudes, starting with early family socialization. Even Adorno, whose austere theoretical orientation had been undeniable, participated in empirical social research. With fellow émigré Paul Lazarsfeld and others, he investigated the new medium of the radio and how it influenced people's listening habits. This turned out to be an unhappy collaboration, and in 1941 Adorno joined Horkheimer and the other members of the Institute who had left New York for Los Angeles because of difficulties they had collaborating with Columbia. In the seaside town of Pacific Palisades – where other German exiles had settled, including the novelists Thomas Mann and Lion Feuchtwanger and the composer Arnold Schoenberg – Horkheimer and Adorno worked on their "dialectics project," the forerunner of *DE*. In 1944 this manuscript was published in 500 copies as a hectographed typescript by the Institute. In 1947 Querido in Amsterdam, an important publisher of German writers in exile, issued a proper book version. It took close to two decades, however, for *DE* to assume its place as the central text of first-generation Critical Theory. In this sense at least it remained, as the authors intended, a "message in a bottle."

In 1950, the Institute returned to Frankfurt and relocated to a new building in the Zenckenbergeranlage adjacent to the university. Horkheimer's and Adorno's lives intersected in many ways. They both remained members of the Institute. Between 1951 and 1953 Horkheimer was rector of the University of Frankfurt and in 1953 stepped down from his directorship of the Institute, a position Adorno inherited while also serving as professor of sociology and philosophy at the university. Horkheimer did not publish much after his return to Germany. Adorno, however, was exceptionally productive, writing some of his best-known books. He also participated frequently in the public intellectual life of Germany.

In the 1960s the Institute became embroiled in controversy as radical students, who understood *DE* as inviting a hands-on reimagining of social order, engaged in mass protests. Horkheimer and, especially, Adorno had considerable sympathy for the students' causes, especially their critique of capitalism; however, they did not accept their demands. The idea, in particular, of uniting theory and praxis by turning academic institutions, including the Institute, into centers for political activity, did not appeal to them. To the dismay of many students, Horkheimer and Adorno fervently believed that theory can only inform radical action if kept above the fray, independent of demands for specific immediate action. Given West Germany's historical role as the successor to a fascist state, they were deeply skeptical of mass mobilization and any call for sudden – perhaps even violent – social transformation. Theory, Adorno went so far as to claim, is today the only form of praxis available. This attitude led Adorno and the students into direct conflict. In one incident, he called in the police to remove demonstrating students from the philosophy department. In another, he felt forced to leave the lecture hall as female students confronted him at the podium, nude to the waist, and pelted him with flowers. He died of heart failure shortly thereafter, in the summer of 1969. Horkheimer followed him in 1973.

* * *

Citations to *DE* are given parenthetically in the text to the English translation, followed by citations to the German original. We have sometimes adjusted translations. The English text is *Dialectic of Enlightenment: Philosophical Fragments*, trans. E. Jephcott (Stanford: Stanford University Press, 2002). The German text is the relevant part of volume 5 of Max Horkheimer, *Gesammelte Schriften*, ed. G. S. Noerr (Frankfurt am Main: Fischer, 1987), on which the Jephcott translation is based. Although not as readily available as are stand-alone versions of the work, this version has the added benefit of excellent editor's notes (also translated by Jephcott). Other versions of the work are Horkheimer and Adorno, *Dialektik der Aufklärung* (Frankfurt am Main: Fisher, 1988), vol. 3 of Theodor W. Adorno, *Gesammelte Schriften*, ed. R. Tiedemann (Frankfurt am Main: Suhrkamp, 1970), and a single-volume edition that is page-identical to the volume in Adorno's collected works, also available from Suhrkamp. Other writings of Horkheimer and Adorno are cited in similar form, with the exception of Adorno's *Negative Dialectics*, which has at present no dependable English translation. English translations from that book are ours.

We have tried to keep the apparatus lean in order to facilitate engagement with the text in hand. Suggestions for further reading appear at the end of each chapter. The bibliography is limited to works cited.

NOTES

1 Adorno is the subject of two extensive biographies, Müller-Doohm 2009 and Claussen 2010. Horkheimer's life is treated with less scope and detail in Jay 1973, Wiggershaus 1995, Abromeit 2011, and Jacobs 2015.
2 Adorno's parentage gave him a complex identity, but by no means one that was unusual in German-speaking lands. His mother was Corsican, so nominally French, and Roman Catholic. His father was German and Jewish, but had converted to Protestantism. Adorno was baptized Catholic and confirmed Lutheran. His maternal grandparents were both Catholic and his paternal

grandparents both Jewish. Under the infamous Nuremberg laws, Adorno was not considered Jewish, as they required at least three grandparents to be Jewish (or two grandparents, if the person in question satisfied various other conditions) in order to count legally as a Jew. Adorno satisfied none of those conditions; so, he was considered – and here is a term so demeaning that it is almost impossible to write – a *Mischling*, a mongrel, i.e., neither Jewish nor "of German blood."

3   We use initial capitals in writing "Critical Theory" in order to distinguish the early philosophy and social theory of what would later become known as the Frankfurt School from literary theory, which is also often called "critical theory."

1
THE HISTORICAL BACKGROUND

By the end of the nineteenth century, German-language social philosophy had developed a rich stock of resources on which to draw. A dominant theme was the importance of history to the formation, use, and theoretical study of concepts. This reversed the standing practice of modern philosophy up to and including Immanuel Kant (1724–1804), in which historical provision played no role in understanding the meaning of concepts, at least not with regard to fundamental ones. Arthur Schopenhauer (1788–1860) could still write that history was *eadem, sed aliter* (loosely and expansively: "the same things happening again and again, only differently") (Schopenhauer 1966: 2.444), but German Idealists increasingly came to the view that history was a form of collective agency directed toward an end, the achievement of which would spell the ultimate in freedom. By the advent of the twentieth century, social philosophy was concerned to account for itself historically as a matter of course, although the progressivism of the Idealist version of historicism fell away, except in certain forms of materialist philosophy.

Early Critical Theory takes its historical situation seriously as a matter of theory and is, for that reason, alive to almost every major trend in Germanophone philosophy dating back to Kant, as well as to several emerging philosophical movements of its own time, many of which were likewise historically minded. Reading the central documents of early Critical Theory, including *DE*, one is faced with what media scholars today call "intertextuality," i.e., texts for which other texts are so important that the content of the texts is more properly thought of as belonging to an ensemble, i.e., multiple texts-within-a-text. This can be vertiginous for the first-time reader.

CONCEPTIONS OF ALIENATION

To gain initial orientation it is necessary to simplify without sacrificing substance and losing sight of scope. To do that, let's focus on a problem that occupied a good deal of nineteenth- and early-twentieth-century social philosophy and was (and still is) central to Critical Theory: alienation.

The word "alienation" has passed into common speech as meaning something like "disaffection" or "disorientation," perhaps pervasive. One might feel alienated from one's family, one's friends, or from an institution, say, one's university. But philosophical uses of the word cut more deeply than those. They emerge in a historical period in which culture itself becomes an object of withering critique. It is striking, then, that the problem of alienation took root in the very soil that had promised liberation, rational self-possession, and untainted progress: the Enlightenment.

The Enlightenment held out that heightened appreciation of the individual's capacity to judge for herself would usher in social freedom. Social relations would not be externally imposed; instead, they would be chosen, endorsed as legitimate. Since choice was an inherent good, so would be chosen social arrangements. At issue is not mere acquiescence to, or even reasonable acceptance of, such arrangements; both are compatible with being subject to external authority. The choice in question had to be elevated, be the product of a fundamental rational procedure, as in Kant, or issue from a "true self," as in Jean-Jacques Rousseau (1712–78).

Either way, it was individuals by dint of something intrinsic to them *qua* individuals who were sovereign.

But a problem arises. For several thinkers, in order to be sovereign, one in principle had to be above the empirical fray. The basis for freedom had to originate from a nonempirical source that did not, for that, undermine the sovereign individual. Otherwise, choice would lack the required ground in some property of the self that was not malleable, at least not under ideal conditions. The close proximity of individuality to this suite of values – authenticity, autonomy, universal rationality – in Enlightenment thought produced a subject that was sovereign *in its potential isolation*, not first and foremost a social self at all. Kant says some stringent things along such lines about possible self-isolation in moral judgment – for instance, that it is more virtuous to have one's duty severely tested and persevere than it is to be naturally dutiful. His moral theory does not require this heroic (or fanatical, depending on one's point of view) element, but such remarks do token high regard for an embattled self, putting down, and in that sense alienating, the empirical portion of its own being. J. G. Fichte's (1762–1814) ethics of conviction continues this trend. To double the irony, the idea that supernatural agency of some sort is involved in this liberation is but a faintly secularized inheritance of the very regime the Enlightenment sought to displace, i.e., Christianity as an ultimate source of authority.

The tenuousness of Kant's position, which enforces a hard break between empirical and nonempirical, "true" character, was recognized almost immediately, and the gap between those two orders, constitutively present in every individual and responsible for individuality, acquired a name: "alienation" (*Verfremdung, Entfremdung*). Kant's contemporaries like J. G. Hamann (1730–88), J. G. Herder (1744–1803), the poet and playwright Friedrich Schiller (1759–1805), German Idealists like Fichte, F. W. J. Schelling (1775–1854), and, most importantly, G. W. F. Hegel (1770–1831), as well as German Romantics like Friedrich Hölderlin (1770–1843), Friedrich von Hardenberg (Novalis) (1772–1801), and Friedrich Schlegel (1772–1829) offered various responses to alienation. Hamann and Herder argued for a turn to language to establish a more basic framework for understanding persons as unified, while

Schiller stumped for an account of various drives operative in human freedom, among which a "play drive" is basic to a harmonized sense of self. The early Idealists sought a foundation for the self in structures of intentionality prior to reflection yet properly autonomous. But this did little to assuage the main worry: that sociality had gone missing and, with it, an essential component of what it is to be human.

Hegel broke from this line in arguing that there was a philosophical perspective comprehensive enough to allow for subjects possessed of Enlightenment conceptions of individual freedom to see themselves as bound together freely only in reciprocal social relations of "recognition" (*Anerkennung*). By construing the main lines of conceptual development in history as a quest for free and full rationality, Hegel thought he could establish that history and reason were one in terms of fundamental structure and, accordingly, that empirical (viz. historical) agency was not only inseparable from freedom, it was the precondition for it. But all that depended upon an ambitious, highly idealized view of history as a progressive closed system. Schlegel, whom Hegel detested but also from whom he drew part of the inspiration for his conception of dialectic, was the antipode, an anti-foundationalist for whom historical instantiations of imagination (not reason) are the vocation of humans. Where the Enlightenment and, by extension, the Idealists sought self-discovery, the Romantics insisted upon self-invention. One overcomes alienation by being, as a self, as potentially flexible as is the empirical world. The prehistory of Critical Theory begins in earnest here, in the aftermath of Idealism and Romanticism in Germany.

It is worth pausing to bring to mind the great historical changes that were taking place in Europe and the world at large in the nineteenth century, changes that would test the mettle of any social theory. The year of Hegel's death saw two slave rebellions, Nat Turner's in the United States and Sam Sharp's in Jamaica, as well as the Merthyr Rising of Welsh coal miners and the first of the Canut silk worker revolts in Lyon. Poland attempted to oust its Russian overlord, and the Bosnians rebelled against the Ottoman Empire. The July Revolution of 1830, which established a constitutional monarchy in France, might have been thought the conclusion of the revolution there that convulsed Europe at the turn of the nineteenth century, but by the late 1840s revolutions had fanned out across Europe, threatening to overturn the French and Habsburg monarchies, the German Confederation, and the Bourbon-held Two Kingdoms of Naples and Sicily. By 1851, all these rebellions had been reversed, often brutally.

Mass media were invented during this period (widespread distribution of newspapers, the introduction of the commercial telegraph), as was mass transportation (the first public rail lines and a global network of long-distance steamships). This was strongly interactive. An example: Time became standardized as a result of better astronomical observation, which in turn standardized railroad schedules via telegraphic communication from station to station. Photographs, phonographs, and telephones were invented, as was electric lighting. But all was not sunny progress. War became a darling of modern technology. The Crimean and US Civil Wars were fought with automatic weaponry (and the first wartime photographs of the legions of dead were distributed via newspaper). The European population swelled and, with it, so did poverty. At the start of the nineteenth century, London's population stood at 960,000; by the turn of the twentieth, it had increased sixfold. When Tsar Alexander II emancipated Russian serfs in 1861, twenty million "souls" (*dushi*) were freed, albeit almost invariably into grim circumstances.

In keeping with this rapid development of society and technology, philosophy as it was traditionally conceived gradually ceded ground to the natural sciences, especially to physics. What had been a main task of modern philosophy up to Kant's time – establishing the conceptual foundations for the physical sciences – was no longer tenable: science seemed self-justifying. Philosophy that mattered turned to questions of value, i.e., to ethical, political, and aesthetic matters. Two distinct lines developed. The first foregrounded the nexus of ethics, aesthetics, and conceptions of life. Its main representatives are Schopenhauer and Nietzsche, both figures of significance in the formation of early Critical Theory and, more specifically, in Horkheimer's and Adorno's versions of it. But the second line is even more important for understanding the background of Critical Theory. Here the main figure is Marx.

HEGEL AND MARX

The Institute for Social Research was founded as a Marxist thinktank. That is not to say that the Institute aligned itself with any one of the many forms of Marxism on offer during those times, nor does it mean that there were no divergent approaches to socialism among its members. But it is to say that all its principals agreed that Marxian thinking was a philosophical reserve from which to draw.

The name "Marx" does not appear in the first published version of *DE*. Moving the Institute to New York and then to Los Angeles required funding from US sources and that, in turn, caused many of its members to downplay the Marxist affiliations of their work. One might think Horkheimer and Adorno would have felt able to speak more freely in a work initially intended for a readership limited to intimates, but they were exercising extreme circumspection. Redactions and substitutions of terms between the 1944 and 1947 versions of *DE* (duly marked by the editors of the English translation to which this Guidebook is keyed, as well as the German version that forms the basis for that translation) attest to the self-editing.

The relevance of Marx for the main line of development in early Critical Theory stems from the importance of Hegel for him. There are three dimensions of Hegel's thought that register, transformed, in Marx, and are transmitted through Marx to early Critical Theory. The first has to do with the nature of thinking itself. For Hegel human thought is essentially conceptual, but what a concept is and, thus, what the qualifier "conceptual" means departs from traditional positions on this question. Hegel holds that thinking works through binary opposition of subjects and objects, where the form of opposition depends on what descriptions or norms are given to both terms in opposition. The stability of overall worldviews depends on keeping these contrasts sharp and in play. But he also holds that such contrasts are defeasible, since the descriptions or norms that underwrite them are due to historical developments in human self-understanding. When components fundamental to the continued existence of a worldview come into express conflict due to the pressure of giving a rationally acceptable account of a changing world, opposition becomes contradiction. It is not "contradiction" in the modern logical sense that is in play; it is, rather, that the worldview is riven in ways that are irreparable. What all of this means is that, at the deepest level, thinking for Hegel is the process of passing from one set of norms to another. He often puts the point in terms of kinetics; thinking just is *moving* from one apparently controlling set of concepts to the next. That is not to say of course that whatever set is at any given point controlling is unimportant; it is very important for those who operate with those concepts (they are basic *for them*, given their historical situation). But for the philosopher the fundamental phenomenon is the building up, breaking down, and building up again of opposites. Hegel argues for a complete model of this process, i.e., for a gapless sequencing of contradictions that forms an ongoing cycle. What does not move is the sequence of the movement. That is, technically speaking, what he means by the term "concept." When he says that thinking is the logic of "the Concept" what he means is that the whole process just described is what a philosopher must posit as thinking. Individual concepts are merely broken-off bits of that, necessary for the process, but not themselves self-standing.

What makes an opposition give way to the next is that, when pressed by its own demands for coherency in the face of more and more telling counterexamples, what seemed to be opposed on certain background assumptions is found out to be not opposed when a more comprehensive background is brought to bear. This is all relevant to Marx, and through him to early Critical Theory, because it tokens the form of dialectic that Marx takes to govern social formation. He holds that this posing of oppositions occurs not merely in thought, but also and primarily in action – specifically, in labor. To overcome contradictions in labor – in particular between producing and ownership – is to increase freedom. One of the main ways in which contradictions seek to maintain a hold over a form of life is by segmenting that form, i.e., presenting it in ways that obscure the complete background against which the practices one might critique and change have meaning. This is the second inheritance of Hegel that flows through Marx to Critical Theory. Concepts and practices have to be understood in terms of the *whole* of background commitments. If one does not take into account the whole of background commitments, many of which are implicit, one both does not understand the reach of the concepts and practices under consideration and will not be able to effectively change those concepts and practices by altering the commitments. Hegel's philosophy is holistic along many dimensions, some of them quite formal. Marx does not really care for the formalities, but it does matter a great deal to him that critique can penetrate what are sometimes very artful ways that the status quo presents the world as broken down into seemingly independent domains. In Marx's estimation, capitalism does just that. We shall return to this point, when our discussion turns to the concept of totality in Lukács.

Third, part of what one might call the "hydraulics" of Hegel's theory of conceptual formation and development is that the content of these whole ways of thinking – what they depend on – emerges more explicitly to those doing the thinking as those ways are put under pressure. The full content of the way of life moves from latent to patent. The idea that there are always, broadly speaking, unconscious elements in thought that need to be made conscious in order to understand and criticize them is powerfully suggestive to Horkheimer and Adorno. It provides a linchpin between German philosophy in its "classical" form and more recent developments in psychology.

In this tradition, "alienation" can be understood as having broad and narrow senses. Broadly speaking, alienation is just thinking; it is something all of us do, splitting the world into dyadic categories that achieve determinacy by exclusion. But, more narrowly, alienation is stuck thinking. It is the experience of not being able to move out of contradiction that causes dissatisfaction and impinges on one's freedom. This is a short-circuiting of the gainful relation between self and world that causes one to regard the world as inimical in principle to self-realization. It is the second sense of the term that is most in play in much of the philosophical and social scientific background relevant to *DE*, but Horkheimer and Adorno presuppose that the narrow sense follows from the broader sense. There is no such thing as no alienation whatsoever, for there must be categorial thought for there to be thinking at all. But, given that, one wants to be able to identify and alter forms of that thought that have become deficient, i.e., those that have turned out to be no longer as sustaining as one previously thought they were.

As we mentioned above, the Marxist credentials of *DE* are left obscure in the 1947 text. One must align it with the 1944 version to bring out the relevant aspects. It is important, however, not to go overboard; the early critical theorists were not traditional Marxists in any case, and nontraditional Marxism admits of extreme variation. Here's an example of overstepping. At first pass one might interpret Horkheimer and Adorno's treatment in *DE* of the forty lines or so of Book 12 of Homer's *Odyssey* that deal with the lure of the Sirens, to be about class conflict: Odysseus is the master who enjoys the spoils of the crew's labor. But the main point of that discussion is not that class is a basic explanatory concept. It is, rather, that class conflict is only a select, modern manifestation of a much deeper process involving the interactivity of myth and enlightenment.

NIETZSCHE

Both Schopenhauer and Nietzsche are precursors to modern accounts of the unconscious, especially important for the extension of the idea of the unconscious to groups and cultures. We are going to set Schopenhauer to the side here, even though he is a continuing presence in Horkheimer's thought and even though he makes a guest appearance in *DE* via turns of phrase, such as the Latin tag "principium individuationis" (the principle of individuation), deployed in Schopenhauer's metaphysics of representation.

Nietzsche is the more direct resource. Hegel holds that human attempts to overcome alienation are both subject to suffering and fueled by it. He does, after all, call history a "slaughter bench" (Hegel 1975: 69, translation emended). But the suffering gets you somewhere final; it is something you fight through in order to arrive at "reconciliation." True, reconciliation for Hegel is, in part, being reconciled to that process and, through it, to the necessity of having suffered. But the point is that suffering can be ameliorated or refined over time, if not eliminated altogether. Nietzsche has a much less sunny picture of the hold suffering has on humans. He inherits this from Schopenhauer – although he never really adhered to the metaphysics that underpins Schopenhauer's pessimism – for whom unconscious forces operating on and from within the psyche essentially qualify any such refinement. Nietzsche concurs but adds that pessimism does not follow from the diagnosis. Pessimism would only follow if you expected matters to be otherwise. But, if you do not make that mistake, the proper attitude toward suffering is one of affirmation, not necessarily of individual cases of suffering, but of the thought that we all suffer on account of being human. The saving point is that we can give meaning to the pain, and that will make it bearable. One must suffer, but one can "love fate" (Nietzsche 2001: 157 [§276] and 1992: 37 [§10]).

As we shall see, Horkheimer and Adorno hold that there is a particular form of enlightenment coping with suffering that is based in a backhanded promise of its amelioration. Enlightenment thinking holds out increased rational control as a panacea, but, they argue, suffering is not limited to pre- or unconscious activities that impact cognition yet evade rational capture and control. The deliberative processes and their products *themselves* cause suffering. Moreover, as they also argue, this enlightenment strain of suffering has always been in place, not just in *the* Enlightenment, but in archaic thought as well. The converse proposition, i.e., that archaic myth is also present in modern times, is also crucial for them.

A second register in which Nietzsche's thought sounds in *DE* has to do with methodology. This, again, is proximal to but in tension with their Hegelian Marxism. All of the argumentation in *DE* is dialectical in that for any apparently well-settled pair of contrasting concepts – say, "myth" and "enlightenment" – Horkheimer and Adorno will seek to show how the concepts intertwine and depend on each other for their content and force. Enlightenment considers itself precisely to be *not* myth, but in fact these concepts are two sides of the same coin. That enlightenment buys its own integrity at the price of a definitive break with myth is evidence to Horkheimer and Adorno that it "doth protest too much." Its attempt to inoculate itself against what it fears still infects it provides a point of entry into the concept.

Now, Nietzsche is no dialectical thinker. But he is very interested in unsettling accepted views on what conceptual options are available and in how conceptions combine in the past to create the illusion of their inevitability and, thereby, their truth. Nietzsche was trained as a classical philologist. Philologists (when they still existed) lived on the borderlands of ancient and medieval languages and linguistics. A standard chore was to deal with incomplete, variable, or even incompatible textual remnants. Based on testimonia, we know that Sophocles authored 123 plays. Seven are extant. There were and are difficulties in the various versions of what remains due to different sources of preservation. The point is that a philologist will be sensitive to the way historical contingency can be forgotten or repressed over time and allow for the historical embeddedness of a text to be replaced by the simplifying idea of a text immemorial. Nietzsche holds that the same sort of forgetting occurs in thinking about values. "Our" values are the true and only ones; all prior values are either false or deficient versions of ours.

The stripping away of such facile, self-aggrandizing historical understandings of concepts is part of a general strategy on Nietzsche's part that he sometimes calls the "transvaluation of all values" (*Umwertung aller Werte*). The apparent correctness of many modern values is largely an artifact of their perceived inevitability. Nietzsche develops an alternative approach to understanding how the values that shape modern European ethics and art have come about: genealogy. If one scrutinizes the formation of values without anachronistically projecting back onto them their present characters, one often finds that their historical antecedents do not follow one another in lockstep and lack a single core content that is preserved through time. One finds instead less well-defined concepts in contingent and indirect relations to one another. One of his main examples is the modern European conception of guilt, which he argues descends in a wayward fashion from premoral conceptions of debtor–creditor relations.

DE marries this genealogical approach to Hegel-inspired dialectical critique. One might think the marriage likely to fail if one has overly strict notions of the characters of the spouses. If one thought of genealogy as aimed at disproving the truth of the values involved, the marriage would not work because dialectic shows how concepts generate successors as of right. If one were to think that dialectic is so tightly structured as to admit of no contingency, then the main advantage of genealogy would be undermined. But these strict understandings are not mandatory. It is a mistake to think of genealogy as aiming at debunking the *truth* of concepts. The debunking aims at their inevitability; whether one accepts or rejects those concepts in light of what the genealogy delivers is a separate matter. The mistaken impression is left, perhaps, by the fact that *in the specific cases he considers*, Nietzsche clearly wishes to reject the concepts for which he is given the genealogy. Likewise, dialectic may display dynamism and resolution and yield meaningful successors to conceptual tensions without presupposing either some underlying form of necessity or a *terminus ad quem*.

PSYCHOANALYSIS

Conceptions of unconscious experience reach back to seventeenth-century rationalism, if not before, but Freud first proposed a *theory* of *the* unconscious, of a psychic realm governed by laws of its own. From its earliest days Critical Theory concerned itself with psychoanalysis, with Erich Fromm appointed as its in-house specialist. His remit was to deploy psychoanalytic resources in order to better understand why European workers had not developed the social self-conception sufficient to form a revolutionary class. Direct physical and psychological coercion may explain some aspects of worker oppression, but the internalization of oppression as non-oppression, as "just what happens to the poor," cannot be explained in that way. Socially directed psychoanalysis promised an account of self-imposed false thinking. It might help one to come to grips with the emergence of fascism as well.

It is surprising that Freud does not make a more concerted appearance in *DE*, although he does crop up every so often; nonetheless, psychoanalytic theory underwrites several key ideas in the text. What conjoins the uses of psychoanalytic theory mentioned above, and what animates Critical Theory's interest in it, is the aspiration to account for the mechanisms that inhibit understanding what can be expected from social life. Not only is the inhibition broad in scope, it also systematically evades correction. Freud's structural theory of the unconscious is well placed to account for both phenomena, although Horkheimer and Adorno in some important cases find Freud's own claims about culture to be "anachronistic" and "too narrow" (7/33, 178/245–6).

Psychoanalysts like Carl Jung and Otto Rank did not shy away from extending depth psychology to cultural matters. Nor did Freud, who wrote several books at the intersection of psychoanalysis, ethnography, religion, and social history. The earliest of these, *Totem and Taboo* (1914), its lovely prose aside, now rates rather poorly on account of both its remoteness from ethnological fieldwork and its simplistic equation of individual psychological development to the development of tribal social structure. Several of its ideas, notably that of applying the Freudian understanding of projection to kinship relations, are important to Horkheimer and Adorno's treatment of antisemitism. But the importance of Freud's ideas for *DE* extends to other of his main cultural works. *The Future of an Illusion* (1927) considers the question of the epistemic and social nature of religious belief. It is productive for Critical Theory on account of its analysis of religious belief as wish fulfillment. Religious beliefs are illusions because they are constitutively nonresponsive to truth. An illusion may turn out to be true – e.g., Freud's famous example is the woman who thinks that in dancing with a prince she will marry him. She *might* marry him of course, but probability is not the point. The point is that the wish that forms the basis for the illusion is insensitive to proof or disproof; the woman is not just miscalculating or gambling. Illusions are false in a special way. Unlike mere mistakes, they have a salvific function. This can cut two ways. One can simply be carried away in the belief; this is not likely to be socially productive. Or the illusion can be recognized as expressing a hope for change. The woman and the prince, after all, might fall in love. What is stopping them? What makes that the stuff of fairy tales and not of realist fiction? The answer is that society will not allow them to break social class to become romantically involved. The utopian content here is wishful; nonetheless, it gestures to a world in which love transcends status. Illusion is an arena in which what would be antisocial if acted upon can be dreamt of as being real and as subject to being, to that degree, mollified and controlled.

Civilization and its Discontents (1930) picks up this thought and runs with it. Societal demands are incorporated into psychic organization. Freud's technical term for this is "introjection." The demands exact a cost in terms of repressing whatever desire is contrary to the internalized rule. But repressing a wish is not extirpating it. Repressed wishes persist at the ready, intensified by their repression. Moreover, the power of repression lasts only as long as there are sufficient superego checks. The best social outcome is to systematically extract from the wish its energy and convert that energy into something socially beneficial. That is culture's job, and the structural theory has a process at the ready: *sublimation*. The mature adult will have adapted to be social and acculturated, i.e., to sublimate libidinal forces in order to better realize what she has been taught to be the social good. The rub is that she is constitutively uncomfortable in doing so. Social coherence exacts a basic cost on individuals. The idea that culture is the outcome of internalized *eros* was not new with Freud; however, he introduces an element lacking in prior accounts, i.e., that culture can *both* inhibit *and* transform primal aggression to its advantage. Civilization coopts the ego's mediation of, and partial resistance to, introjection.

For Freudians who were also Marxists – e.g., Otto Fenichel, Fromm, and Wilhelm Reich – introjection was important on additional grounds. First, some Marxists reject the idea that economic relations cause each and every bit of social structure and, instead, treat culture as a primary social scientific category. This allows a better response to a perennial problem for late-nineteenth- and early-twentieth-century Marxist theory that not only Fromm but Institute social scientists Friedrich Pollock and Franz Neumann discuss at length: Why does capitalism not only persist but also intensify? Why is there late capitalism at all? It is open for the Freudian Marxist to reply: because there are ideological features of capitalism that insinuate themselves into the unconscious and are, because of that, very difficult to identify, let alone eradicate.

By the same token, a Freudian understanding of acculturation might be put to work to give an account of fascism and its modern European twin, antisemitism.

OTHER PROXIMATE TWENTIETH-CENTURY INFLUENCES

There are three more proximate influences on early Critical Theory whose thought merits separate synoptic treatment: Max Weber, Georg Lukács, and Walter Benjamin.

WEBER

Accounts of alienation are tempered by their connection to conceptions of dialectical rationality that do not motivate Weber. Accordingly, neither the concept nor the phenomenon of alienation figures in his sociology. Nevertheless, Horkheimer and Adorno find in Weber's diagnosis of modern malaise a sociological complement to approaches to alienation that stem from German Idealism and Marxism. "Disenchantment" (*Entzauberung*), a Weberian term of art, holds pride of place in the third sentence of the first paragraph of the first chapter of the work, setting the tone for what comes after (1/25). The controlling concept in Weber, however, is "rationalization" (*Rationalisierung*) to which disenchantment is subordinated (see Weber 2004). Rationalization is a process in which "purposive rationality" (*Zweckrationalität*) gradually displaces "value-rationality" (*Wertrationalität*). Purposive rationality says that any end is sufficient to determine the rightness of the means to it, so long as the concept of an end is determinate enough to direct the action. The issue here is not that ends determine means; that is a truism. It is, rather, that ends, so construed, are themselves nothing but means to other possible ends (which are also means). They have only extrinsic legitimacy, authorized by yet further purposes. Value-rationality, by contrast, treats some ends as intrinsically valuable. Such ends are not merely further means; they establish the value of any means rationally connected to them relative to a course of deliberation or action. The default premodern source for such values for Weber is religion. But religion effects its "buck stops here" status by what can only seem as fiat to a modern sensibility:

appeal to supernatural authority, unquestionable and final by dint of metaphysics and faith. Of course, purposive rationality had a role to play in the everyday premodern life, but it was considered secondary to and constrained by its transcendent counterpart.

One of the mainsprings of modernity is a widespread translation of value from otherworldly to worldly sources; that is largely what "disenchantment" is. Kant's moral theory stands at the crossroads of the two forms of valuation in virtue of its attempt to preserve value-rationality over and against purposive rationality. It rests on the proposition that there is one end that is intrinsically good, good in itself: subjecting oneself to the moral law, which amounts to having a good will. There is no recourse to purposes in establishing the legitimacy of that. For Kant, it is morally impermissible to treat persons merely as means; one must always treat another as an end, and that means as an end in itself. There is a price to pay for this saving maneuver: a thinned-out appeal to supernatural agency in the conception of acting from duty. Depending on one's point of view, Kantian ethics tokens enchanted disenchantment or disenchanted enchantment.

For Weber, rationalization characterizes modern Western society generally, but he is adamant that there are several lines of its development in Europe that differ significantly from one another. One such line stands out in the reception of his work. *The Protestant Ethic and the Spirit of Capitalism* (1905) is a sustained consideration of a surprising case of rationalization, one that has as its helpmate, not as its adversary, religion (Weber 1956). In Weber's reckoning, Protestant denominations that accept the theological doctrine of predestination – more precisely the doctrine of double predestination, i.e., that God chooses whom to bless and whom to damn before their births and, in some versions, before all time – are specially placed to be at the leading edge of capitalism, a purposive rational regime if ever there was one. Predestination places a strict block on human knowledge of divine purposes. No one can know themselves or others to have been saved (or damned). To even so much as to attempt to transgress this constraint is sinful. Weber argues that such groups develop interpretations of work and economic value that see in the former a calling and in the latter a sign that one has been saved. Producing economic value through work does not earn one salvation; to be predestined is always already to have been saved or not. Rather, work reflects one's belief that positive engagement in the things of this world and economic success are not futile when it comes to one's existence in the next. Capitalism proper – capitalism as a way of life – is not possible until mercantile exchange is married to the idea that work is a good in itself. Calvinism and other forms of Protestantism that came to dominate Northern Europe provide the conceptual resources (i.e., the 'spirit') for this valuation. Weber argues that this pursuit of economic value leeches more generally into society and is secularized. Weber was a realist when it came to the eclipse of the social force of intrinsic value. Rampant purposive rationality is here to stay. In his famous formulation, modern humanity is domiciled in a "steel-hard carapace" (*stahlhartes Gehäuse*) that not only protects but also imprisons.

LUKÁCS

Although *DE* leans on several ideas that originate in Marx, the onus is more on ideas in Marx continuous with Hegel than on *Capital*.[1] We have chosen in this introductory chapter to focus on one such idea, alienation. But Horkheimer and Adorno make use of many of Marx's ideas by dressing them in more acceptable Hegelian clothes. One concept that is crucial for them that does not submit to this change of costume is that of a commodity. Fortunately, the work of Hegelianizing the concept of commodity was already done for them by one of the Marxist thinkers in the line of reception that Horkheimer and Adorno favor, the Hungarian philosopher Georg Lukács.[2] Lukács also goes unmentioned in *DE* – all the more reason to come to grips here with his importance for the Frankfurt thinkers.

Lukács foregrounds two structures, jointly constitutive of alienation under conditions of advanced capitalism: (1) *reification* and (2) failure to adequately grasp *totality*. "Reification" (*Verdinglichung*) is a process in which social relations and products are viewed by default as things (*res*, *Dinge*), more specifically as commodities. This is a matter of form and experience, not of simple mistake. Marx uses the concept without much fanfare in his discussion of commodity fetishism, and that is as good a place as any to try to get a grip on the concept (Marx 1993: 3.969–70; see also Marx 1993: 1.163–77; cf. Hegel 2019: 302 [¶ 520]).

The most familiar contexts in which one comes across the idea of a fetish are in religion or psychology. Generally speaking, a fetish is a form of metonymy, i.e., the shorthand representation of a thing by one of its aspects, which creates a focal point for veneration (religion) or obsession (psychology). To treat a thing as a commodity is to treat it as having value in terms of its possible monetary exchange. But monetary value is only a part of the value of products and, if Marx is right, a superficial part at that. Thus, the aspect-for-whole substitution: products are monied objects, i.e., commodities. Commodities operate in terms of the forms of sociality that matter most in capital markets: seamless fungibility of products. Such sociality is depersonalized. Exchange has little to nothing to do with the product as a bearer of whatever self-expression a laborer achieves through her production, because the quality of what is produced is generic, made only in order to exchange. Reification for Lukács, then, is a basic phenomenon of capitalist *culture*, sociality overrun by the idea that anything might be bought or sold.

This sets the stage for a calculative, instrumental orientation. What matters is not primarily the object, action, or human relation as such but what they can mean for an agent in terms of maximizing monetary value.

Reification affects product, producer, and user. Abstractly, the fact that products are made by humans – however indirectly that may be under factory conditions – is registered of course. But Lukács's principal idea is that the capitalist economic life overtakes the rest of culture in European late modernity to such an extent that all artifacts are understood on the order of objects of exchange. That means that all objects are taken as they are given by a process of making that is impersonal and, because impersonal, not subject to intercession and change. Think of the helplessness that someone nowadays with social democratic leanings in the United States might feel when confronted with the increasing oligarchy that neoliberalism recommends on a daily basis. In the estimation of many, the United States is entering what one might call a Second Gilded Age. Who could change *that* without changing *everything*? And who can change everything?

Reification impacts the maker as well; she becomes merely a consumer with regard to her own work, viewing it as detached from her even in its making. Even though people are not artifacts, one can come close to reifying them as well; one can view others such that their self-expression through work doesn't matter, even (or especially) to themselves. Reification might be reversed in direction as well: to treat things as people. One names one's car not because one recognizes in it the value of the labor it expresses, but because one's affective relations in general are at such a low ebb due to commodification that a car can be easily personified. It is really a way to identify with the car, which is after all a machine. Most important, however, is that reification is a property that affects whole social systems, not merely their individual components. Capitalism is an artifact writ large. It is a human creation after all, and what can be done can be undone, even if with great difficulty. But capitalism appears to many to be as inalterable as the Milky Way.

The word "reification" appears often in *DE* and so does "totality" (*Totalität*), a term Lukács introduces in his early essays on aesthetics. It also has provenance in Marx, who used the term memorably when speaking of how a rich man is in need of all activities of life, not merely a select few. The concept first gains systematic purchase, however, in Lukács's monograph *Theory of the Novel* (1916), a seminal text for Adorno especially. Totality is a complicated and unruly idea. At times Lukács uses the concept functionally. To say that an individual, an artwork, or a society is a totality is to say that it is akin to an organism in that its various parts have their defining features only as they operate together as a whole. Greek life as Homer portrays it is a totality. Agents of that world experience themselves and each other as having meaning in terms of the whole of that world, well-constituted as it was to them. Modern European societies lack totality. The norms and mores that govern them do not bind agents to wholes; such societies are constituted by alienation. The early Lukács sometimes puts this point in the following way: form and life (or "soul") do not coalesce. On this basis, he argues that the modern novel is the key art form. All novels are melodramas; they cannot mirror totality as totality, as could ancient epic and tragedy. Characters in modern novels do not find social existence to be immediate or obvious; instead, they are withdrawn and reflective. Even the best of novels is limited to showing the lack of totality for what it is (Lukács 1972: 56). The novels of which Lukács most approves are ironic in structure: straightforward on the surface, with distance and critique provided by tried-and-true devices like indirect free discourse.

Used in this way, totality is a social-ontological category, predicated of individuals and whole societies. But there is a second way that the concept of totality figures in Lukács, i.e., as a methodological desideratum. The social philosopher, even (or especially) when encountering a society that lacks "totality" in the ontological sense, should view the society under the ideal of totality. This means two things. First, the social philosopher must not take for granted the segmentation of the parts of society accepted by that society. An alienated society will falsely silo phenomena in order to preserve itself as alienated. The social philosopher instead must treat all the parts of a society as thoroughly connected and reciprocating. At times, Lukács suggests something even stronger, i.e., that *any* part of a society is essential to the whole of it. The take-away is that the social scientist or philosopher must keep an eye out even for what might at first seem to be an unremarkable interconnection as crucial for the social whole. The thought might be taken to Leibnizian extremes: each part expresses the whole and, in virtue of that, all the other parts. A change in one ripples through all the others. But such methodological flourishes do not carry one very far into what makes Lukács's conception of totality distinctive and appealing to critical theorists. Anyone of a Hegelian bent will insist on both these points.

The duo of reification and totality provide a key premise for Horkheimer and Adorno's account of what they call the "culture industry." The form that cultural products must take is highly generic, commodity-like, although they must not seem so to their consumers.

BENJAMIN

Walter Benjamin, a friend and intellectual mentor to Adorno, was formally never a member of the Institute but received funding from it for some of his projects. His writings are dense, elusive, and highly original. Of first importance to *DE* are his accounts of what concepts are, how they behave in complexes, and what overall interpretative regimen is proper when investigating them philosophically. Benjamin's views on these matters provide Horkheimer and Adorno with a vehicle for loosening Hegelian conceptions of dialectical reason. Benjamin was no Hegelian, and it is not immediately clear that splicing Hegel's and Benjamin's conceptions of dialectic will work, but those are questions we leave to the side.

We have already encountered what by modern lights is a non-standard theory of what a concept is: Hegel's view that a concept is a sequential process of overcoming opposition. The ordinary modern philosophical view of concepts is that they are either representations or rules that order otherwise disparate items in terms of what they share. The concept "Bernese Mountain Dog" picks out, from among the many individuals, standard features in terms of which they may be grouped in that breed of dog. There are many general properties such dogs may have that are made irrelevant in such a procedure, depending on the concept that controls the sorting. But no matter how many properties one truly predicates of subjects, one will not arrive at what the subject is in its singularity. Properties are by definition generalizations; individuals are specific. Conceptualization is a matter of determination to the modern way of thinking, of bringing a case under a rule or law. How determining a concept needs to be in order to function in a given context is a matter of what the context demands. Mathematical concepts must be definitive; they must fix meaning rigorously. The same is true of concepts in sciences that deploy a great deal of mathematics to model and achieve results. Even the relatively inexact life sciences require a good deal of fixity from generalizing terms. But everyday speech is less demanding. One doesn't order lunch by means of definitions, axioms, and postulates.

That said, if one holds, as Horkheimer and Adorno do, that scientific modes of thinking set the bar for more ordinary modes in modernity, one might be concerned that concepts tend to reduce experience toward strict determination. And if one holds, as they also do, that commodification generally characterizes the way objects are experienced, so that they appear generic at base, then one might be concerned as well that concepts reduce phenomena toward the ever-same. You regard the knife you use for specific tasks in the kitchen by default as a commodity when you regard it as a representative of the brand of knife it is. Say it is a knife of Japanese origin, a luxury item. Even in the kitchen use of the knife you are in mind of its power to signify social status, which depends on its branding that, in turn, tokens conformity to a generalized way of life hinted at in advertisements. These concerns multiply when concepts, understood in this way, combine into large structures. Theories are hierarchies of concepts and laws, arranged in terms of their power to categorize. The more fundamental the concept or law, the more categorial.

Benjamin considers concepts to be grounded in a more basic form of cognition, which is fundamentally *reactive* and *expressive* (Benjamin 2004ff.: 2.720–27). Cognition initiates by having to situate oneself in a natural environment full of other entities and processes. The world does not simply fall under human control and cannot be assumed to easily submit to one. After all, entities and processes have their own powers, which may or may not be averse to one; one is but one among many. The natural human response to this primordial scene has two, interactive dimensions. One possible reaction is to minimize generalization in an attempt to meet the thing on its own ground. This cognition is immersive, a kind of mental camouflage, whereby one attempts to become "the same" as another thing. It is possible to think of this as identifying with the objects, but there is a caveat. This is creative in its way; it is not merely passive. And because humans are beings who are at base conceptual, such identification can never be complete; there will always be a residuum of considering the object as other than one and, thus, as a candidate for general thought. Note the subtle slide above in speaking of becoming "the same as" or "like" the object: Those are comparatives and involve generalization.

That brings one to the second possible reaction: one can try to make the object more like oneself. One does this through generalizing. One molds the experience of the other thing in terms of the categories with which one is outfitted, and, if one is successful, the other thing becomes predictable to that extent and its foreignness is overcome. Things become *objects*. If one builds out from there and deploys schemes or theories of ordered reactions of this sort, one has developed a powerful means to control nature.

Benjamin can seem to favor immersion over capture, but it is important to keep in mind that they are both creative and both means of control. Likewise, it is key to think of these reactions not as opposed to one another absolutely, but to exist on a continuum of response. There is no pure immersion, if one means by that a complete evacuation on the part of the subject of categorization, and there is no pure conception, if what one means by that is a complete overrunning of the impulse to merge with nature; they are always present together. The important thing from Benjamin's perspective is that the balance between them can be struck more in favor of one than the other. Here Benjamin is clearly on the side of immersion: Smoking hashish, Dada poetry, and surrealism are all attempts to beat back conceptual regimes in order to reveal more of the primordial relation of mind to nature. This entire primary process on the subject of negotiating nature is what Benjamin calls "mimesis." Mimesis is a concept that is extraordinarily important for Horkheimer and Adorno in *DE*, threading itself through almost every discussion, sometimes by name, sometimes implicitly. It is not going too far to say that Adorno's career is spent adjusting the implications of mimesis for critique.

There is an additional aspect of Benjamin's account of mimesis that is important to take into account for understanding *DE*: his idea of a "constellation" of thought. Here we shift from philosophy of mind to ontology. Benjamin is broadly speaking a nominalist. For him, things considered as they exist apart from human experience are unique beings. Humans cannot experience them as such – in all their singularity – but we can use approaching the condition of their singularity as a desideratum for thinking about them. When Horkheimer and Adorno deploy the Latin tag *hic et nunc* (here and now) (6–7/32), they allude to what European medieval philosophers called "haecceity": that in virtue of which this thing is this thing and no other. The cardinal mistake according to Benjamin is to regard the general as the essential. Generalization is conventional by its very nature, and ignoring the conventional element in any particular generalization is to treat that generalization ahistorically.

Given that we are bound to think of anything to some degree generally and, thus, in tension with its singularity, which admits of no generalization, how is it that we can get closer to the things themselves? Benjamin's answer cribs from Schlegel: we do so by modeling within our conceptuality what transcends it (cf. Benjamin 2004ff.: 1.116–200). Such modeling must be indirect. In Schlegel's case, this is done by irony and related strategies. In Benjamin, it is done by thinking of groups of concepts as constellations instead of as theories *in potentia* (see Benjamin 2019: 1–39). He is working with an extended analogy here. A constellation of stars is not a natural phenomenon. Stars have positions relative to one another in space. If by "position" one means physical distance from one another, then the position of stars to other stars is independent of the perspective from which they are viewed. But, if by "position" one means "place in a pattern," position is relative to vantage point, since pattern is. Constellations are patterns that are relative to point of view. If one were able to look at the sky from the position of Proxima Centauri b – the closest known exoplanet to Earth – there would be no Big Dipper, no Sagittarius, and no Orion. If one thinks of groupings of concepts that way, one keeps front and center that the things that they group in terms of likenesses and differences depend on which likenesses and differences are deemed salient. There are no strictly universal concepts, nor everlasting ones; none is a priori, all are a posteriori.

If one can register within a conceptual complex not only its own perspectival nature but also the additional truth (according to Benjamin) that there are potentially other groupings of the very same things, one could give such an indirect model of how things surpass any description in the very act of description. The idea that a group of concepts is a constellation, rather than a theory, helps because theories increase in power to the extent that they gain in scope and in conceptual closure. The idea of a constellation of concepts, by contrast, leaves the complex open to even radical reconfiguration. Benjamin seems to extend this idea to scientific theories as well as to philosophical, social scientific, and aesthetic theories. But it is more friendly to interpretative regimens than to explanatory ones. In any case, he deploys a concept he takes from theology to keep the theorist honest: *naming* (Benjamin 2004ff.: 1.62–74).

Benjamin's account of primordial names is the last of his troika of main concepts: mimesis-constellation-name. Benjamin is not here talking about common proper names like "Jules," "Jim," or "Saul." Those are words that purport to refer to single entities and, if Kripke is right, do so without descriptive content; they directly pick out individuals. To that extent they are not concepts; they do not operate to group individuals in terms of shared properties. Still, "Jim" is an ordinary name and can be used to refer to lots of different individuals. That is true even of an unusual name, for instance, "Methuselah." What Benjamin means by a name is what some philosophers call a logically proper name, a name that can be used to refer to one and only one entity. Such a name is like an ontological tag, and every entity has its own. He finds precedent for such names being ontologically primary in the Genesis account of creation.[3] Primordial names are godspeak, the language of the creator in its act of creating (calling forth entities) and perhaps of the first human language, gifted by the creator, which needs no general terms. Adam and Eve's language, then, does something no natural language can do: it expresses without any conceptual overlay exactly the way things are. In other words, it is completely and purely mimetic, at the furthest point on the immersive end of the register. This aboriginal language would not be a natural language in any standard sense, as it would consist solely of isolates. There would be no relations between terms, merely parataxis. Concepts are for Benjamin "fallen" names that have lost, over time and under social pressure, their power to immediately refer and have been forced into indirect, representational relations with things.[4]

Benjamin holds then that categorization is an important human capacity – to arrange the world in terms of types – but it is derivative of non-categorial thinking. If one wishes to think along with Benjamin's use of myth to make his point, postlapsarian humans have always been categorizers. Part of God's punishment for the rebellion in Eden is to fate humans to conceptualize, to have to approach creation through their cognitive limitation. Modern European life is awash in concepts, to the diminishment of the singularity of experience. At an extreme – and it is an extreme Benjamin holds is realized over and over again in modern culture – this can amount to a thought-prison.

THE IMMEDIATE CONTEXT: HORKHEIMER'S EARLY ESSAYS

Last, let's turn to work in early Critical Theory that led up to the main positions in *DE*. We must be selective, for there are very many essays from the 1930s by various members of the Institute that provide needed background. Horkheimer's essays prior to emigration to the United States form a reasonably integrated whole that stakes out distinctive positions on many of the philosophical and social scientific debates of the early twentieth century. A synopsis of Horkheimer's work from this period is, however, too complex a task for present purposes. It is best for us to look at the programmatic result of those essays, which is another essay (and Horkheimer's most famous), "Traditional and Critical Theory" (1937) (see also Horkheimer 1993: 1–14/1985a: 3.20–35).

Theories are human artifacts and, accordingly, are creatures of their times (Horkheimer 1995: 216–17/1977: 549–50). As such they are not to be spared social contextualization. A theory is critical if it is self-aware of this status. It must be bifocal; because its theoretical activities are themselves fully social acts, it must both study whatever social formation is in question *and* keep an eye out for the social context in which that study takes place (Horkheimer 1995: 229/ Horkheimer 1995: 561–2). This is what Horkheimer calls "developing an existential judgment with a historical dimension" (Horkheimer 1995: 238/ Horkheimer 1995: 570).

Traditional theory does not conceive of the theory-society relation in this way. It claims to represent the world as it is, i.e., independent of the representational medium. Critical theory makes no such assumption; it treats the structure of the world as dependent upon the means of representation. When discussing what makes a theory traditional, Horkheimer stresses the centrality of observation to physical theory and, by extension, to social and philosophical theories. By the lights of traditional theory, observation is the primary epistemic ingress to the world. That presupposes that the instruments of study do not change the nature of what they study. One advances hypotheses, crafted to extend a fund of knowledge already established, and tests them against facts, i.e., phenomena taken to be independent enough to prove or disprove the hypothesis. If verified (or not falsified) the results gained from the hypotheses join the fund, providing the basis for further hypotheses. The fund is never completely stable perhaps, but it is replete enough to support a deductive structure internal to the theory. The problems with traditional theory do not stem from its uses of inference: deductive, inductive, or abductive. Critical theory also makes use of all three (Horkheimer 1995: 226/ Horkheimer 1995: 558–9). The problem from Horkheimer's perspective is encapsulated in the phrase "knowledge already established." Although traditional theories may pay lip service to the historicity of theories, this is limited to pointing out the failings of prior theories, failures that do not call into question the social contexts in which those theories were developed, but rather have to do with the inadequacy of the theory by present lights. The thought that current theories express historically contingent social imperatives is missing (Horkheimer 1995: 194–95, 244/ Horkheimer 1995: 527).

Horkheimer's discussion of the conclusions to draw from the distinction between traditional and critical theories is not as perspicacious as one might like. He leaves open an important question of scope. What exercises him most is the idea that the social sciences are modeled on the physical sciences, a hot-button issue for neo-Kantians in the generation prior to the development of Critical Theory. There is an extra urgency in Horkheimer's formulation, not only because the Institute was engaged in empirical as well as "pure" theoretical work, but also because of what he saw as the continuing encroachment of reification, rationalization, and bureaucracy in general culture, science included (Horkheimer 1995: 228–9, 239/ Horkheimer 1995: 560–1, 571).

It is worth noting that insisting that social theories be critical and not traditional is compatible with saying that theories in the physical sciences are properly traditional. Or, to put it in a slightly different way, the distinction between traditional and critical theory operates within the domain of social theory alone; it does not touch on the physical or biological sciences. But Horkheimer can seem to slide into broader territory to challenge the very concept of observation operative in the sciences at large. Key here is the question of whether observation can be neutral. Horkheimer's claim seems at times to be that observation or, even more primary, perception is theory-laden – it involves unremarked upon theoretical commitments that affect data, in fact, affect the very idea in such theories of what a datum is (Horkheimer 1995: 37, 43/ Horkheimer 1995: 57–8, 63–4). This both prefigures a later debate in Anglo-American philosophy of science and rehearses an earlier discussion in German sources over the line to draw between the natural sciences, on the one hand, and human sciences, on the other.[5]

We won't discuss this aspect of Horkheimer's critique further, except to note that its payoff is mostly rhetorical. If he can sow doubt about the status of observation in the natural sciences, he can argue that they are not really the sort of role models that some social scientists take them to be. The empirical results of natural scientific theories are objective (Horkheimer 1995: 204–05/ Horkheimer 1995: 537), but that those results were sought out, that instruments were constructed to pursue them, and, most importantly, what those results mean for society in general are social scientific matters (Horkheimer 1995: 200–01/ Horkheimer 1995: 533–4) and involve a standing concern for totality (Horkheimer 1995: 25–7, 31, 206–07, 211/ Horkheimer 1995: 46–8, 51–2, 539–40, 543–4).

Traditional theory is, then, both reified and ideological (Horkheimer 1995: 194/ Horkheimer 1995: 527); therefore, it can have no independent and impartial vantage point on its status as a social product. It unreflectively takes itself to be exemplary because it is blind to its social character. The prominence of traditional theory in modern society is the result of balkanization of theoretical pursuits in general, which reflects advancing division of labor and the resulting alienation that is typical of capitalism. Traditional theories are inherently socially conservative (Horkheimer 1995: 210–11/Horkheimer 1995: 543–4). (It is an irony, then, that some members of the Vienna and Berlin circles of what Horkheimer, somewhat misleadingly, calls "positivism" were themselves communists.) A critical theory by contrast has a dialectical understanding of the innerworkings of societies and of social development, its eye trained not only on totality but also on how totalities can shift over time and circumstance. In particular, the tendency of modern totalities to support themselves ideologically – to hide their true totality under a false totality – should receive primary attention. But, unlike Hegelian dialectic or "vulgar" dialectical materialism, social formations will be treated as open-ended with regard to the future.[6] There is no strict dialectical necessity; that would be to try to fashion traditional theory out of Hegelianism, which would be a cardinal mistake. Gaps, repetitions, and equivocality are all possible, and that is what opens the door to a rapprochement with genealogy. Critical theory as well must be interdisciplinary: it comprises philosophy, sociology, anthropology, psychology, economics, political theory, history, and aesthetics. But it will be unlike contemporary calls for "interdisciplinarity" because each of the disciplines conjoined will itself be reformed critically. No critical theory could come from the mere conjunction of several traditional theories at work in related disciplines.

There is sometimes the worry – it is one of Habermas's complaints – that the position of *DE*, or of early Critical Theory more generally, supports no positive, progressive direction. That is true, but is it a good objection? Adorno especially might counter with these lines from Eugenio Montale's poem "Do Not Ask for the Word" ("Non chiederci la parola"): "This, today, is all that we can tell you / that which we are *not*, that which we do *not* want" [Codesto solo oggi possiamo dirti, / ciò che *non* siamo, ciò che *non* vogliamo]. To the extent that critique establishes what has not worked, so long as background conditions remain fairly consistent, it *has* established something going forward, namely what *not* to do. One might even argue that it is a category mistake to expect a dialectical investigation to be prognostic without importing a teleological vanishing point. Such an importation could only be non-dialectical, a mere assertion. Can philosophy be predictive if one does not model it on the explanatory sciences? Or do critics like Habermas fall back into traditional theory? We pick at this thread more intently at the close of this book.

FURTHER READING

Jay 1973 is still the best intellectual history of the Frankfurt School up to Habermas. Wiggershaus 1995 is also very good but can be a bit too meticulous for the non-specialist and is dismissive of Adorno. Held 1980 and Benhabib 1986 are philosophical introductions to the major figures. The first chapter in Rush 2004 provides a comprehensive and more technical overview of the conceptual roots of Critical Theory in the 1930s, focusing on Horkheimer, Marcuse, and Adorno. Scheuerman 1994 is excellent on the empirical side of early Critical Theory. Geuss 1981 is a concise, rigorous account of what makes Critical Theory critical. For those with German, Theunissen 1969 is a difficult but typically brilliant consideration of various aspects of Critical Theory.

For guidance with Hegel, Pinkard 1994 is a detailed study of what has come to be considered Hegel's main work, *Phenomenology of Spirit*. More comprehensive, and crucial to the reception history of Hegel in the anglophone world, is Taylor 1975, a bit dated now but still valuable. Beiser 2005 is also a good omnibus treatment. Pippin 1989 is the trendsetter for subsequent Hegel scholarship in English, but is an advanced study.

Wood 1981 is the best synoptic philosophical treatment of Marx. Elster 1985 is a very clear and to-the-point introductory text from the "analytical" Marxist perspective. Berlin 1978 is a classic in intellectual biography and worth looking into. Avineri 1968 can also be recommended.

Scholarly work in Nietzsche's thought is vast, uneven, and almost always polemical. It is difficult to recommend treatments that are balanced enough to benefit the newcomer. Kaufmann 2013 [1st ed. 1950] opened Nietzsche to serious philosophical consideration to anglophone audiences, and although no longer current scholarship, is still worth consulting. Schacht 1983 is reliable. Deleuze 1984 is of great interest but is subject to the author's own philosophical predilections. Nehamas 1985 is by some measure the most important book on Nietzsche since its publication but is demanding.

Wollheim 1971 and Lear 2005 are both excellent philosophical overviews of Freud's thought. Whitebook 1995 is the best source for the role of psychoanalysis in Critical Theory.

On Lukács, there are a few worthwhile collections of essays. Mészáros 1971 is especially good, and Parkinson 1970 and Heller 1983 are also worth consulting. Parkinson 1977 is a solid overview of Lukács's thought and Löwy 1979 a more specialized account of his philosophical development. Bernstein 1984 is a thorough assessment of Lukács's aesthetics, focusing on *Theory of the Novel*. Goldmann 1977 is something of a classic and has dated well.

Bendix 1977 is still the best introduction to Weber. Part 3 of Giddens 1971 also contains much of interest. For those with German, Köhnke 1986 is an excellent overview of the development of neo-Kantianism and Dahms 1998 valuable on the debate within and without Critical Theory on what counted as "positivism." On this, see also Adorno 1978. For the development of the Vienna School and its contribution to analytic philosophy in the United States, see the outstanding Coffa 1991.

Pensky 2001 provides a firm overview of Benjamin's thought, with special attention to his dissertation on the German Trauerspiel. Buck-Morss 1977 is strong especially on the subtle differences between Adorno and Benjamin, and Buck-Morss 1991 is likewise with regard to Benjamin's later thought. Stern 2019 is the best treatment of Benjamin's philosophy of language in its historical context.

Although a discussion of his very difficult thought was not practical in this overview, Bloch 2000 was a significant influence on early Critical Theory.

NOTES

1 The two dominant lines of Marxism at the time of the writing of *DE* track whether one gives precedence to the early or to the late Marx. Because several key documents from Marx's early period were not published until much later (or, if published, difficult to access), dialectical materialism, which views late Marx as official, first gained prominence. It stems from Engels and several dominant thinkers of the Second International. Dialectical materialism predicted the demise of capitalism as necessary and imminent according to

economic law. Workers were to have risen up and "proven" these facts by their deeds. This is to be contrasted with another approach to Marx that holds his later works to be canonical and relegates the early work to being merely Young Hegelian, that of Louis Althusser. Althusser held that Marxism was a science, that any science worth the name was not a matter of generalizing from empirical experience but one of introducing an "epistemological break" (*coupure épistémologique*) by means of a central organizing concept that, in advance, changed the kind of phenomena that could count as significant. See Althusser 2006. (He takes the concept of such a break from the idea of the scientific "obstacle" in Bachelard 2000). Althusser continually changed his mind concerning which concept marked the break but, all told, it seems to have been that of surplus value. The other main line of Marx reception, so-called "humanistic" Marxism, grew as an attempt to understand why capitalism persisted past such obituaries and was willing to reformulate Marxism in ways that could not help but be unorthodox to the dialectical materialist. Humanistic Marxism's chief concern was to investigate more than did the later Marx what one might call the libertarian aspects of socialism, i.e., the psychological, sociological, political, and philosophical role of individuals in revolution and counterrevolution. Marx's work prior to *Capital* is central to this approach.

2   In what follows, we limit discussion to Lukács's work prior to 1930. Lukács had an agile philosophical mind, which was put under pressure by various political changes in Hungary and the USSR. His work went through discrete stages: neo-Kantian, Hegelian, humanistic Marxist, and Marxist-Leninist. In his last period he was also for a time active in the Hungarian government and supported the failed rebellion of 1956. During this time, he renounced or radically recontextualized his earlier work. It is difficult to parse genuine from forced recanting. One might say that Lukács was a philosophical version of the composer Shostakovich in this regard, except that we do not have any private statement by Lukács like the String Quartets.

3   See Gen. 1: 3–27. There are complications. The Abrahamic God does create by saying, but the text leaves open whether God creates Adam by saying "Adam." Moreover, it is Adam, not God, who gives names "to all the cattle, and to the fowl of the air, and to every beast of the field"; all of which God creates *after* he creates Adam, and puts them before Adam in order that he, Adam, name them. Gen. 1: 19–20. There are of course exegeses to back every sort of position one might take on the meaning of this gnarly text. Perhaps the language that Adam uses is God's, shorn of its creative power. Perhaps the names Adam gives to the less wild creatures are conventional; God has already named them into being after all and seems to permit and then endorse Adam's naming of them. None of this needs to be settled to appreciate Benjamin's main point.

4   Benjamin is indebted here to a line of late-nineteenth and early-twentieth-century Jewish philosophy that attempts to marry Kant, German Romanticism, and German Idealism with negative theology. Martin Buber,

Gustav Landauer, Fritz Mauthner, Franz Rosenzweig, and Benjamin's close friend, Gershom Scholem, are representatives.

5 For the Anglo-American debate, see Hanson 1958, Kuhn 1962, and Feyerabend 1975. Hacking 1983 is the best synopsis of this line. It should be said that this more modern philosophy of science is concerned with scientific foundations to a degree that would be foreign to Horkheimer and Adorno. For someone like Kuhn science normalizes not because it stultifies, but because it becomes extraordinarily good at achieving results. Only when it loses apparent accuracy or predictive power due to new data will science turn to its theoretical foundations. That turn is something only a sociology of science can chart. For the German dispute over *Naturwissenschaften* versus *Geistes-/Kulturwissenschaften*, see Windelband 1919 and Rickert 1986a and 1986b. Dilthey 1991 and 1993 are also relevant.

6 The humanist Marxist charge that dialectical materialism is "vulgar" originates with Korsch 2013. Lukács adopts the phrase, and Adorno's *Minima Moralia* is peppered with it. What is vulgar about dialectical materialism according to humanistic Marxists is the idea that culture can be reduced to economic causes, i.e., that culture is epiphenomenal. It is less well known that "vulgar" was an epithet common in leftist political philosophy of the time. Plekhanov and Lenin both deployed it. Lenin used "vulgar socialism" to refer to Narodism (Lenin 1964: 6.261–8). For Plekhanov it referred to evolution-based historical theories (Plekhanov 1976: 3.140f.) Plekhanov does not have in mind here Darwin, but rather loose uses of the concept of evolution in sociology, e.g., Spencer.

2
THE DIALECTIC OF ENLIGHTENMENT

A common and persistent view of the *DE* has been that it aims to offer a devastating critique of enlightenment thinking or at least of its guiding and fundamental aspirations. Critics have surmised that by "enlightenment" Horkheimer and Adorno must have meant the European Enlightenment and, with it, the mentalities and commitments that emerged between, say, 1680 and 1800. This was the historical period in which an aspiring bourgeoisie came to replace the old aristocracy as the hegemonic social class, thereby bringing about a new, liberal order and a capitalist, technologically oriented society. To the extent that *DE* was read along these lines, it naturally became associated with *anti*-enlightenment thinking and, hence, with a rejection of many of the values that crucially animated modern European progressive movements. A recent exponent of this reading, Steven Pinker, thus declares the *DE* to be a book that "impugns science (together with reason and other Enlightenment values) for crimes that are as old as civilization, including racism, slavery, conquest, and genocide."[1] While Pinker focuses on commitments associated with open scientific inquiry, claiming that Horkheimer and Adorno are dismissive of those, a long tradition of conservative anti-Enlightenment thinkers – de Maistre et al. – have attacked ideals such as freedom, equality, and progress, arguing that they undermine social cohesion and, when combined with liberal individualism, the very possibility of leading a fulfilling life in an orderly society. If Horkheimer and Adorno criticize enlightenment ideals, and the European Enlightenment espoused those ideals, so the argument goes, Horkheimer and Adorno must be *against* the Enlightenment and all that it stood for. Being anti-Enlightenment is in some sense to be "anti-modern," even reactionary.[2] That is hardly a position that two neo-Marxist thinkers steeped in Kant-scholarship, modern music, and critical sociology would endorse.

Outside Germany, the anti-Enlightenment reading of *DE* was especially prevalent during the 1970s and 1980s. Perhaps because of the instinctive hostility among many of its then left-leaning readers toward the bourgeoisie, the historical agent of the Enlightenment, such a reading seemed to make sense. However, more recent interpretations have largely disconnected Horkheimer and Adorno's use of the concept of enlightenment from *the* Enlightenment considered as a historical epoch. It is now widely accepted that the book is not an anti-Enlightenment tract. What interests its authors are not the social and cultural developments in Europe between 1680 and 1800 that historians refer to by the terms "Enlightenment," "*Aufklärung*," or "*siècle des Lumières*," but, rather, a certain way of thinking which, while interwoven with actual historical forms, is best viewed as free-standing and present throughout the very history of mankind.

At least two considerations speak in favor of this broader interpretation of the authors' conception of the Enlightenment. First, in other writings both Horkheimer and Adorno characterize the Enlightenment as a period in history in quite positive terms, praising its commitment to science, freedom, reason, and secularization, and viewing it as an essentially progressive and liberating period.[3] In *DE* itself they admit that "freedom in society is inseparable from enlightenment thinking" (xvi/18). The Enlightenment period, they argue, harbors the tendencies they analyze and criticize; however, it is not reducible to them. A second reason to discard the narrow anti-Enlightenment interpretation is that *DE* is intent on exploring enlightenment as a fundamental commitment, ideal, or norm and hence as more general in scope than the particular tendencies and orientations historians typically ascribe to the historical period. While embedded and expressed in all sorts of activities, institutions, and practices throughout history, the enlightenment commitment can be individuated, defined, and itself be made the object of philosophical scrutiny.

The understanding of enlightenment as an ideal has a long and celebrated history in German letters. Leibniz, Lessing, Goethe, and Mendelssohn each formulated such ideals, and in his 1784 essay "An Answer to the Question: 'What is Enlightenment?'," Kant offered an influential and celebrated definition of the ideal: "*Enlightenment is man's emergence from his self-incurred immaturity*. […] The motto of enlightenment is therefore: *Sapere Aude*. Have courage to use your own understanding!"[4] To be enlightened is to apply this principle to oneself; it is to think for oneself and be disposed to do so, independent of prejudice, dogma, received opinion, or external authority. Kant distinguishes between "an age of enlightenment" (what he also calls "the century of Frederick," referring to the then-king of Prussia) and "an enlightened age." While we live, according to Kant, in an age of enlightenment, the ideal of being able to use one's own understanding confidently and well, without outside guidance, has not yet been fully implemented. An enlightened age is therefore outstanding, a historical goal yet to be achieved.

Given their consistent emphasis on the threat to autonomy in modern, highly organized societies, both Horkheimer and Adorno were deeply sympathetic with the spirit behind Kant's account of enlightenment as an ideal. They repeatedly emphasize that the very possibility of social critique – and hence of a Critical Theory – is predicated on the commitment to use one's own understanding to break through ideological obfuscation and dogmatic thinking. Absent enlightenment in this sense, or at least the ability to say "no," there can only be immaturity.

Yet Horkheimer and Adorno's formulation of the ideal is more Hegelian than Kantian. In his *Phenomenology of Spirit*, Hegel considers the form of consciousness "Enlightenment" to embody the norm "*Be for yourself* what you all are in yourself – *rational*."⁵ Kant conceives of the norm as expressive of pure practical reason, which as such has no inherently historical character. Hegel formulates a version of the same as unfolding dialectically in history. For Hegel, the injunction "be rational!" serves as an ideal for the worldview named "Enlightenment" – likewise not identical with the historical period of that name – the content of which is due to what Hegel takes to be the necessary series of attempts to think of the world in terms of that ideal. As the dialectic of Enlightenment (in Hegel's sense) unfolds, it turns out that the ideal is significantly empty: in its relentless call for abstraction, and in reason's criticism of everything given to it as subject to it, Enlightenment finds itself forever striving to hold on to a content that can never be made as determinate as it itself requires. Enlightenment's efforts to gain in integrity by sharply distinguishing itself from religious belief (the companion worldview that Hegel terms "Faith" [*Glaube*]) – the typical target of enlightenment criticism – must come to naught. Both Enlightenment and Faith are radically alienated from their designated objects of truth.

Horkheimer and Adorno do not adopt the precise details of Hegel's view, but in formulating their conception of enlightened thinking, they make use of some key Hegelian assumptions. First, they carry over from Hegel the stipulation that enlightenment, rather than a historical epoch or an abstract principle, is a *Weltanschauung*, i.e., a way of relating to oneself, others, and the world in terms of a reasonably cohesive set of background principles and practices, which permeate and define a way of life. Speaking loosely and in the vernacular of contemporary ethics, they display a meta-normative status, staking out what actions and self-interpretations one ought to see as valuable. As a matter of experience, such principles also form what phenomenologists would call a horizon of intelligibility within which particular human endeavors appear coherent and meaningful. To be initiated into enlightenment thinking is, then, to reach the point at which its totality of cognitive responses, evaluations, and interpretive schemes is taken for granted. They will not be questioned.

A second Hegelian assumption is that, in order to understand this *Weltanschauung* and its practical implications, it must be situated within a larger historical context that displays a fundamental human effort to achieve certain overarching goods. For Hegel that overarching human good is freedom. By searching for a way to liberate herself from the self-alienated world of European aristocracy, the proponent of Enlightenment understands a certain interpretation of reason to provide the road to freedom. If reason never accepts what is given merely as it is given but always keeps asking critical questions, always asking for more and better evidence, reason, so the stipulation goes, may take itself to be free.

Third and finally, Horkheimer and Adorno adopt Hegel's idea that enlightenment displays a characteristic dialectic and, as for Hegel, that dialectic reveals how the set of ideals defining the enlightenment harbors a contradiction and collapses ultimately into their opposite. "Myth is already enlightenment, and enlightenment reverts to mythology" (xviii/21).

Like Hegel, Horkheimer and Adorno are generally quite skeptical of the employment of definitions in philosophical texts. Philosophical concepts, Adorno argues in *Negative Dialectics*, attain meaning not through abstract stipulations but, rather, through their use in the overall unfolding of the text. It is the sum total of conceptual relations within which concepts are situated that determine how concepts should be understood; definitions as such create abstractions that prove incapable of engaging with the concrete historical reality that philosophy, on their view, purports to grasp.

Bearing that in mind, *DE* specifies enlightenment thinking as follows: "Enlightenment thinking, understood in the widest sense as the advance of thought, has always aimed at liberating human beings from fear and installing them as masters" (1/25). What is generally feared and what one must master is nature; *enlightenment is the process of humankind's liberation from nature* or, more specifically, *from the experience of adversity that characterizes our relationship to nature*.

On this view, and with the emphasis on the overriding goal of "being installed as masters," enlightenment immediately takes the form of a *project* – not just any project, but one that is fundamental to a comprehension of human history. We are here far removed from any traditional reconstruction of the period of the Enlightenment or from the mere formulation of a social desideratum. Horkheimer and Adorno treat enlightenment as an anthropological process in terms of which history develops. Enlightenment is the engine of progress, the ongoing effort to distance oneself from nature and establish mastery over it. Enlightenment's ultimate aim is domination (*Herrschaft*), the transformation of nature from sublimity to subservience. Power will be a crucial notion in this account. Thus does Nietzsche join Hegel.

Consider Genesis 1:26 in which God, after creating man, decrees, "let them have dominion over the fish of the sea, and over the fowl of the air, and over the cattle, and over all the earth, and over every creeping thing that creepeth upon the earth." A similar thought, one might say. Yet in Horkheimer and Adorno's account, there is, beyond the consolidation of dominance, no ultimate purpose or intention *behind* the process of enlightenment's unfolding – no authorizing gesture or guarantee. Rather than a well-meaning God vouching for the separation from nature, the starting point and driver is *fear*, a feeling of being overwhelmed by nature, both within and without oneself, i.e., a fear of heteronomy.

The fact that enlightenment thinking responds so directly to fear (of sickness, suffering, weakness, death, etc., all the ways in which nature underwrites our finitude) – compensates for it – suggests that Horkheimer and Adorno's conception of nature carries very distinct and dramatic implications. Compared to Marcuse, for example, who in *Eros and Civilization* and elsewhere formulated a philosophy of liberation that directly associated emancipatory potential with nature, *DE* sees in nature a threat to human subjectivity – at least to the extent that nature is a source of hunger, pain, etc. As the Other of enlightened mastery, nature threatens to overwhelm whatever attempts there may be to distance, render intelligible, predict, and control. Thus, at the end of a process of enlightenment – the late modernity of our time – nature is pacified or dominated by technology and industry and, thereby, forgotten, repressed, or destroyed. In *Aesthetic Theory*, Adorno proposes that nature nowadays can be experienced mainly as ravaged by industrial capitalism; its appearance has "graduated" from being, in its early phase of being mastered, beautiful to, in the late phase of mastery, being ugly.[6]

Nature in its unsubjugated form is a domain that stands opposed to enlightenment thinking. The prospect of controlling it may promise a release from domination and, thereby, what Horkheimer and Adorno think of as happiness. The claim has the ring of paradox. Only those who have managed to establish sufficient distance from nature can truly appreciate its beauty and the happiness it promises.[7] However, that very distance precludes the promise from ever being kept; it can only appear as *Schein*, an illusion oblique to reality.[8] In Adorno's aesthetics, moments of such illusory (*scheinhafte*) exposures to nature are rare yet are potentially cognitively and ethically transformative. Beauty pauses, as it were, the history of domination to offer a glimpse of the utopian and transcendent. In that sense beauties count as metaphysical remembrances of nature. Schopenhauer is in view.

This conception of nature includes not only external but internal nature as well: psychic drives and libidinal forces. The fear of nature on which the process of enlightenment is predicated includes our inner nature and, in particular, the archaic dimensions of the human psyche that Freud identified. Mastery of nature in general would not be possible unless instincts could be repressed, a stable ego established, and respect for reality necessary for observation and theorizing be made to triumph over the raw immediacy of desire.

Enlightenment thus targets ourselves – it is a work of ourselves on ourselves – just as much as it targets, and transforms, the external world. In their reading of Homer's *Odyssey*, which will be examined in the next chapter, the complementarity of internal and external domination becomes a central topic. For now, it should be noted that any significant regression beyond the external nature we can know – the nature which we find ourselves controlling – is only available to us as semblance (*Schein*), in unguarded aesthetic moments. By the same token, any return to the internal nature we can know would in reality be impossible. Such a return would involve nothing less than a complete restructuring of the human psyche. It would be utopian in the strict sense of the word: a no-place.

Unlike Kant, who interprets enlightenment thinking in terms of the exercise of autonomy – which in his view requires transcendental freedom, the capacity to act and think spontaneously by determining oneself in the light of self-chosen a priori principles – Horkheimer and Adorno take a predominantly naturalist view of human capacities. Enlightenment liberates; however, the act of liberation is itself a response to the pressures placed on humans by nature, generated ultimately by the natural need for self-preservation. Consequently, the means of domination necessary for liberation must themselves be viewed as mere instruments, tailored to secure survival yet without any serious claim to universality.

Yet Horkheimer and Adorno are not reductive naturalists. Their naturalism is more akin to that of Darwin, Nietzsche, or Dewey; there is continuity between nature and subjectivity. Our rational capacities depend upon our biological makeup and are accounted for in functional terms. Here is one formulation:

> Precisely by virtue of its irresistible logic, thought, in whose compulsive mechanism nature is reflected and perpetuated, also reflects itself as a nature oblivious of itself, as a mechanism of compulsion. Of course, mental representation is only an instrument. In thought, human beings distance themselves from nature in order to arrange it in such a way that it can be mastered. Like the material tool which, as a thing, is held fast as that thing in different situations and thereby separates the world, as something chaotic, multiple, and disparate, from that which is known, single, and identical, so the concept is the idea-tool [*ideelle Werkzeug*] which fits into things at the very point from which one can take hold of them.
>
> (31/62–3)

Absent additional explanation, this might seem like an untenable view of mind and thought. If thought were *wholly* under the sway of nature (including a reified social world) considered as a "compulsive mechanism," i.e., as a causal order, then reasoning and critique would become extraordinarily difficult to account for. The imagery suggests a machine or zombie, incapable of responding rationally, imaginatively, or creatively to the world. Even if the imagery holds some plausibility when looking at the uncritical mass behavior that Horkheimer and Adorno find so prevalent in late modernity – that of individuals being pushed around by social forces over which they exert no control – it runs into serious philosophical difficulties if understood more broadly. Human beings, one might argue, act on norms. In light of evidence and standards of epistemic assessment, we commit ourselves to the truth or falsity of propositions – and that commitment is an act that cannot be viewed simply as caused by a "mechanism of compulsion." Genuinely holding a proposition to be true or false is not something that can be wrung out of us. We do that when weighing what the reasons tell us we *ought* to commit ourselves to. As Wilfred Sellars writes, we place an episode or a state "in the logical space of reasons, of justifying and being able to justify what one says."[9]

In his later writings, Adorno forwards a less stark view of thought. In *Negative Dialectics*, for example, while he continues to emphasize the functionality of thought, he also argues that the genesis of reason has created for thought a relative autonomy, thereby removing it from immediate subjugation to natural constraints.[10] A question remains, however, as to whether relative autonomy of this sort is real or just an illusion generated by our concern, due to the instinct for self-preservation, to see ourselves as independent of nature. In any event, Adorno's preoccupation in that work with what he calls "identity thinking" – with how thinking, especially in modernity, detaches itself from the task of being responsive to experience in order to secure a space of pure ideality governed by strict norms of universality and generality – seems open to some degree of autonomous rational activity and self-determination. The emphasis, however, continues to be on constraint and necessity, whether natural or social. Adorno's subject enjoys none of the freedom or spontaneity that became the hallmark of philosophical conceptions of the self in Kant and German Idealism.

MYTH

From what has been said so far it should be evident that the liberation promised by enlightenment thinking comes at a price.

As we have seen, one of the leading ideas in *DE* is precisely that enlightenment – and in particular the freedom that comes with it – reverts to necessity and heteronomy. While constituting the baseline for human progress and, thereby, offering the promise of freedom and happiness, enlightenment also contains a regressive, if not tragic, element, one that taints human history and challenges the optimism of canonical philosophies of history, most pointedly Hegel's. Not only does enlightenment *contain* such a regressive element, enlightenment is also in and of itself *reversible*. Its progressive and regressive elements, enlightenment and its opposite, can in some cases ultimately be indistinguishable.

The idea that enlightenment can be regressive (and only regressive if progressive), which the authors mine from Benjamin's essay "On the Concept of History," is, to say the least, counterintuitive. How can freedom and liberation involve being subjected to compulsion? How can something that counts as progress at the same time count as regress? In order to get a grip on this idea, it is necessary to examine Horkheimer and Adorno's conception of myth and their idea of the interdependency of it and enlightenment.

Nineteenth- and early twentieth-century accounts of the relationship between myth and enlightenment argued for a linear and largely irreversible movement from myth to enlightenment. For example, numerous recountings of the cultural history of ancient Greece would start with the world of myth, expressed in the Homeric epics, Hesiod, and the early tragedies, and, culminating with the emergence of philosophy in Xenophanes, Heraclitus, and the Eleatics up through Plato and Aristotle, trace the increasing rationalization of the mythical worldview. Myth is typically staged as concrete, static, and irrational, enlightenment as abstract, dynamic, and rational. Enlightenment liberates the mind from its erstwhile subjection to projected natural powers; it sets people free to think and act autonomously. On a grand scale, Hegel's philosophy presents just such a reassuring history of "Spirit" (*Geist*). In its world-historical development, Spirit overcomes all forms of self-inflicted dependence and achieves free and fundamentally complete self-actualization. The story is old, flattering, and was left unchallenged pretty much until Nietzsche, Benjamin, and the authors of *DE* started to question it.

In the Preface to *DE*, Horkheimer and Adorno claim that the enlightenment "relapse(s) into mythology" (xvi/18). Joined with the comment already cited that "[m]yth is already enlightenment, and enlightenment reverts to mythology," this is a frontal attack on the linear "from myth to enlightenment" narrative. Yet what exactly do they mean by "myth"? How can myth be a form of enlightenment and at the same time something to which enlightenment reverts?

On a first reading, it is difficult to get a firm grip on Horkheimer and Adorno's concept of myth. Throughout the first chapter of *DE*, they offer several characterizations of myth – some they ascribe to the Enlightenment (i.e., the historical epoch) and others evidently represent their own views. The Enlightenment took the view that myth (understood, for example, as superstition or silly stories) was the adversary that had to be overcome. Enlightenment thinking interprets the mythical worldview as based on fantasy and superstition, "the projection of subjective properties onto nature" (4/28–9). Moreover – and this is how our authors start chiseling out their own view – myths operate within an enchanted world, a world of spirits and forces endowed with inscrutable intentions.[11] This is an animistic world. Opposed to enlightenment, which sees death as the default position, informed as it is by natural science, the mythical mind assumes the existence of life in every thing and every process. Horkheimer and Adorno's preferred term for the spiritual nature of things in the world of myth is *mana*; and mana, they claim, constitutes the object's "aura," a concept that they adopt from Benjamin.[12]

The principal meaning of the Greek noun *mythos* is "a telling," and how a myth tells is central to mythic thinking. Myths narrate events of particular significance for a community. These include: the founding of the community in some immemorial past; actions relevant not only to the founding but to the ultimate fate of the community, undertaken by gods and demons; and the role of near-supernatural humans (heroes, sorcerers, priests, prophets) in establishing and maintaining an acceptable and productive relationship to the divine. The social function of the telling is not just to narrate an interesting story; it is to embed and re-embed the community in its roots. The telling, that is, is ritualistic.

According to Horkheimer and Adorno, myth achieves a qualified distance between human beings and the powers of nature;

it is in this regard that myths are "already enlightenment." For myths are meaning-making devices. While largely pictorial and lacking in complex reflective structure, myths do "narrate, record, explain" (5/30). As Hans Blumenberg would later also emphasize, something as simple as naming contains an element of enlightenment, an idea we have seen that idea at work in Benjamin as well.[13] Once a phenomenon receives a name, that name can be communicated to others and deposited in memory to be drawn on later. The name pins down, determines, what is otherwise unwieldy, heterogenous, and threatening, giving it an identity. As an example of this process of minimal rationalization, Horkheimer and Adorno point to how, in the development of ancient Greek culture, local spirits and demons were first identified with places and then with the elements generally – sea, sky, earth, and water. The Olympian gods, in turn, no longer were themselves the powers or the elements; instead, they *represented* powers and elements. Knowing that an order exists, and that both gods and men have designated places within it, creates a sense of acquaintance and belonging and, on that basis, a space in which to act meaningfully.

Myths thereby liberate us from fear and, in so doing, create the necessary conditions for generating further comprehension and meaning. That is the progressive dimension of myth. However, as Horkheimer and Adorno also point out, myths are fundamentally inert: their structural form is repetition. Two thoughts motivate this claim. First, the mythical worldview remains in thrall to a conception of the world as ultimately static, bound to repeat itself in accordance with a fixed pattern that reflects the divinely sanctioned order of the universe. To understand such a world is ultimately to understand that pattern and, in particular, to understand it as repeated for all time. This is why the notion of fate is so central to the mythical worldview. Whatever happens because of fate happens inevitably, out of intrinsic necessity, and outside any possible human intervention. The second motivating thought concerns how humans existing within such a dispensation represent themselves as incapable of reflection and as unfree. What has authority is the absolute past, "absolute" because the past will be the present and the future and always has been for as long as time has and will structure the world. While it is open for humans to understand and act with effect within the horizon disclosed by myth, we are powerless to change any of its fundamentals: "The postulation of the single past event endows the cycle with a quality of inevitability, and the terror radiating from the ancient event spreads over the whole process as its mere repetition" (21/50).

Rituals externalize the mythical urge to repeat, thereby enacting mythical content. They instruct by instantiation that myth has an insurmountable hold over the community. Rituals are precisely *not* supposed to change in form or content; the very idea of innovation is incomprehensible to the mythical worldview. In some cases, however, rituals do permit instrumentalization. According to Horkheimer and Adorno magic and sacrifice are not merely enactments of myth and acts of obeisance; they can also be means to obtain ends set independently of religious belief. Although steeped in the authority of ritual, both magic and sacrifice foreshadow a more objectifying attitude toward what is thought to be fundamental about the world.

This emphasis on myth as involving repetition was central to the early Adorno's philosophical essays and especially to his habilitation thesis on Kierkegaard. It is also an important concept in Benjamin's literary criticism, which profoundly influenced both Adorno's thesis and his philosophical conception more generally. For Benjamin, myth signifies an order of immanence, characteristic not only of pagan religious systems but of life in general, governed by a network of domination and misfortune. As the "always-the-same" (*das Immergleiche*) of "empty time" – time as a mere medium for repetition – myth forms the basis for his interpretation of Marx's notion of prehistory (*Vorgeschichte*). On Marx's account, history is nonetheless prehistorical when the tensions, suffering, and irrationality of class division keep returning as if a natural process. This idea also informs Adorno's conception of natural history (*Naturgeschichte*), the reification of nature as abstract, meaningless, and foreign.

ENLIGHTENMENT, CONCEPTS, AND LANGUAGE

In *DE*, then, myth both liberates and returns humans to the never-changing natural processes to which they are habituated.

Myth explains and generates intelligibility yet does so by invoking a regularity whose authority is represented as oblivious to reflection and, therefore, to critique.

One might think that enlightenment is therefore substantially and even essentially different from myth. Enlightenment is by definition a liberation from hearsay about the powers of nature. It conceives of human agency as controlling, indeed dominating nature. That is what modern subjects are for enlightenment, not subject to nature but only to themselves as free rational agents. How, then, can enlightenment revert to myth? In order to make good on such a claim, Horkheimer and Adorno must show that even enlightenment is fundamentally repetitive, that the overwhelming subjection to fate and the "mindlessness" that characterizes mythical thought must be central to enlightenment thought as well. It is important to appreciate just how provocative such a claim is. The idea lies at the heart of what this book is about, and for the book to make sense, the idea must be taken seriously. For those who cannot accept it, the overarching conceptual framework of *DE* has little to offer. Again: Is not all human progress in some sense predicated on enlightenment and enlightenment thinking? How can the liberation *from* nature return individuals *to* nature?

Horkheimer and Adorno offer their response by way of formulating a genealogical account of rationalization. Unsurprisingly, given that it is supposed to elucidate and perhaps even explain the nature of progress, the process of civilization, *and* enlightenment in the widest sense of humankind's liberation from nature, the account has several parts and can easily appear sprawling and disjointed. As many commentators have noted, the understanding of rationalization draws quite extensively on Weber's theory of the same, extending the conceptions of purposive rational action and disenchantment, which for Weber are defining marks of modernity, to history as a whole. However, it also carries forward ideas from Nietzsche's *Genealogy of Morality*, especially with regard to the constitution of inner mental spaces structured around guilt and repression. Yet the details of Horkheimer and Adorno's narrative are entirely their own.

In its original, "pure" state, the mythical mind sees itself as merged with nature and as wholly dispossessed. A sovereign authority – expressed in *mana* and articulated in religious cultic ritual – ties members of communities to each other and to the animistic natural world. Ritual, costume, dance, and adornments create an experience of kinship with things. At this point in the development of human actions with regard to nature, there was no substitution of like for like: "the rites of the shaman were directed at the wind, the rain, the snake outside or the demon inside the sick person, not at materials or specimens" (6/31). What Horkheimer and Adorno call "the sanctity of the *hic et nunc*" (6/32) is respected. The immediate present is all and categorical thought merely latent, a regime of numinous singularity in which no two things are exchangeable.

The sanctity of the *hic et nunc* plays a crucial role in Horkheimer and Adorno's reflections on knowledge in that it recognizes and respects the uniqueness of each thing and experience. Although classification must be considered a condition of knowledge and concepts are needed in order to make judgments, the *ideal* of knowledge is tied to sustaining at least in part a non-subsumptive relationship with the thing in its uniqueness. The respect for and recognition of the uniqueness of each and every thing is largely a matter of nurturing a non-discursive relation to the world: mimesis.

Adorno returns to the concept of mimesis in several of his key later works; despite this, definitions of this concept are few and far between. In *Negative Dialectics*, the mimetic element is characterized as an "elective affinity" (*Wahlverwandtschaft*) between the knower and the known.[14] In *Aesthetic Theory*, Adorno presents it as a "nonconceptual affinity of the subjectively produced with its unposited other."[15] *DE* glosses mimesis as

> a tendency deeply inherent in living things, the overcoming of which is the mark of all development: the tendency to lose oneself in one's surroundings instead of actively engaging with them, the inclination to let oneself go, to lapse back into nature.
>
> (189/258–9)

Benjamin supplies the common thread. In mimesis the subject assimilates itself to what it takes to be opposed to it, its Other (think of a chameleon's skin altering to blend into surrounding foliage). Such activity responds to the Other in terms set by the Other and is, accordingly, receptive to the Other without intervening classification. While the subject respects the otherness of the thing, its difference from itself, it does not strive to create any distance. Instead, it lets the thing "express itself" freely.

Note that the notion of mimesis complements that of *mana*. Mimetic cognition responds to the world also as though each and every thing is alive. Imbued with power, it is a world which myths, rites, and customs mirror and consciously or unconsciously represent. While modern agents think of themselves as encountering the world in terms of objective categories that are the result of dispassionate observation and assessment, the mimetic response displays a profoundly evaluative character, taking directly from the engagement with the Other. Each tree, rock, or field requires solicitous regard from whomever experiences it. In Horkheimer and Adorno's vision of archaic existence, to know the world is to know prereflectively how to respond to it in its own terms.

At some point, however, more division and separation occur. The shaman becomes a technician endowed with a special ability to move between the living and the dead; the magician identifies ends to be pursued, using mimetic action as a means to secure them; the priest specializes in performing sacrifices. In all three cases, naming becomes important, as well as substitution of meanings. Note that these names are now *not* Benjamin's Adamic names; these are "fallen" names, mere denotations. If a hind is going to be offered up for one's daughter, or a lamb for one's son, then the receiving power must be able to appreciate the sacrificial gift as such and in its uniqueness (6/16).[16] *Only* the offering of Iphigenia appeases the wrath of Artemis. *Only* the sacrifice of Isaac answers Yahweh's command. Nature or the gods require *specific* thoughts and actions from us.

Yet, as Horkheimer and Adorno point out, the very idea of substitution presupposes an appeal to the *genus*, that which can represent other entities, allowing for the exchange. Iphigenia is giving her life *so that* the conditions are met for Agamemnon's troops to set sail *in order that* his honor is preserved in the battle for Troy. Rather than a royal life of unconditional worth, she becomes fungible, a means – endowed with something like an exchange value – to obtain an end. Her life is, to put it flatly, traded away. What was supposed to be unique and specific is, in fact, a token exchanged for a result.

As already mentioned, naming creates distance and narrative mastery. Its ideal of singular reference suggests a respect for the object as unique, but also transient. As the name gets repeated, it starts to function as a concept. You see your new friend Jim today and say "hi Jim," and do the same thing tomorrow and next week. A name is such that it can pick out its referent in an indefinite number of new contexts, allowing generality and creating unity among uses of the name. According to Horkheimer and Adorno, discursivity, the ability to think, is fundamentally dependent on abstraction. While concepts are able to refer to particular entities, they do so by sorting them according to what they share with others of their kind, i.e., by category. When it is conceptualized, the sensuous thing of which one is aware becomes intelligible via the application of abstract content. The unequal becomes equal. Everything becomes repeatable.

Conceptualization made possible by abstraction affords the cognitive distance required for observation. Rather than being exposed to the threatening immediacy of teeming, undifferentiated nature, agents are able to impose order by detecting identities and differences among the things they encounter. And armed with a sense of order, humans can act more systematically. Objects can be manipulated in accordance with principles and procedures that have increased scope, and domination over nature intensifies on that count. In fact, thinking in terms of identities as between things rests on domination:

> The generality of the ideas developed by discursive logic, power in the sphere of the concept, is built on the foundation of power in reality. The superseding of the old diffuse notions of the magical heritage by conceptual unity expresses a condition of life defined by the freeborn citizen and articulated by command.

(10/36)

This is of course somewhat speculative, and Horkheimer and Adorno do not offer a very original account of this early stage of reasoning. They gesture broadly to the transition from a Paleolithic to a Neolithic social order, from what they call "nomadism" to a world of "fixed property." The introduction of agriculture and domesticated animals – and with that property, centralized authority, and social stratification – marks this transformation. Societies become more hierarchical, and rulers and ruled, power and labor, diverge. This was all quite standard fare even in Horkheimer and Adorno's time.

As a general theory of concepts, however, Horkheimer and Adorno's view may seem problematic, resting as it does on an appeal to abstraction and something akin to essences (albeit constructed ones). Essences, Wittgenstein argued, are neither necessary nor sufficient for determining the correct application of a concept. They are not necessary because correct application does not require the presence of an essence before the mind. And they are not sufficient because the essence itself, which is general, cannot specify how correct application should take place in individual cases. If, rather than appealing to abstraction and essence, language is viewed as something that speakers *use* so that practice becomes more crucial than knowledge in accounting for conceptual mastery, then Horkheimer and Adorno would have to restrict their conception of identity thinking to contexts in which concepts are used in *overly* subsumptive ways. They would have to distinguish language as a vehicle for identity thinking from language as a vehicle of meaning-making and communication and, in so doing, they would have to sacrifice at least some of what they take to be the diagnostic scope and power of the idea of identity thinking.

Since Horkheimer and Adorno do not draw this distinction in the *DE*, they risk – like the *Lebensphilosophie* of their own generation represented by Klages and Spengler – having to condemn or at least be skeptical of all conceptual thinking. While pragmatically useful in constituting order and continuity in nature, concepts are without genuine reference, locked inside what Fredric Jameson once called "the prison-house of language."[17]

Much ink has been spilt on this particular worry. Albrecht Wellmer and Habermas have accused Horkheimer and Adorno of harboring an irrational stance – of being more Nietzschean than

Hegelian. When considering this issue, however, it is worth noting that a majority of the contexts in which Horkheimer and Adorno discuss language in *DE* focus on how the drive for power and domination motivates agents to use language in an identifying, subsumptive, merely classifying manner. Obviously, since in their worldview power and domination are ubiquitous, there can be few or perhaps no contexts in which language is used exclusively for benign, cooperative purposes. Nevertheless, the inherently implausible idea that language is mainly a tool of domination would, if we adopt a more nuanced reading of their philosophy of language, become less central or apply exclusively in contexts of overt or demonstrable uses of power, and, therefore, less damaging to their overall view. It would also allow more consistently for a view of conceptual thinking as crucial to reflection and critique – and this is precisely the view that Adorno ends up espousing.

There is, however, no easy escape from the reifying effects of conceptuality in our authors' view. Conducting a form of "self-critique" of the concept, while also realizing that this critique is done conceptually, becomes a central part of especially Adorno's endeavor in *Negative Dialectics*.

ENLIGHTENMENT, RATIONALIZATION, AND CULTURE

DE tells a multifaceted story of rationalization. We just saw that the primary vehicle of identity thinking – conceptual determination via reduction – plays a crucial role. Yet the emergence of cultural forms, including philosophy and science, testify to the consolidation and importance of identity thinking as the supreme form of meaning-making in the Western tradition: Pre-Socratic cosmologies conceptualized "the positions which had once been occupied by Ocnus and Persephone, Ariadne and Nereus" (3/28). Images of generation from water and earth, familiar from archaic cyclical visions of nature, became in time hylozoic elements that ultimately would be interpreted as "the pure form of ontological entities" (3/28). The gods of the Olympus "were finally assimilated by the philosophical logos as the Platonic forms" (3/28). Leaving behind anthropomorphism the early philosophers formulated accounts of extreme generality, geared to convey a sense of cosmic unity. In the classical period Plato and Aristotle rationalized the mythical worldview to an extraordinary degree; however, they retained, so Horkheimer and Adorno argue, traces of the mythical conception of unruly power in their own accounts of matter (*hylē*). Take Aristotle. For him there are immanent powers and properties in things; as their principle of change, *energeia* is the end toward which natural processes are directed.

With Francis Bacon and the modern rise of the scientific method, this view is called into question. Knowledge in classical Greek philosophy is grounded in the noetic grasp of essence, itself based on an appeal to mimesis, of the mind making itself adequate to forms of reality. In sixteenth-century Europe, a conception of knowledge emerges in which *power* is the key explanatory factor. According to Bacon, power not only results from knowledge, knowledge *is* power. Experimental science obtains its predictive knowledge from acts of manipulation; rather than attempting to disclose essence by means of sheer insight, the natural scientist intervenes experimentally in nature, with the sole aim of disclosing causal laws, thereby allowing for further interventions and, with them, manipulation. The value of scientific concepts and theories on such a view is determined not by whether they are true, i.e., correspond to reality, but by the extent to which they are useful, i.e., support prediction. The connection with human wisdom that was central to archaic myth and classical Greek metaphysics is lost, "forgotten." Science strips away the qualitative in favor of the quantitative, dealing only with what can be expressed in mathematical form. Abstraction becomes total and totalizing; events are now at their core "calculable." Moreover, these laws form the basis for technology and its indicative form of rationality. The ultimate purpose of modern science is no longer merely to understand but, rather, to increase and enhance human dominion over nature. Discovery and invention are but two sides of the same coin.

The idealization of nature intrinsic to mathematization makes human orientation – ethically, cognitively, even existentially – difficult. While resting on value commitments, natural science is silent about questions of value. In the scientifically understood universe value can only be a subjective projection that expresses human desires, preferences, and aspirations.

To be sure, science must be granted its self-constituted domain of truth, in which objectification, generalized explanation, prediction, and control reign supreme. But detaching so radically from human life thins out the experience both of subject and object. The subject is no longer situated as an evaluative agent embedded in concrete social and historical contexts and able to act on non-instrumental conceptions of the good. Rather, she appears as an incorporeal and detached capacity for procedural, subsumptive thinking. The object of experience, mathematized nature, becomes intelligible only in terms of its most abstract qualities, and everything that falls outside its scope – the "incommensurable" – is left opaque and potentially incomprehensible.

Horkheimer and Adorno point to Kant's Transcendental Idealism (as they understand it) as an expression of this process. According to Kant, human knowledge is in principle able to comprehend all of nature due to nature's dependency on formal a priori features of mind. Humans will never know everything, but we can know anything (except things-in-themselves, but they are not cognitively accessible, thus, not natural). In stark contrast with classical epistemic paradigms that pertain to the real, for Kant nature is the sum total of appearances, i.e., what can stand under natural (viz. scientific) law. Horkheimer and Adorno especially target an interpretation of Kant associated with the Marburg School of Neo-Kantianism, whose architect was Hermann Cohen and whose adherents included Paul Natorp and Ernst Cassirer. On this interpretation Kant's account of human experience can be reduced to his account of scientific experience. The reduction of nature to whatever might be an object of science renders qualitative experiences arbitrary. The Kantian natural world of mathematized facts undercuts giving a plausible account of human subjectivity. As readers of Kant will know, the subject is for him in the final instance simply the immutable, formal, and entirely self-identical ego-point – the transcendental "I think" which must be able to accompany any representation. How the subject may be situated more concretely and with more content became a puzzle that subsequent thinkers, including Hegel, struggled with and tried to piece together.

Kant makes an appeal to a noumenal world, opposed to the order of appearance, in an attempt to account for how the subject is able to determine itself freely according to laws that satisfy "pure" (i.e., non-empirical) rational constraints. Yet interaction between the noumenal world of rational self-determination and the world of empirical experience remains highly problematic, despite Kant's best efforts in the *Critique of the Power of Judgment* to demonstrate such a connection.

Horkheimer and Adorno are not claiming that Kant's view is correct of course; rather, they view him as a diagnostician *malgré lui* of the flaws in the purported gem of the modern world. Reading him against the grain – as Adorno was taught to do very early on by Kracauer – the paragon of the German Enlightenment emerges as a finely calibrated barometer of the commitments that the new world of science, machines, and capitalism demand.

Unfortunately, Horkheimer and Adorno do not engage with realist views of natural science. The physicist Roger Penrose claims that physicists have always felt that "[n]ature herself is guided by the same kind of criteria of consistency and elegance as those that guide human mathematical thought."[18] While it is still a puzzle that they do, mathematical laws "apply to the world with [...] phenomenal precision."[19] Far from a stipulation or mere tool, arising to epistemic prominence as a result of the all-too-human need for mastery, mathematics, Penrose claims, *is* the "language of nature," and there is a pre-established harmony between representation and reality, ruling out any noumenal world set in contrast to the level of appearances.

How might Horkheimer and Adorno respond to such a claim? Perhaps the most effective response would focus on how the object of scientific explanation gets constituted. They do not, after all, deny that such explanations have tremendous power. To the contrary, their view is precisely that the systematically unified method of natural science allows for an enormous increase in human knowledge and that science's claim to objective truth *within its purview* must be respected. They differ sharply from scientific realists like Penrose, however, who claim that scientific practices presuppose a metaphysical view of nature as including *only* that which is mathematizable, i.e., meaningful *exclusively* in terms of ideal continuities. Whether being itself, or nature, really is only what science takes it to be is not itself a scientific question. Unlike

Penrose, Horkheimer and Adorno provide a social scientific account – grounded in their anthropology – of the constitution of scientific data. If that account can be defended, then scientific realism of the metaphysical kind must be rejected. While the natural sciences operate successfully within what phenomenologists would call their "regional ontologies," the question of nature and what agents can reasonably view as real within the framework of human experience as such is philosophical.

Another challenge to Horkheimer and Adorno's position comes from that phenomenological quarter. For Husserl and Heidegger human beings – even in modernity – always find themselves within a concrete lifeworld in relation to which the formal knowledge provided by science must be viewed as an abstraction. Husserl and Heidegger, each in their own way, view the objectification and abstraction prevalent in modern forms of experience as deeply concerning and call for critique and intellectual resistance: a more inclusive, non-reductive vision of the mind/world relation is needed. Nonetheless, they never go quite as far as do Horkheimer and Adorno, for whom the functionality and abstract quality of human thinking imply that modern experience is devoid of virtually all the qualities that once gave one a properly responsive orientation to nature.

It is important to note that, while largely unthematized in *DE*, Horkheimer and Adorno accept the proposition that no cognition of any sort would be possible unless agents are able to relate attentively to at least some aspects of the concrete particularity of their immediate surroundings. Adorno, especially in *Negative Dialectics*, claims that were the mimetic, qualitative element of knowledge entirely lacking, "the possibility that a subject knows an object would be completely incomprehensible."[20] But just stating this does little more than reiterate the problem. In the absence of a more developed account, Horkheimer and Adorno's view of cognition may easily come across as inadequate.

To repeat a point, Horkheimer and Adorno might argue in response that, rather than providing a complete representation of the conditions of human orientation, their goal in *DE* is to foreground in unmistakable terms the *dominance* of abstraction, how the calculative behavior of mere subsumption and classification, while an inherent dimension of historical progress and an emblematic expression of science and technology, has invaded the everyday and become the most striking aspect of rationality in general. On this reading, there would be room for a phenomenological or pragmatic theory of more informal modes of meaning-making and action. It would not, however, play an important role in the book's critical project.

THE RETURN OF MYTH

Enlightenment returns to myth. Self-preservation, adaptation to challenges individuals meet due to nature, was what enlightenment turned out to be. Individuals increasingly find themselves trapped in self-perpetuating cycles of repetition, unconscious biases, and unacknowledged falsehoods even in their enlightened situation. In Horkheimer and Adorno's view, this process is relentlessly dissimulating (enlightenment is supposed to be an escape from, not a more efficient form of, myth) and profoundly alienating:

> The more completely the machinery of thought subjugates existence, the more blindly it is satisfied with reproducing it. Enlightenment thereby regresses to the mythology it has never been able to escape. For mythology had reflected in its forms the essence of the existing order — cyclical motion, fate, domination of the world as truth — and renounced hope. In the terseness of the mythical image, as in the clarity of the scientific formula, the eternity of the actual is confirmed and mere existence is pronounced as the meaning it obstructs. The world as a gigantic analytic judgment, the only surviving dream of science, is of the same kind as the cosmic myth which linked the alternation of spring and autumn to the abduction of Persephone.
>
> (20/49–50)

In modernity the process of rationalization that started with the first efforts to gain mastery over nature returns human beings to the nature from which they sought to escape. It is not that we have become closer to nature thereby; rather, it is that the freedom we sought is illusory, itself an expression of nature. Since mastery was always predicated on the ability to marshal the most systematic assemblage of means to gain control, we have reified thinking, turning it into an unreflective creator of identity akin to myth. In every aspect of life we are beholden to established procedures over particular differences. And where particular differences are only variables in a repeating sequence, there is little room for imagining them as initiating a different form of life.

Everywhere they look Horkheimer and Adorno see domination. Thinking and rational action in general are instrumental, able, based on a knowledge of causal relations, to recommend a means, a course of action, given the existence of a stipulated end.[21] About the authority of ends reason must be silent, as Weber thought. Of course, ends can figure as means in new plans, but rather than solving the problem of end-indifferent reasoning, this only threatens regress. Their claim is not that, in modernity, agents *tend* to reify and instrumentalize their relations to objects and others. That would be a factual, sociological claim. Rather, it is that modern agents do not, at least for the most part, possess any modes of evaluation other than those that are involved in instrumentalizing things by fitting them into categories. Science, technology, and administrative techniques have expanded their range and power enormously at the cost of shuttering the end-oriented and object-attentive range of human possibilities.

DE offers a philosophy of history grounded in the projection of this anthropologically formulated conception of rationalization onto the past. In sharp contrast to the interpretations emerging out of bourgeois and Whig views of history, which see progress developing along a linear axis, according to Horkheimer and Adorno history in the West has from the very beginning been set on a path of "self-enslavement" and "self-destruction." Modernity for them displays virtually no potential for progressive social transformation. While central to the early Frankfurt School, the Marxian dialectical materialist idea that changes in a society's structure and means of production inevitably bring about progressive changes in the relations of production and, hence, in class-relations, finds no foothold in this dystopian vision of modernity. For Horkheimer and Adorno, history – as it was for Benjamin – is a "permanent catastrophe" (Adorno 1978: 192).

In modernity, human consciousness is reified *in extremis*, and that means that it cannot easily see or think beyond given historical constraints. This indicates that Horkheimer and Adorno's diagnosis of modernity will simply present the culmination of a structure that was always present in history. Like Hegel, but in an inverted sense, the very logic of history becomes the key to deciphering its particular manifestations. It also suggests – to the consternation of many of the book's critics – that seemingly crucial political differences largely disappear. What seemed to the members of the early Frankfurt School as a historically decisive battle waged between capitalist liberal democracy, communism, and fascism becomes less important when one appreciates the "deep grammar" of modernity: universal reification, domination, and violence.

The variations of identity thinking that play themselves out and inform each other in Horkheimer and Adorno's account of modernity are many. They accept Weber's conception of the growth and intensification of bureaucratic and formal exercises of power. Bureaucracies, whether in liberal or non-liberal systems, subject individuals to procedures that treat them in terms of generality. While early Frankfurt School research had been tracking a transformation from liberal to more organized forms of capitalism – e.g., during the New Deal, but also in fascist Germany – in Adorno's work after the war the process of bureaucratization takes on an increasingly dark hue. Especially after Stalin's accession to power the illiberal systems of the Soviet empire displayed pronounced totalitarian features, prioritizing the collective while largely treating individuals as disposable. And, of course, as Adorno and many other researchers would claim, the Holocaust was to a considerable extent made possible by large-scale bureaucracy. Auschwitz, he came to argue, represents a satanic unity of identity-thinking and instrumental reason, systematically murdering individuals based on nothing but membership in a "racial" group. Its perverted conceptions of integration implied a total disregard for individual lives and demonstrated the extent to which the social can come to dominate individuals completely.

Identity thinking finds many other outlets. In liberal capitalist systems, markets have their own, apparently inexorable logic grounded in economic laws of exchange. As Lukács claimed, the near-universal commodification taking place in advanced capitalist systems – the commodification of labor power and hence of individuals, but also of virtually all things – means that agents, in order to act rationally, must display a calculative, instrumental attitude toward their surroundings. Indeed, as agents view an entity in terms only of its exchange value, they inevitably understand it to be at base fungible – means rather than ends. According to classical economics, commodity exchange tends to be highly efficient, responding quickly and predictably to human needs and interests. However, the drive toward commodification can also be deadly. Everything becomes a "resource," an investment, from which individuals expect a calculable profit. Horkheimer and Adorno provide abundant examples of what this means socially. While explicitly commercial activities are typically viewed as being "for profit," the profit motive invades even the most existentially and intimately important aspects of one's life: Art is product, science is business, marriage is merger. One's whole life becomes a project aimed at increasing one's value, i.e., one's *exchange* value. "What's in it for me?" tends to be the decisive question at this level.

If self-preservation can be said to be the number-one priority for individuals, it follows that successful adaptation to the socially prevalent norms associated with their function and position will be crucial to the outcome they manage to procure for themselves. According to Horkheimer and Adorno modern societies become increasingly oriented toward standardizing behavior and making sure that individuals react conventionally to the expectations that are being placed on them. Indeed, as the liberal era of Western capitalism reaches its end in the politically and economically turbulent 1920s and 1930s, and the United States, Europe, and Soviet systems place their bets on greater concentration and intensification of administrative power, the space for individually initiated reflection and action diminishes, making adaptation to the powers-that-be not only instrumentally effective but socially unavoidable. All is predictable, and predictability is all. The classical bourgeois individual, able to make semi-autonomous decisions in light of rationally binding norms reflective of non-instrumental considerations, is doomed. In its stead ascends the merely adaptive individual, who molds itself "to the technical apparatus body and soul" (23/52). The self-alienated, adaptive individual has relinquished the claim to individual or personal freedom, familiar from Kant's practical philosophy, that arose with liberal capitalism. Rational behavior now equates with standardized behavior.

"Choice" becomes a mantra, but the framework within which choices can be made is limited and limiting so that real choice is all but ruled out. In corporate America individuals act in accordance with the demands placed on them by advertising. In the more overtly authoritarian systems of fascism and state communism, they follow orders or simply align their behavior with that of the collective.

A dire and depressing picture, but does it leave any room for resistance? Let's take stock. At times, especially in their account of mass culture, Horkheimer and Adorno seem to propose that virtues such as spontaneity, imagination, and intellectual independence have gone missing completely. Concern of this sort and magnitude echoes widespread sentiments about mass society and its consequences around the time of writing *DE*. The First and Second World Wars had convinced many that there was something deeply wrong with the modern world. Some of those sentiments had their home on the right side of the political spectrum. Thinkers and writers like Spengler, Heidegger, and Eliot denounced "mass behavior," arguing that it precludes the formation of individual judgment, stifles ethical responsibility, and renders the cultural past impotent. The picture seems to have little place for any commitment to collective political action. Adorno, in particular, argued that collective mobilization of the kind seen in Marxist politics, rather than functioning to liberate individuals from oppression, would just create more of the mindless and irresponsible behavior that he already believed had become standard fare in liberal societies.[22]

Adorno's view of resistance remained staunchly individualistic, condemning all forms of collectivism. A truly reconciled, rational society would present to the individual for her authorization candidate conceptions of community. However, current liberal societies serve to integrate individuals into society by simply eliminating their claim to uniqueness. Agents in late capitalist and state communist societies, Horkheimer and Adorno argue, are at best pseudo-individuals.

When such pseudo-individuals think systematically, the result is *positivism*. Unlike critical thinking, which would utilize reason to identify ideology and seek to disclose truth and rational potential for social change, positivism succumbs to the pressure to conform, equating reality with fungibility and technical control. Unsurprisingly, given their emphatic commitments to social critique and reflection, Horkheimer and Adorno reject positivism understood narrowly: the Vienna Circle and its verificationist theory of meaning.[23] Recognizing no other form of reality than that of scientifically gathered facts would be inconsistent with their view that Critical Theory aspires to critical distance across the totality of phenomena. However, Horkheimer and Adorno mostly use the term "positivism" in a wider sense, including the panoply of ways in which human thinking finds itself being reconciled – falsely, in their view – to how the world is interpreted in modern circumstances. Positivism in this wider sense restricts thought to the reception and ordering of what is given in observation without questioning the conditions under which it is given, i.e., that it can show up *as given* in the first place. For them givenness is never a given; rather, it presupposes context.

Positivism, Horkheimer and Adorno argue, is the epitome of what enlightened thinking becomes once it has succumbed to and been transformed into myth. Its prevalence calls into question not only the normative and value-oriented thinking in virtually all areas of human concern, except perhaps those of simple acts of instrumental reasoning and classification in organizational and scientific endeavors. Its pervasive return to myth also seems to preclude the kind of Critical Theory to which the two authors are committed from being even so much as possible. Prominent critics, starting with Habermas, have argued that criticism of the vast scope that we find in *DE* is self-defeating. Like global skepticism, it implicates Horkheimer and Adorno in a performative self-contradiction: One cannot dismiss reason and still be committed to a form of critique that appeals to reason.[24] The position taken in *DE*, Habermas argues, is simply too extreme. Moreover, they fail to recognize the various ways in which modern institutions have utilized and been shaped by forms of reasoning that are both ends-oriented and universalist.

The question whether conceptual resources may exist for the kind of criticism that Horkheimer and Adorno practice is complex and difficult and will be dealt with more extensively in the final chapter. To be sure, *DE* may well be the darkest work to come out of the classical phase of the Frankfurt School. But that is in keeping with its central aim: to accentuate the negative in order to shake people up. As Horkheimer and Adorno move forward in the 1950s and beyond, the search is on for some foothold from which to generate positive critique. Adorno in particular, while continuing to subscribe to the fundamental vision of *DE*, initiates the practice of "micrology," which attempts to excavate traces and fragments in existing culture from which to develop more adequate practices. They can involve simple, everyday actions such as how we treat children or non-human animals. Or they can involve challenging encounters with complex works of modern art. In general, it seems clear that while Adorno, in particular, does hold that reification has reached near-universal proportions, it can be resisted. A resistance that made a decisive difference, however, would have to vault over modernity, indeed over history as we know it. No such leap seems within reach and, even if it did seem to be, chances are that it would *merely* seem to be. What one thought was a leap would be in actuality a fall, a fall back into catastrophe. Whatever hope there is must be indexed to the most fugitive experiences. "Perspectives must be produced," Adorno writes in the final section of *Minima Moralia*,

> which set the world beside itself, alienated from itself, revealing its cracks and fissures, as needy and distorted as it will one day lay there in the messianic light. To win such perspectives without caprice or violence, wholly by the feel for objects, this alone is what thinking is all about.[25]

FURTHER READING

For those with German, Früchtl 1986 is a systematic study of mimesis in Adorno's thought. Thyen 1989 discusses the concept of the non-identical in Adorno's *Negative Dialectics*, a concept in close proximity to Adorno's later conception of mimesis. Halliwell 2002 discusses the origin of the concept of mimesis in ancient philosophy and literature, as well as its subsequent development in Europe.

NOTES

1 Pinker 2019: 396.
2 For a study that emphasizes the influence of reactionary thinkers – e.g., Oswald Spengler and Ludwig Klages – on Horkheimer and Adorno, see Immanen 2025.
3 In a joint discussion in 1946, Horkheimer refers to the idea of writing a second volume, describing their shared effort not as a rejection of the Enlightenment but as its "rescue" (*Rettung*). Horkheimer 1985a, 12.593–605.
4 Kant 2005: 54.
5 Hegel 2019: 313.
6 Adorno 1997: 46: "The impression of ugliness stems from the principle of violence and destruction. The aims posited are unreconciled with what nature, however mediated it may be, wants to say on its own. In technique, violence toward nature is not reflected through artistic portrayal, but it is immediately apparent."
7 Stendhal 1975: 66 n.: "Beauty is only the *promise* of happiness" (*la beauté n'est que la promesse du bonheur*). There are several interpretations of the formula. The one most pertinent to *DE* is Nietzsche's favorite: beauty is incomplete in an important sense. It cannot in and of itself reconcile one with the world; it only expresses such reconciliation. See Nietzsche 2007: 75 [III. 6]. Horkheimer and Adorno would have no doubt also known of Baudelaire's qualified acceptance of the thought. See Baudelaire 1962: 456.
8 The German word "Schein" is cognate to English "shine." The term plays a significant role in German aesthetics. In that tradition, *Schein* is not mere semblance; rather, it is appearance in which the property of being manifest is especially striking, so striking that one cannot help but be put in mind of what is behind such appearing. In other words, *Schein* gives the sense of something being more-than-natural, of manifestation that exceeds the capacity of its object to contain it.
9 Sellars 1997: 76.
10 Adorno will occasionally go so far as to see "thought as such, before all particular contents, [as] an act of negation, of resistance to that which is forced upon it […]." While presenting an idealized view of thought, an emphatic idea of cognitive processes far removed from the cynical picture of thought as exclusively in thrall to natural and social pressures, the passage does suggest that Adorno is ready to attribute at least some autonomy to human thinking. See Adorno 1970: 6.30.
11 As noted in chapter one, the concepts of enchantment and disenchantment are central to Weber's account of rationalization. See Weber 2004: 13–14: "[The growing process of intellectualization and rationalization] means that in principle, then, we are not ruled by mysterious, unpredictable forces, but that, on the contrary, we can in principle control everything by means of calculation. That in turn means the disenchantment of the world."

12 *Mana* is a concept in Melanesian-Polynesian religions that refers to the spiritual force with which a place, an object, or a person may be imbued. It is often associated with healing. Horkheimer and Adorno may have become familiar with the concept from reading Marcel Mauss's *Esquisse d'une théorie générale de la magie* (1902). Mauss's discussion is indebted to the primary research presented in Robert Henry Codrington, *The Melanesians: Studies in their Anthropology and Folklore* (1891).
13 Blumenberg 1988: 35: "All trust in the world begins with names, in connection with which stories can be told."
14 Adorno, 1970: 6.55. The concept originates in Goethe.
15 Adorno 1997: 54/1970: 7.86–7.
16 Horkheimer and Adorno write "lamb" (*Lamm*) here, not the word ordinarily used in German Bibles "ram" (*Widder*) that is closer in meaning to the Biblical Hebrew *ayil*. Standard Christian biblical interpretation holds that Abraham's attempted sacrifice of Isaac prefigures the agnus Dei, i.e., the lamb as a symbol of Christ. See John 1:29 (*agnos tou theou*). One might remark that the transition from ram to lamb – from the assertive leader of the flock to the docile baby sheep – is typical of a difference in mood of the Old to New Testament, from the sublime to the user-friendly.
17 Jameson 1972.
18 Penrose 2004: 60.
19 Penrose 2004: 21.
20 Adorno 1970: 6.55.
21 See Horkheimer 1974b: 3–4:

> But the force that ultimately makes reasonable actions possible is the faculty of classification, inference, and deduction, no matter what the specific content – the abstract functioning of the thinking mechanism. This type of reason may be called subjective reason. It is essentially concerned with means and ends, with the adequacy of procedures for purposes more or less taken for granted and supposedly self-explanatory. It attaches little importance to the question whether the purposes as such are reasonable. If it concerns itself at all with ends, it takes for granted that they too are reasonable in the subjective sense, i.e., that they serve the subject's interest in relation to self-preservation – be it that of the single individual, or of the community on whose maintenance that of the individual depends. The idea that an aim can be reasonable for its own sake – on the basis of virtues that insight reveals it to have in itself – without reference to some kind of subjective gain or advantage, is utterly alien to subjective reason, even where it rises above the consideration of immediate utilitarian values and devotes itself to reflections about the social order as a whole.

And on p. 5: "Ultimately, subjective reason proves to be the ability to calculate probabilities and thereby to co-ordinate the right means with a given end."
22 For an account of Adorno's view of politics, see Hammer 2006.

23 Horkheimer and Adorno's understanding of the Vienna Circle is coarse. The members of the Circle preferred the designation "logical empiricism." Verifiability as the criterion for meaning was subject to ongoing debate within the Circle and, at different phases, there were different contestants. The main debate was about the breadth of verifiability. In time, Carnap dropped the idea in favor of confirmation.

24 Habermas 1993a: 126–7: "Horkheimer and Adorno find themselves in the same embarrassment as Nietzsche: If they do not want to renounce the effect of a final unmasking and still want to continue with critique, they will have to leave at least one rational criterion intact for their explanation of the corruption of all rational criteria. In the face of this paradox, self-referential critique loses its orientation."

25 Adorno 1978: 247/1970: 4.283 [§ 153].

3
ODYSSEUS BETWEEN MYTH AND ENLIGHTENMENT

With its vast repertoire of apparently discrepant themes and topics, *DE* contains plenty of surprises. Yet no other section of the book may strike the reader as more immediately puzzling than *Excursus I: Odysseus or Myth and Enlightenment*. An excursus is a digression, a journey of sorts, that nevertheless contains further exposition of a topic previously treated. The first excursus obliges by following a thread already introduced: the relationship of myth to enlightenment. As enlightenment turns into myth, that uneasy relationship – chiasmatic as it is – becomes defining for modernity. But why an excursus on the eponymous hero of Homer's *Odyssey*? What could this epic poem – 12,109 lines in dactylic hexameter, originating most probably in an oral tradition that dates back to the Late Bronze Age (*ca.* 1400 BC) and eventually written down in columns on rolls made from papyrus (or possibly some kind of animal skin, such as vellum or parchment) – possibly have to do with modernity?[1] How can such an archaic source illuminate the central topic, i.e., the ineluctable interconnectedness of progress and regression more than three millennia later? It does not help much to be told, as we are in the Preface, that the *Odyssey* is "one of the earliest representative documents of *bourgeois* Western civilization" (xviii/6) (emphasis supplied). What could possibly be less bourgeois than the attitudes, virtues, and actions of heroes, gods, and demi-gods in the aftermath of the battle of Troy?

Let's begin by noting how utterly central the *Iliad* and the *Odyssey* are not only to cultural and literary history but also to philosophical reflection.[2] For Plato, Aristotle, and other thinkers of ancient Greece, they formed the mythological, theological, and ethical background of their way of life, instructing people in how gods and heroes act while setting up and articulating ideals that range from the mastery of context-specific virtues such as seafaring and battle to concern with the management of one's passions. Even while questioning the received authority of some of these virtues, as does Plato, ancient philosophers never rejected the Homeric celebration of strength, perseverance, glory, and communally oriented self-sacrifice.

Medieval Christian culture tended to be more focused on the *Aeneid* and its dutiful hero Aeneas, veteran of the battle for Troy and founder of Rome (itself later the source of Roman Catholic Europe). In the eighteenth and nineteenth centuries, however, Homer's epics regained centrality, especially in German philosophy. Goethe, Schiller, Hegel, Schelling, and, later, Jacob Burckhardt and Nietzsche are close readers of Homer. They analyze such features as the Homeric virtues, the presence and immanence of the divine, the experience of fate, destiny, shame, and belonging. Nineteenth-century philosophical readings typically see Homer's commitments as being profoundly communitarian, understanding the individual exclusively within the framework of social expectations constituted by the sacred, founding nature of myth itself. As the twentieth-century approaches, interest in the politically constitutive nature of myth as the framework of the community intensifies as themes from the Jena Romantics to Nietzsche are picked up by conservative theorists and poet-philosophers such as Alfred Rosenberg and Stefan George and, through them, spread more generally in Germanophone intellectual circles.[3]

A NEW APPROACH TO THE *ODYSSEY*

As Horkheimer and Adorno turn to Homer, it is reasonable to assume that they appreciate how fraught with philosophical implications the history of these readings has been.[4] No understanding of these epics can extricate itself completely from their "effective history" (*Wirkungsgeschichte*), the history of interpretations in their organic, internally self-referencing development.[5] That said, both Horkheimer and Adorno are skeptical of the concept of *the* classics, associating the idea of a canon with unreflective, dogmatic reading practices, as well as with the unwillingness to consider classical works independent of their historically constituted frameworks.

In his writings on music Adorno sometimes offers aggressive, anachronistic, and seemingly counterintuitive interpretations that prioritize "truth-content" over immediate contexts of meaning. For example, while the Baroque Bach, being hyper-attentive to formal principles of composition, is viewed by Adorno as modern, a composer such as Stravinsky, emphasizing rhythmic practice over expressive timing, counts as hieratic, trapped in a tonal sarcophagus and composing music that only sounds progressive to the unschooled ear.[6]

Adorno – the primary author of this excursus – brings this attitude to bear here. He clearly wants to challenge the deference encountered in the standard treatments of Homer.[7] He is cognizant of how ideas of "eternal literary value" and "the authority of the classics" can inform contemporary social and political narratives, with unduly conservative results. The alternative reading he gives to Homer bears unmistakable marks of the approach to texts that, for more than fifteen years, he had largely adapted from Walter Benjamin's literary criticism. In writings such as *The Origin of the German Tragic Drama* and "Goethe's *Elective Affinities*," Benjamin would dislodge the work from its own historical context by subjecting it to a strictly immanent reading. Such readings – which Benjamin, inspired by Schlegel and other German Romantics, called "criticism" (*Kritik*) – seek to redeem moments of truth in texts that would otherwise be overwhelmed by their standard reception histories. Criticism, in this sense, reveals discontinuities and caesurae that permit one to pierce the beautiful illusion that shrouds the classics.[8] In what is another important inspiration from Benjamin, Adorno's approach to the *Odyssey* may also be thought of as "constellational." To rehearse the main point from Chapter 1: Just as images in the stars come into being due to the conventional configuration of their elements, so ideas emerge when material elements of phenomena are regrouped in a new philosophically informed pattern. The ideas release the phenomena from the meaning they would have had otherwise.

The methodological commitments associated with Benjamin's notions of truth-content, redemptive and immanent criticism, and constellational reading inform the choices made by Horkheimer and Adorno in the excursus. They focus almost exclusively on individual episodes in the poem and reconstrue them as forming a novel conceptual series. That is, they isolate each episode from the epic as a whole and, thereby, create self-standing fragments rather than constituents of a pregiven unified totality. By reading these fragments against the grain, sometimes violating traditional expectations of what constrains their meaning (surely, Odysseus cannot be so mundane as to be bourgeois; he is an *epic hero* after all), Horkheimer and Adorno construct a constellation that not only surprises but purports to reveal the phenomena truly at stake for the first time. If there is truth to be found in the poem – and they believe there is – it is demonstrated repeatedly as each episode takes its place in the new configuration.

As we saw in the Chapter 2, myth displays features of enlightened thinking, and enlightenment may revert to myth. Whereas the first chapter of *DE* draws on readings of such thinkers as Bacon, Kant, Hegel, and Weber, the first excursus is deeply and explicitly indebted to Nietzsche. As Horkheimer and Adorno recognize, Nietzsche is far from being an easy and reliable ally in the project of unmasking enlightenment. Rather than subtly thematizing the ambiguities of enlightened thinking, we find in Nietzsche a "blind eulogy of blind life" (36/68), and in particular an invocation of the life-affirming powers of Dionysus, familiar to readers of Nietzsche from both *The Birth of Tragedy* and the late writings. Nietzsche wishes to debunk all forms of enlightenment in favor of an anti-modern celebration of strength and conquest. Homer viewed through this lens, Horkheimer and Adorno argue, results in an "ideology [...] which imposes a praxis by which everything living is suppressed" (36/68). The poet Rudolf Borchardt, they claim, follows this thread, "idolizing" (37/69) the naked force of the mythic. Such "cultural fascists" (36/68) do recognize aspects of enlightenment in archaic sources like the *Odyssey*. Yet, unlike Horkheimer and Adorno, who insist on the "intertwining" (*Verschlungenheit*) of enlightenment and myth, these conservative critics see such elements as wholly inauthentic and as threats to the beauty and glory of the poem's heroic force. For the fascist, mythic *thymos* (vitality) is a good in itself and enlightenment rationalism an interloper. While there may be an ongoing contest between the two impulses, the only applause is for the complete victory of myth.

Horkheimer and Adorno would agree that in modernity myth (or ideology) prevails; however, this is not due to the *triumph* of myth over enlightenment. As already indicated, Horkheimer and Adorno adamantly oppose any simple, nondialectical valorization of either term in that dyad. The relationship between the two is Janus-faced: enlightenment (in the form we have come to know it) *is* myth, and myth *is* enlightenment. If the dominant forms of meaning that the critical thinker detects in the modern, purportedly enlightened world is best characterized as nothing but mythical (whether in the direct, viz. fascist, or the dialectical sense), then modernity is in deep crisis. Because Horkheimer and Adorno always keep open the possibility that "enlightenment [...] reflect[s] on itself" (xvii/20), and that "freedom in society is inseparable from enlightenment" (xvi/18), critical distance becomes an option. And with critical distance, one may hope for social change.

Nietzsche is as far from a Hegelian as one might like. Nevertheless, he not only castigates proto-fascism as a simple-minded reaction to enlightenment, but also recognizes the interactivity of enlightenment and myth. In *On the Genealogy of Morality* – the work that Horkheimer and Adorno highlight – he claims to have discovered an intimate connection between enlightenment and power, how enlightenment always comes with regimes of discipline whose constitution rests on domination. For Horkheimer and Adorno, however, the most fertile ideas in the *Genealogy* are nested in its account of the relation of renunciation to conscience. *Contra* thinkers who hold that conscience is a given – in Kant's case a "fact of reason" – Nietzsche understands conscience to emerge historically from relationships of power. The feeling of guilt (*Schuld*) arises from a feeling of owing someone something, i.e., being in someone's *debt* (also *Schuld*), rather than from some spontaneous expression of moral responsiveness.[9] That is, conscience originates in exchange. If a subordinate is to survive, he has to offer compensation for his guilt. Guilt can of course be objective, such as when a jury makes a finding based on evidence that a person has broken the law. That person will "have to pay" by undergoing punishment. However, punishment and the fear it invokes may also lead the subjugated to *internalize* the debt, allowing it to structure the psyche in the form of aggression directed against oneself, bringing about what Horkheimer and Adorno refer to as renunciation (*Entsagen*). The guilty individual desperately wants to pay his way out; however, the one very effective form of payment is to turn his instincts inward and give up his self-sufficient agency, thereby renouncing any claim to happiness and satisfaction he might have. "I pay," the guilty agent thinks, "by letting a key part of me – my most essential wishes and aspirations – go." The guilty even finds a backhanded form of freedom in this self-denial.

While, according to Horkheimer and Adorno, hardly an agent marked by the deep sense of guilt that one finds in Abrahamic figures, Odysseus exemplifies the case. Take his famous cunning (*mētis*), by means of which he repeatedly defies his enemies. It transcends myth through rationality. But no matter how shrewd Odysseus may be, his cunning is more than just strategic. It implicates him, subjectively, structuring how he appears, not only to others but to himself. Like Nietzsche's agent of guilt, Odysseus renounces his claim to his own happiness. In return he achieves an instrumentally defined goal.

The best case for this claim is Horkheimer and Adorno's interpretation of the episode of the Sirens. Recall that these mythical, all-knowing creatures sing an irresistible yet mortally dangerous song. No one who hears it can escape their destruction. Flaunting Circe's warning, Odysseus and his men sail safely by. Yet how? Odysseus reasons that even if one accepts the mythic premise and the implicit contract presented by the Sirens (hear the beauty and die), there are two options open to avoid ruin. One of them consists in plugging his men's ears with wax and ordering them to row on with all their might. They renounce. He chooses the second option for himself. He has himself tied to the mast so that he can hear the song but is unable to act on the compulsion to give himself over to them. On Horkheimer and Adorno's interpretation the scene allegorizes the dialectic of enlightenment. The sailors are made to repress and control nature (the Siren song) through work (rowing). Sacrificing whatever immediate desire for happiness they may have, they must work in order to survive. While socially subjugated and objectified, forced to repeat the movements of the rowing and, in this sense, acting not freely but under constraint, they are sheltered from the necessities of fate, myth, and nature. Enlightenment supplants myth. However, in the mindless, forced repetition enacted in the rowing, they cannot help but return to myth. The freedom they have is reduced to self-preservation, little more than an escape from death. Moreover, it is stultifying, having been bought at the expense of a more dignified, satisfying form of existence than what repetitious manual labor can offer. Odysseus, on the other hand, experiences the riveting beauty of the Sirens' song but only "as a mere object of contemplation, as art" (27/57). Temptation has been neutralized; there is no erotic lure, no *Liebestod*. Rather, Odysseus, the "bourgeois," anticipates the experience of the modern concert-goer who, while enjoying the music "disinterestedly," as Kant would put it, sits immobilized before it, thereby endorsing the distance between himself and the object of his admiration. Odysseus defeats the mythical creatures, but only at the expense of his naturally constituted claim to happiness. (The view of art as succumbing to the dialectic of enlightenment – of promising a form of redemption that its rational form and conditions of viewership deny it – plays an important role as well in *DE*'s chapter on the culture industry and in Adorno's later aesthetics.)

The image of oarsmen and helmsman suggests how the division of labor eventually segments humanity into those who work without enjoyment and those who enjoy without working. This is the only reference to class in the revised 1947 edition of *DE*.

Both servant *and* master are alienated (echoing Hegel's master/bondsman dialectic in the *Phenomenology of Spirit*). The servant is alienated from his body and soul; he works under compulsion. The master's enjoyment is mediated by the servant's work and is only nominally "his." For both, the control of nature appears inescapable, operating within as a compulsion.

Involved in all this maneuvering is an unexpected form of sacrifice. According to Horkheimer and Adorno, sacrifice in the *Odyssey* is a form of fraud. Odysseus dupes deities by offering them gifts, a practice at which he is an expert at this point in his career.[10] Sacrifice is transactional; it always involves instrumentality. One gives up to get back.[11] Yet he is offering not just any gift. Unlike the more primitive blood sacrifices, in which an animal is ritually slaughtered in order to please and appease the gods, Odysseus sacrifices *a part of himself*. Now Freud joins Nietzsche as a guide. Odysseus sacrifices a part of himself by suppressing his own impulses, i.e., his *inner* nature. In this he is both priest and offering. The sacrifice, in other words, is "introverted," performed on oneself. Considered as a sacrificial victim, Odysseus not only overcomes blood sacrifice (which itself is a major civilizational event), he displays a form of selfhood or subjectivity that depends on suppressing nature, in this case, his own.

In Chapter 2, we encountered the notion that enlightened thinking is by and large instrumental, oblivious to final ends. This reading of the *Odyssey* adds to that the proposition that enlightened thinking requires rational *self*-mastery. Ancient philosophy has much to say about rational self-mastery, centered on being virtuous, i.e., ethical excellence in character required for flourishing (*eudaimonia*). Odysseus is a hero who clearly displays excellence in a number of pursuits; however, his self-mastery, especially when battling mythical beings, is to a considerable extent a matter of renunciation and domination. That is how he establishes distance and control. Drawing upon Freud's *Civilization and Its Discontents*, Horkheimer and Adorno generalize the impulse to establish self-mastery through renunciation to history as such:

> The human being's mastery of itself, on which the self is founded, practically always involves the annihilation of the subject in whose service

that mastery is maintained, because the substance which is mastered, suppressed, and disintegrated by self-preservation is nothing other than the living entity, of which the achievements of self-preservation can only be defined as functions – in other words, self-preservation destroys the very thing which is to be preserved. [...] The history of civilization is the history of the introversion of sacrifice – in other words, the history of renunciation.

(43/78)[12]

Selfhood as self-sacrifice, as the introversion of sacrifice, is a notion on which Horkheimer and Adorno stake not only their readings of the *Odyssey* but their understanding of civilization more generally. Civilization depends upon the thwarting, deflection, redirection, or sublimation of individual desire.

This view has been criticized as excessive and ultimately misleading. Habermas, for example, holds that the self should be understood along communicative lines, as the result of interaction which presupposes that what is expected of one as a conversant is reflectively internalized.[13] Horkheimer and Adorno appeal exclusively to the idea of a "mastery over nature" (*Naturbeherrschung*) and confuse, Habermas argues, the complex process in which the ego attains an identity with the practices in which agents engage in order to control and master the world. The former is grounded in relationships between ego and alter ego, presupposing a conception of intersubjectivity; the latter is a subject-object relationship involving instrumental thinking and identity-oriented categorization.

As already indicated, Horkheimer and Adorno's account is indebted to Freud's structural theory of the psychic apparatus. For Freud, the ego (*Ich*) is governed most fundamentally by considerations of safety. In response to an often hostile and dangerous environment, the ego seeks self-preservation, the maintenance of its self-identity. It mediates two demanding masters: the natural, archaic id (*Es*) and the social, inhibiting superego (*Überich*). The id is the domain of libidinal energy and aggressive impulses. While governed by the so-called pleasure principle, it is typically in conflict with the ego on account of the destabilizing force of thinking and acting impulsively and unrealistically. In the interest of not coming to grief on harsh reality, to ensure the psyche's preservation, the ego must reject those demands – or, as Horkheimer and Adorno put it, "sacrifice" them. The superego, made up of internalized social demands, observes, judges, and seeks to constrain the ego. The root of conscience (*Gewissen*), it instills guilt and intensifies the fear of being deprived of love and social recognition. In the form of the "ego ideal," the superego supports the ego's efforts to stave off the excessive demands of the id. However, the superego's demands are themselves excessive. To respect reality is to give up on purportedly unrealistic and antisocial desires (some of which may be unrealistic and antisocial only from the standpoint of how society is currently organized).

It seems clear, then, that Freudian metapsychology informs Horkheimer and Adorno's reading of the *Odyssey*. Odysseus and his men respect reality by instrumentally mastering it. However, in doing so they need to introvert the sacrifice – refrain from acting on the impulses that threaten their chances of survival. By making the satisfaction of those impulses impossible, they "destroy" their own natures. They survive as a result of Odysseus's shrewd cunning, but surviving means living without self-actualization. The archaic claim to happiness on which that concept of self-actualization is premised has been rejected. They are now saturated with an inextricable feeling of guilt and hence of aggression: the impulses *cannot be accepted, cannot be acted upon*. Odysseus is thus the model of the agent of progress as Freud portrays it in *Civilization and its Discontents*. Ultimately, the aggression which drives human mastery of the environment becomes indistinguishable from the aggression with which the psyche controls itself.

Appreciating the Freudian background helps to explain why Horkheimer and Adorno insist on viewing human interiority as a battleground rather than a playing field. For Habermas the relationship between individual and community is in the end fundamentally harmonious. The internalization of normative expectations takes place through communicative interaction, which is grounded in recognitive relationships between ego and alterego. On Horkheimer and Adorno's Freudian account, however, the superego is thoroughly alien, theorized as "blindly, unconsciously internalized social coercion."[14] Odysseus's rowers can testify that there can be no unconstrained communication and interaction; integration takes place exclusively through subjugation and violence. The id, moreover, appears equally foreign. As Odysseus himself experiences, its claim to happiness can never be reconciled to reality. Instead, the claim must remain utopian, "only a promise of happiness." Habermas has it that one might safely pay the Sirens a visit by chatting with them, but Horkheimer and Adorno would flatly reject this notion. Sirens simply are *not like that*; it is not their *nature*. This nature cannot be changed through negotiation, although it may be circumvented or tamed through cunning. Promise happiness they may, but fatal they remain.

THE LOTUS-EATERS AND CIRCE

The episodes with Calypso, Circe, and the Lotus-eaters explore experiences that, from the vantage point of enlightenment thinking, are regressive yet not life-threatening. The Lotus-eaters, Odysseus says, "had no intention of killing my companions, not at all, they simply gave them the lotus to taste instead [...]."[15] Inducing stupor and forgetfulness of the pained yearning home, they offer a form of somatic happiness. Horkheimer and Adorno, however, dismiss their bliss as illusory, "a dull aimless vegetating, as impoverished as the life of animals" (49/86). Like Marx's critique of religion, which he compares to opium, that happiness is, they think, at best compensatory, a way of "enduring the unendurable in ossified social orders" (49/86). Real happiness, they claim, is always the result of some historical process of alleviating pain and dissatisfaction. It is an achievement of winning through suffering and, therefore, is deserved. The problem, of course, is that such processes commit agents to accept the imperatives of enlightenment. The price of this type of happiness is high and may even, as the episode with the Sirens demonstrates, be unattainable. The tension between immediate, bodily happiness and mediated, historically achieved happiness cannot be denied. In later works, such as *Negative Dialectics*, Adorno seems more prone to think of happiness in the former sense. Happiness, he writes there, "aims at sensual fulfillment and obtains its objectivity in that fulfillment."[16] Here, however, perhaps because of the association with drugs, he rejects immediacy.

Odysseus's encounter with the enchantress Circe also confronts him and his crew with the implications of regression to a nonthreatening, pre-civilized form of happiness. Unlike the episode with the Lotus-eaters, in which the cause of regression is drug-induced, the encounter with Circe involves magic and, thus, complex and ambiguous *craft*. We must remember here that Horkheimer and Adorno understand magic to be an instrumental use of mimesis. She transforms Odysseus's crew into swine. Yet Hermes has provisioned Odysseus with a protective herb, thanks to which he resists her spell. Before they leave her to travel to Hades, he feasts, Odysseus and Circe have sex, and he convinces her to transform his crew back into men in an improved state, with bodies that look younger, stronger, and more beautiful than before.

As swine, Odysseus's men have been abandoned to instinct. The linear time of the civilized self – the time in terms of which work is parsed – has been suspended. Reduced to animality they are consigned to immediacy, to inarticulate nature, and thus to myth. Horkheimer and Adorno point out, however, that their existence as swine carries an element of reconciliation – they have been recalled to an "idealized prehistory" (55/94), their way of being is "idyllic," reminiscent of the "wild animals which listen to the playing of Orpheus" (55/94). They are "at one" with nature, reconciled with it. But this remains, as in the Lotus-episode, semblance. The men, after all, have lost their human form; changing from human to pig involves a loss of something higher, more developed, and must be rated a "calamitous collapse" (55/94). Yet the element of unmediated happiness cannot be entirely discarded as a simple illusion. There *is* something about these creatures, grunting, snuffling, and glutting, that deserves to be thought of as joyful.

In *Aesthetic Theory* and elsewhere, Adorno elaborates on the Proustian suggestion that olfaction is the most archaic of the senses, a form of perceptual intake that depends on and is experienced as being in proximity to the object, and yet, unlike touch, seeing, and to some extent hearing, is indiscriminating. Because of its ineluctable exposure to the unclean and animalistic, smell has been suppressed by civilization in favor of auditory and visual perception, which by contrast promise objectivity and function at a distance. In *DE* however, the emphasis is firmly on the inevitability of enlightenment, and mere regression is deemed unacceptable: "In the image of the pig, [...] the joy of scent is distorted into the unfree snuffling of someone who has his nose to the ground and has renounced the upright posture" (56/95). Despite their apparent contentment, there is something fundamentally despicable and shameful about these pigs who once were the proud companions of Odysseus.

In Horkheimer and Adorno's deliberately anachronizing reading, Circe is a prostitute (*hetaira*) – a courtesan who in exchange for a victim's loss of autonomy offers happiness. She does not kill; rather, in the service of nature, of myth, and of radical heteronomy, she aims to return her "victims" to that which has been repressed within them. Odysseus realizes that in order to overcome her he must succumb, while at the same time resist the pull of heteronomy. So, he sleeps with her; yet the herb permits him to both accept and refuse what is fundamentally on offer. As in so many of the key episodes of the *Odyssey*, it is heroic to knowingly and instrumentally use regression in order to secure autonomy and, thus, selfhood. By pretending to be pure nature – by heeding, i.e., the implicit demands of the mythical contract – he avoids nature and strengthens his enlightened identity. Nature once again is bent to Odysseus's will. Of course, the pre-enlightened, mythical world of Circe knows neither contract nor any other formal relation between human beings. That only becomes possible due to Odysseus's uncanny ability to disenchant nature. Circe recognizes this: "You have a mind in *you* no magic can enchant."[17] What she represents is the law of repetition associated with myth. For those who live in a mythically structured universe, individuals have no choice but to act in accordance with the law. Odysseus does that. But, because he with the same gesture fools her, he manages to break free from mythic power and have it both ways.

PENELOPE, LOVE, AND MARRIAGE

Comparing Circe with Odysseus's wife, Penelope, permits Horkheimer and Adorno to deliver some rather sobering reflections on the nature of marriage. The relationship with Circe comes across as patriarchal. Representing nature, the suppressed Other, she appears irresistible. Nevertheless, she weakens when confronted with the counter-magic with which Odysseus manages to subdue her. Penelope has traditionally been viewed as the epitome of fidelity and monogamous love. Over many years she never once gives in to any of the suitors who crowd her hall. A veritable emblem of resistance and domesticity, she waits and weaves. Horkheimer and Adorno, however, see her as a woman for hire who sells pleasure for the property and protection she receives from her spouse: "Harlot and wife are complementary forms of female self-alienation in the patriarchal world: the wife betrays pleasure to the fixed order of life and property, while the harlot, as her secret accomplice, brings within the property relationship that which the wife's property rights do not include – pleasure – by selling it" (57–8/97). Rather than a spontaneous upsurge of feeling, Horkheimer and Adorno see in the famous recognition scene a scheming woman "determined to avoid a mistake, which she can hardly afford under the weight of the order bearing down on her" (58/98). This seems not only harsh but inadequately supported by the text. Yes, Penelope is determined not to put a foot wrong, but, given that the suitors have been lounging around, hounding her with marriage proposals, and depleting Odysseus's stores for years, she has good reason to be on guard. She requires proof of Odysseus's identity – that he knows the history of the marital bed. After receiving the "living proof,"

> Penelope felt her knees go slack, her heart surrender,
> recognizing the strong clear signs Odysseus offered.
> She dissolved in tears, rushed to Odysseus, flung her arms
> around his neck and kissed his head and cried out,
> "Odysseus – don't flare up at me now, not you,
> always the most understanding man alive!
> [...]
> In my heart of hearts I always cringed with fear
> some fraud might come, beguile me with his talk;
> the world is full of the sort,
> cunning ones who plot their own dark ends."[18]

Given how much the reader (or listener) already knows about Odysseus's cunning, the passage may seem unintentionally ironic.

Odysseus's history with other women is, after all, filled with deceit. Yet there is no suggestion that Penelope is left cold by his return. Indeed, what could be more obviously characterized as a "spontaneous upsurge of feeling" (58/98) than the vivid description of her crying and kissing, knees going slack, her heart in surrender? Horkheimer and Adorno's misreading underscores the risks involved in even intentional anachronism. Were Penelope truly bourgeois, caring mainly about her self-preservation and position within the socio-economic hierarchy, their reading might make sense. Her priorities are evidently more complex though, and ultimately Horkheimer and Adorno do indeed recognize that her marriage to Odysseus, while mediated by necessity and account-balancing, is grounded in love – or at least to what they refer to as "solidarity and steadfastness in face of death" (59/99). The wife, in particular, ties the marital bond to myth, the pre-historical and mimetic promise of happiness whose signification in a successful marriage counterbalances socially dominant masculine discourse. Like Circe, Penelope is a fundamentally ambiguous figure: faithful lover, wary *hetaira*. Conceived in such terms, she conforms to the will of the male in a patriarchal order, yet also acts as a cipher of happiness in that tough, cold world.

These reflections on sexual difference position Horkheimer and Adorno perilously close to a form of traditional essentialism in which women, while capable of enlightened thought, are at base irrational. Calypso, Circe, and Penelope – Odysseus's three women – are beings largely of myth. That means that, unlike Odysseus, they must appear as primarily responsive to a pre-civilized, inscrutable domain, the chthonic; even if they display capacities for autonomy and rational planning, deep down they are heterogenous. What they will and want is determined by forces external to them.

Similar views of sexual difference appear in Kant, Fichte, Hegel, and Nietzsche. They were entirely mainstream in nineteenth-century bourgeois culture. Nowadays they are considered ignorant and antiquated. In Horkheimer and Adorno's defense, it is worth keeping in mind that their central aim in the first excursus is to elaborate the braided concepts of myth and enlightenment. The three women and Odysseus are caught up in and defined by the dialectical interplay of these concepts. That tension plays through the women, and because they do not reduce to either one of its components, they are able to challenge the paternalism which would so reduce them. Take Penelope. Her fidelity, while grounded in myth, sets her against the strategic rationality of the suitors, who act for the sake of glory in an antagonistic – indeed agonistic – social reality. To be sure, this serves Odysseus's paternalistic interests. He wants to own her; she allows him to subjugate her. Yet her unwillingness to let the memory of him fade anticipates a more civilized, perhaps even utopian, form of togetherness based on respect for the uniqueness of the Other. Perhaps it is this, and not her bourgeois coldness, that ultimately explains Penelope's obsession with getting his identity right: there can be no substitute for Odysseus! True love cannot help but be exacting.

THE CYCLOPS

The ambiguity of marriage – its mythic grounding and its genuine anticipation of civilized life, with the dialectic between the two being mercilessly exposed to the norms of strategic rationality – stands in sharp contrast to the barbaric and uncivilized world of the Cyclops. This group of one-eyed, cannibalistic monsters, to which Polyphemus, Odysseus's most dangerous adversary, belongs, accepts the norms of kinship – especially the patriarchal bond – but suppresses the physically weaker. Devoid of property relations, the Cyclops have neither law nor any other organized way of thought or action. They live in anarchy; far from being cunning, they are stupid and easy to fool. Despite being a son of Poseidon, Polyphemus is utterly disrespectful of the gods, believing that he and his kin are stronger and older than they. The main deceit in this episode revolves around Odysseus's use of a Greek word that sounds somewhat like his proper name in response to the giant's demand to identify himself. That word, which Horkheimer and Adorno transliterate into German as *Udeis*, means "no one."[19]

When Polyphemus tells the tribe that Udeis is to blame for the attack in which he lost his one eye, they just shrug their shoulders and laugh. Odysseus in effect has used Polyphemus as a marionette; he has put into the giant's mouth the claim that he has been harmed by no one.

Horkheimer and Adorno, however, offer a considerably more complex reading. One of its strands takes up the question of the stratagem of the name and of naming more generally. Odysseus, they claim, is a radical nominalist. In a way, that cannot be true. As we saw in Chapter 1, linguistic nominalism can be construed as the doctrine that at base language is made up of names with single references, no general terms allowed. But, as opposed to the stupid giant, who cannot help identifying a thing with its name, Odysseus is able to deploy the conceptual nicety that the same thing can have different names or descriptions, each of them conventional, provisional, and perspectival. That is not nominalism of this minimal kind. But Odysseus does exploit a kind of naïve nominalism *on the part of the giant*. Odysseus detaches vocalization from the world and crafts out of it a tool, language unyoked from direct and singular reference. Polyphemus can be duped because he is unable to entertain even the possibility that Odysseus could call himself by another name. Naively, he thinks that Udeis must be another person. (That *Udeis* and "Odysseus" sound similar is likely to have provided a comic effect to the epic's audience, given how closely the arrogant Odysseus gets to revealing his real name and being chased by the whole tribe.[20])

Another strand of Horkheimer and Adorno's reading returns to the theme of self-renunciation. Odysseus is an effective agent only to the extent that he denies his identity in the very act of naming himself "nobody." In adopting a designation indicating his non-existence, i.e., his death, Odysseus adapts himself to nature and, at the same time and with the same gesture, cheats and defeats nature. Odysseus satisfies his demands, "but in such a way that by conceding their power he deprives them of it" (46/66). As already indicated, Horkheimer and Adorno think of this as a form of self-sacrifice that ultimately allows Odysseus to win himself back again as the rational subject he aimed to be all along.

As he and his men scramble to escape the Cyclops's lair, Odysseus, unable to help himself, reveals his true name.

> I called back with another burst of anger, 'Cyclops –
> if any man on the face of the earth should ask you
> who blinded you, shamed you so – say Odysseus,

> raider of cities, *he* gouged out your eye,
> Laertes' son who makes his home in Ithaca!'[21]

The act is superfluous and dangerous. Polyphemus, with Poseidon in support, hurls a boulder that barely misses the ship. Like so many heroes of adventure stories, Odysseus wants to be admired and have as many as possible know of his identity and glorious feats. To Horkheimer and Adorno this self-identification is not just bragging; it is a manic form of *hubris* (arrogance, sometimes with an element of impiety). Odysseus knows well the power of the primeval world, and this is what causes him to so vehemently assert his identity. Fear of nature *qua* nature and of the possibility that he really could become Nobody – regress to a pre-individual, pre-rational level – impels him to reestablish himself by naming himself truly. Without knowing it, Odysseus thus becomes stupid at the very moment when he most needed to be smart.

It is possible to read this as a comment on the fragility of enlightenment. The hero, Horkheimer and Adorno write, "is driven objectively by the fear that, if he does not constantly uphold the fragile advantage the word has over violence, this advantage will be withdrawn by violence" (54/92). We have seen that, given its natural mode of development toward greater abstraction, more instrumentalization, and a concomitant withdrawal from the concrete world of mimetically engaging objects, enlightenment may revert to myth. Enlightenment embodies its own forms of violence, but so does myth. Violence of one kind may work to escape violence of another, but violence is involved either way. On Horkheimer and Adorno's account, rational identity is fraught with uncertainty, a tenuous achievement easily revoked.

UNDERWORLD AND HOMELAND

Hades represents the most extreme and irreversible manner in which myth, according to Horkheimer and Adorno, is associated with stasis, muteness, and primeval repetition. The *Odyssey* deals with numerous exotic and foreign lands, but none is farther away from Odysseus's homeland than this. The dead, after all, are banished from the land of the living; there is no return for them to any semblance of home. They are but shades (*skiai*), forever condemned to darkness, insubstantiality, and silence.

Horkheimer and Adorno understand homeland (*patris*), Odysseus's ultimate goal, not as linked to soil or geography but, rather, to a rejection of myth. A homeland allows one to lead a civilized life – a life in which one can both act in worldly affairs and have the leisure to reflect. To yearn for such a place is to anticipate a condition in which "settlement" and "the fixed order of property" (60/85) prevail and nomadism has been overcome. The thought, perhaps surprising coming from two thinkers indebted to Marx, must be that a home is a determinate place that, as with property, is socially recognized as "objectively" yours. It is the place at which you are yourself and recognized as such by others. This is precisely not the phantasm of an original state, conjured forth by the mythical imagination.

Central to this rejection of mythical thought is the phenomenon of language.[22] Language bears with it the capacity to remember, re-experience, and resist: "Speech itself, language as opposed to mythical song, the possibility of holding fast the past atrocity through memory, is the law of Homeric escape" (61/102). The object of these activities is violence.

In an effort to exemplify how language, here poetic utterance, bears witness to evil, Horkheimer and Adorno draw attention to the harrowing scene in Book 22 in which fifty women slaves (*dmōiai*) of Odysseus's household have been summarily hanged outside the palace for having had sex with the now-dead suitors.[23] In a manner that would not be completely foreign to a Zola, Homer describes the women as having their "heads [...] trapped in a line, nooses yanking their necks up, one by one/ so all might die a pitiful, ghastly death [...]/they kicked up heels for a little – not for long."[24] There is some solace to be had, Horkheimer and Adorno claim, in the sense we may have as readers that this is long past – the "once upon a time" of the fairy tale. Yet, while there is hope in the fact that the event represented is long past, memory carries an ethical injunction: this must not happen again![25] Of course, as Horkheimer and Adorno know perfectly well, it has happened again – and will happen for as long as there are people left to perpetrate such misdeeds. Civilization is joined at the hip to barbarity – at least until nature becomes something other than an object of anxious domination. However, the act of witnessing offers the semblance of freedom; rather than being viewed as fated, as a constant in human history that is forever bound to repeat itself, there is hope that "inhumanity" (*Unmenschlichkeit*) can be resisted.

This is speech that engages the shades of the underworld. As Odysseus sacrifices to the dead and addresses them, they start to speak, creating "mental forms" out of the inchoate power of myth, revealing themselves as *having been* unique and vulnerable individuals, real human beings. The pluperfect is crucial here: they once were what they are not now, and they carry that with them. The word makes the duality of this spectral realm snap into place: the shades are unreal, set in sharp contrast to the living, but, as they reawake to speech, they hold forth the promise, however faintly and vainly, that life can prevail over death even in the realm of the dead. This, to be sure, is yet another expression of the redemptive power of naming due to Benjamin. Speech may unduly categorize particulars at the expense of their singular existence; nonetheless, to the degree that language can be turned to particularity as such, it may be to that extent redemptive. It is as such a redeemer that Odysseus addresses the dead. His talk stirs them toward the beings they once were. But since he cannot truly bring them back to life, the linguistic mood that holds sway must be the optative.

The theme of *nostos*, of the homeward journey, structures the *Odyssey*. Odysseus may meander and find himself waylaid, but he never relinquishes the aim to return home and reunite with Penelope, Laertes, and Telemachus. Even when Calypso offers to make him "immortal, ageless, all his days"[26] in exchange for staying with her, he does not falter. He does of course return, in the sense that he repossesses his property and reasserts his position as head of the household and as king. Although Horkheimer and Adorno do not make the point explicit, Odysseus triumphs over all the mythical powers that in various ways try to prevent him from returning to civilization, a place where moral and juridical order exists and where a man of enlightenment may rule. Yet the return exacts a high price. The Odysseus who comes home is radically self-alienated. He has had to harden himself immeasurably, weaponizing his desires, that part of himself that more than anything else connects him to his body and, through it, to nature. The man who now shares Penelope's bed is – they imply – shrewder and colder, a man of relentless, even fanatic, grasping, who eschews any impulse that does not conform to what he deems useful. Unlike a modern agent, who faces daily a disenchanted reality completely devoid of mythical authority, their Odysseus knows the price he has paid. He is not blind to the many temptations and snares he has had to finesse. Although he is hardly the proto-bourgeois that the authors cast him to be, Odysseus does anticipate Marcuse's "one-dimensional" man.[27] Unlike the other rationalist of the Greek mythical imagination, Pentheus, who comes to a very sticky end for trying to outsmart Dionysus, Odysseus is thoroughly "successful."

TOO MUCH OF A BAD THING?

Horkheimer and Adorno's iconoclastic reading of Homer's epic raises many questions. How, for example, is Odysseus supposed to have single-handedly neutralized the Weberian nature's "enchanted garden" (*Zaubergarten*), transforming it so thoroughly that the very nature of sacrifice, which had been the key means to appease mythic powers and make them amenable to human interests, invades his identity, making him *for himself* the instrumental agent they claim he is?

DE's chapter on the concept of enlightenment introduced the idea of fear as the motivation that explains the distancing required. Yet because he always already finds himself at the necessary psychic distance from mythic powers, Odysseus seems to be distinctively fear*less*; he never, even in Hades, faces the horror of what Blumenberg calls "the nameless," i.e., the fear of the monstrous, of the abysmally strange.[28]

How does the idea so much as occur to Odysseus that he can trick the gods by means of strategic self-alienation? Horkheimer and Adorno's reading of the *Odyssey* neglects the fundamental issue: how can Odysseus be *so* different, not only from mythic powers but from men of his own standing? Why were not Ajax and Agamemnon, both of whom Odysseus visits in Hades, equally shrewd in their dealings? Why were they subject to those powers? One might argue that Odysseus's supposed enigmatic freedom, which to a large extent breaks with the epic world, would be more conceivable in the subsequent "axial age." According to Marcel Gauchet, while the sacred complex (to which the Homeric epics belong) does not leave the human subject with any other opportunity but to dispossess itself of distance from the collectively accepted teaching and reality of the sacred, what Karl Jaspers called the axial age opens distance between nature and the divine, leaving the immediacy of the mythic experience to be replaced by a more rational attitude.[29] With the slow but persistent emergence of monotheism, religious authority becomes the prerogative of interpretative experts (priests in particular), and nature is divested of the ferocious powers that dominated the religious imagination of the earlier period. The earlier predominance of a founding past, celebrated and expressed by the community in ritual, which encourages social equality (as well as social immobility), gives way to societies that are more stratified and dependent on rational norms of governance. Statehood emerges.

It would be tempting to contextualize Horkheimer and Adorno's approach to the *Odyssey* as introducing a tension not only between the world of the hero and the world of the unknown but also between two *social* worlds, each structured by presuppositions. Hegel's celebrated reading of *Antigone* provides a model.[30] Rather than focusing exclusively on the irresolvable conflict between two individuals – Antigone and Creon, the first representing the authority of the gods of hearth and home, the second representing the values and principles of the rational politician of the *polis* – Hegel holds that their "collision" displays a more fundamental social division for which ancient Greek society possessed no remedy other than dissolution. When Horkheimer and Adorno flirt with the idea that Odysseus is a prototype of bourgeois subjectivity, they introduce an even more seismic cleft. A bourgeois *hero*? Even a proto-bourgeois one? Is that even a coherent thought?

One might reply: well, there is at hand a replete tradition of interpreting the poem as being so unlike the *Iliad* that significant adjustments have to be made to conceptions of heroism in order to size it up as epic. Perhaps Horkheimer and Adorno are merely ringing changes on that. Yet the point remains that the oddity of Odysseus, that he stands out as a new kind of lord of nature and, therefore, of his peers as well, is left undeveloped. To put the point another way, the formulation that "myth [is] already enlightenment and that enlightenment reverts back to myth" presupposes *overlap* of the world of myth and of reason. This is the border Odysseus seems to be able to traverse at will, although not, as we have seen, without burden. In a sense, he even sets the border. That kind of agency is so outsized in comparison to other accounts of Greek heroes that it is difficult to generalize as any sort of trend.

Horkheimer and Adorno do successfully establish that, while steeped in the world of myth, the *Odyssey* contains a not-insignificant element of enlightenment. The Odysseus they are analyzing does, at least to some extent, manage to objectify and control natural *qua* mythic powers. He is, after all, the man "of many turns," the "much travelled," "shifty," "complicated" (*polytropos*) one who evades the set ways of nature. Fate transmutes to necessity, something that is immovable but can be worked with or around. The idea of enlightenment vetted in this excursus is consistent with the claim in *DE*'s first chapter that enlightenment is ultimately equivalent with being independent from extrinsic power.

But do Horkheimer and Adorno prove that enlightenment becomes myth in the *Odyssey*? Doubtful. The best-case scenario depends on accepting their idiosyncratic, Benjaminesque definition of myth. Surely, Odysseus does not succumb to myth if this means that his actions are, in the final analysis, determined by mythic forces. That is precisely what Horkheimer and Adorno claim he escapes. The view must rather be that, as a result of his perpetual and systematic self-sacrifice in the endeavor to deceive the mythic powers, Odysseus creates his own counterworld of myth. In this counterworld heteronomous repetition is all but irresistible, but what resistance there is requires pure instrumentality and, in its own sphere, is compulsory. To live in this counterworld is to detach from others and from any positive, nurturing relationship with nature as a matter of reflex. Odysseus is *homo oeconomicus*, always ready to engage in exchange. He is as alone as Crusoe; both he and Defoe's character deal "in total isolation from all other human beings, who appear to both men only in estranged forms, as enemies or allies, but always as instruments, things" (49/86). Both give something of themselves, but only in order to realize a return. Ultimately, it is repetition and compulsion that imprison Odysseus in his own subjectivity of false, self-alienating necessities that align him with myth. Just as Tantalus, Sisyphus, and the Danaids are "figures of compulsion" (45/82), so Scylla, Charybdis, Circe, and Polyphemus are "constituted by repetition: its failure would mean their end" (45/82). Such beings can do only one thing, play one trick indefinitely. This is precisely why Odysseus can fool them.

All that said, one might argue that Odysseus is more internally complex than this and insist that his unwavering commitment to *nostos* reveals a man of extraordinary fidelity and genuine love. The Odysseus who "wept as he held the wife/he loved, the soul of loyalty, in his arms at last"[31] – can he really possess such *sang froid*? Conversely, doesn't the mythical worldview harbor more than brute repetition and compulsion? In order to make out the claim that enlightenment reverts to mythology, Horkheimer and Adorno overlook key features of the mythical worldview: its concreteness and its power to integrate societies by providing a realm of sanctity. For all the talk of myth in *DE*, even when "myth" connotes "ideology," one cannot help being surprised by how little attention they actually pay to the real nature of myth (as well as to the copious literature on myth in several of the major European languages). The more one does pay attention to such things, the less plausible it becomes that Odysseus manages to instrumentalize mythic power.

In the end, then, it is inadvisable to read Horkheimer and Adorno as claiming to have offered a comprehensive reconstruction of *Odyssey*. Their goal was never to position themselves in the field of Homer scholars. Rather, as they make clear in the 1944 Preface, the aim was to "pursue" (*verfolgen*) the dialectic of myth and enlightenment as it plays itself out in the *Odyssey*. Tying the thesis of the dialectic to a fundamental document of Western civilization gets one's attention, but at least one important purpose of their reading is somewhat more modest: they want their reader to take seriously the notion that the ills often associated with late modernity did not just appear out of thin air a couple of centuries ago.

FURTHER READING

For accounts of the German reception of Homer, Bleicher 1971 and Marchand 2003 are both valuable. Wellmer 2000 provides an interesting approach to the reading of the Sirens episode.

NOTES

1. See Vermeule 1972.
2. See, e.g., Ahrensdorf 2022 and Haines 2005.
3. See Frank 1988.
4. For a reading of Excursus I that emphasizes the German reception's nationalistic and occasionally antisemitic character, see Fleming 2012.
5. The term is due to Gadamer. For him 'the classical' is not primarily a descriptive term handled by an objectifying historical consciousness. Rather, being a historical reality to which the historical consciousness belongs and is subject, it is saddled with normative implications: "The classical is something that resists historical criticism because its historical dominion, the binding power of the validity that is preserved and handed down, precedes all historical reflection and continues in it." Gadamer 1975: 287.
6. Adorno 1982, 135–46/1970 10.1: 138–51.
7. In a letter to his mother from February 10, 1942, Adorno claims to have drafted the chapter before carefully going through it with Horkheimer. See Müller-Doohm 2009, 281.
8. Benjamin 2019: 23:

    Criticism, together with the criteria of a terminology – the sounding board of the philosophical theory of ideas in art – take shape not according to the external standard of comparison but immanently, in a development of the formal language of the work, in such a way as to bring out the content of that language at the expense of its effect." It is likely that by "content" (*Inhalt*), Benjamin here means "truth-content" (*Wahrheitsgehalt*).

9. Nietzsche 2007: 45:

    The feeling of guilt, of personal obligation, to pursue our train of thought again, originated, as we saw, in the oldest and most primitive relationship there is, in the relationship of buyer and seller, creditor and debtor: here person met person for the first time, and measured himself person against person. No form of civilization has been discovered which is so low that it did not display something of this relationship.

10. He has already masterminded the Trojan Horse, which allows the Greeks to finally conquer Troy. This is not mentioned in the *Iliad*, but is at *Odyssey* 4.271–4 and, more fully, at 8.492–520. All citations to the *Odyssey* are keyed to Homer 1996.

11 One doesn't get back exactly what one gives up, but there are relations of equivalence that govern the transaction. The brilliance (and inside anti-Hegelian joke) of Kierkegaard's Knight of Faith (*Troens Ridder*) is that, in his sacrifice, precisely what he believes in is that the sacrificed will be returned as such. But that is not possible, since what is sacrificed, even if returned, would have to be returned as having-been-sacrificed-and-returned. What is returned would not be the selfsame thing, as it would have that additional property.

12 Cf. Freud 1989: 84:

> His aggressiveness is introjected, internalized; it is, in point of fact, sent back to where it came from – i.e., it is directed toward his own ego. There it is taken over by a portion of the ego, which sets itself over against the rest of the ego as super-ego, and which now, in the form of 'conscience', is ready to put into action against the ego the same harsh aggressiveness that the ego would have liked to satisfy upon other, extraneous individuals. The tension between the harsh super-ego and the ego that is subjected to it, is called by us the sense of guilt; it expresses itself as a need for punishment. Civilization, therefore, obtains mastery over the individual's dangerous desire for aggression by weakening and disarming it and by setting up an agency within him to watch over it, like a garrison in a conquered city.

13 Habermas 1993: 153: "Individuality forms itself in relations of intersubjective acknowledgment and of intersubjectively mediated self-understanding." The passage leans heavily on the account provided in Mead 1967, with which Habermas is familiar.

14 Cf. Adorno 1970: 6.269.

15 Odyssey 9.104–05.

16 Adorno 1970: 6.202.

17 Odyssey 10.365.

18 Odyssey 23.230–5, 242–5.

19 Odyssey 9.366f. While occasionally consulting the Greek original (judging from the quotations and the footnotes), Horkheimer and Adorno seem to be primarily working from a German translation. Which translation they use is never made explicit. However, as Backhuys 2017 points out, it is most likely the standard Voß translation. Backhuys also notes the discrepancy between what Horkheimer and Adorno remember the Greek word to be and the actual occurrence of the word in the poem. Homer uses the word *outis* (compound of *ou*, 'no' and *tis*, 'somebody', nominalized with changed accent). The word Horkheimer and Adorno recall is *oudeis* (interior elision of *oude*, 'but not' / 'not' and *eis*, 'one'). Homer never uses *oudeis* and, in any case, it would not fit metrically in the relevant lines of the poem. *Oudeis* occurs seldom in epic, but is prevalent in tragedy and prose. Backhuys suggests that what we have is a case of faulty back-translation.

20 But see note 19 above. Would *outis* sound enough like *Odysseus* to support Horkheimer and Adorno's contention? Recommendations about how to pronounce ancient Greek are tendentious, never mind its Homeric variant. If Allen 1968 is accepted as a guide (even though focused on Classical, not Homeric, Greek), the sonic difference between *oudeis* and *outis* might be bridged. He suggests French *d* for δ and French *t* for τ. To complicate

matters, there are two other bits of linguistic context to consider. Homer also uses the construction *mē tis* ('no one'), playing off *outis*, which is homonymous with the word *mētis* ('crafty'), which is a description of Odysseus. See *Odyssey* 9.410. This is a clearer case of sounding alike uniting meaning in terms applicable to Odysseus, the crafty no one. The second component of the context is more speculative. At 9.460 Polyphemus, again referring to Odysseus, says that he is *outidanos*, a 'good-for-nothing', in this context a weakling or even a coward (in the *Iliad* it is what Achilles calls Agamemnon when he wants to belittle him). This epithet is repeated at line 515. This sounds a bit closer to *Odysseus* and contains the *outi-* root as well. So, even though Horkheimer and Adorno are wrong about *oudeis*, and even if *outis* does not sound enough like *Odysseus* to ground their claim, the context in which *outis* occurs sports several sound semblances that intersect meaning and play on "nobody."

21 Odyssey 9.558–62.
22 The distinction between a mythical homeland of the soil and a historically and socially constituted homeland may be seen as bearing some similarity to the distinction between earth and world (*Erde* and *Welt*) in Heidegger 2002: 1–56. But, while Heidegger understands a people (*Volk*) to inhabit the tension (*Riß*) between the two dimensions of disclosing Being, i.e., earth and world, the more urbane Horkheimer and Adorno insist on the complete rejection of the mythical dimension of earth. In subsequent work, Adorno argues that the very notion of being-at-home, with its implication of the suspension of alienation, is deeply problematic.
23 For a synopsis of the various, often overlapping sectors of labor in Homer's poems, see Finley 1979: 51–73.
24 Odyssey 22.497–500. It is the "not for long [...] which lays bare the unspeakably endless torment of the single second in which the maids fought against death" (62/87), that moves the authors the most. "The exactitude of the description, which already exhibits the coldness of anatomy and vivisection, keeps a record, as in a novel, of the twitching of the subjugated women, who, under the aegis of justice and law, are thrust down into the realm from which Odysseus the judge has escaped" (61–2/87).
25 The idea of remembrance as a source of ethical obligation makes a famous and much discussed return in the passages of *Negative Dialectics* in which Adorno discusses the convergence of specific materialism with social criticism and change. There he writes that Hitler has imposed "a new categorial imperative on humankind: to arrange their thoughts and actions so that Auschwitz not repeat itself, so that nothing similar happen" Adorno 1970: 6.358.
26 Odyssey 5.151. Odysseus repeats the story to Arete at 7.296.
27 Marcuse 1964.
28 Blumenberg 1988: 34.
29 Gauchet 1997; Jaspers 1953. For an excellent contemporary introduction to the concept, see Habermas 2023: 1.321–36.
30 See Hegel 2019: 251ff.
31 Odyssey 23.260–1.

4
FROM KANT TO SADE

The second excursus is an extended discussion of the relation of Kant to enlightenment, where "enlightenment" this time refers both to a period in European intellectual history, *the* Enlightenment, as well as to the conceptual complex that is the subject matter of *DE*'s first two chapters. Specifically, the topic here is Kant's role in the Enlightenment conception of reason, with ethics as the main focus. The arresting claim is that Kant's Transcendental Idealism, in spite of itself, is allied with the thought of two figures it would have to view as inimical to it: Sade and Nietzsche.

AN IMPERFECT PAIR

Excursuses are sidebars and, as such, might seem to be relatively self-contained. But it is clear that this second excursus is an inversion of the first. Excursus I, as we just saw, investigates the interactivity of enlightenment and mythic thinking in a source rooted in archaic narrative. The dialectical partner to this claim – that myth is housed in enlightenment as well – is less well developed. The second excursus follows from the first in the sense that it takes up and develops this aspect of the dialectical balance: the question of what is mythic about enlightenment. And, as we shall see, it leaves less explored the obverse: the question of what is enlightened about myth. As a pair, one might say, the two excursuses complete a dialectical analysis. What Odysseus is to Excursus I, Juliette is to Excursus II. They are an imperfect pair.

The two excursuses not only structurally complement one another, they are also similar in temperament. Both exaggerate their cases, and intentional overstatement is deployed as an attention-getter. Portraying Odysseus as a traveling salesperson and Kant as a not-too-distant relative to Juliette is meant to make you sit up in your chair.

Kant is by some measure the philosopher who receives the most extensive treatment in *DE*. The way Horkheimer and Adorno write this chapter assumes a familiarity with doctrines and some of the details of *The Critique of Pure Reason*. We will, therefore, have to go into some of those details, not in order to determine whether their interpretation of Kant is defensible, but to see in the first place where they are coming from philosophically.

They open their discussion with what they know to be the most accessible thought of Kant's, a passage we have already discussed: "*Enlightenment is 'man's emergence from his self-incurred immaturity*. [*selbstverschuldeten Unmündigkeit*]. *Immaturity* is the inability to use one's own understanding [*seines Verstandes*] without the guidance of another'" (63/104).[1] Horkheimer and Adorno agree with the sentiment (see 90/138) but not with the execution. What they intend to do with this definition of enlightenment is telegraphed right away when they add that "'understanding without direction from another' is understanding guided by reason (*Vernunft*)" (90/138). Reason for Kant is the capacity for ordered, systematic thinking, which is more or less the same thing for him as saying for thinking period. Reason's a priori structure sets the base conditions for the most complex and abstract forms of conception: theories. Theoretical reason in turn orders the deliverance of the understanding (*Verstand*) – the faculty of the application of concepts, pure and otherwise, to intuitions, the result of which is experience (*Erfahrung*) – and sets methodological conditions for discovery. Reason is constrained only by logical principle and, on its own, does not take account of material possibilities. (It only does so secondhand, in ordering what the understanding provides by way of knowledge.)

What Horkheimer and Adorno – both of whom wrote dissertations on Kant with this emphasis – are indicating right at the start is that the means for the emergence from "self-incurred immaturity," according to Kant, is to liberate reason from nature and deploy a priori principles that gain force precisely by not being subject to nature, in order to subjugate that very nature. Kant's account of pure reason sets the terms for his entire philosophy; it is thinking with the greatest compass. It expresses an impulse or conatus to categorize and to elevate rule above instance that pervades from the top down every aspect of his thought. This is the antithesis of materialism, which takes nature prior to all thought to set the conditions on what can count as experience.

In this, Kant is indebted to the early modern rationalists. Like Descartes and, especially, like Leibniz, he conceives of the world as coterminal with a tiered system of concepts. But he outdoes his rationalist predecessors in joining that to a radical conception of autonomy as individual sovereignty. Not only must the world conform to the dictates of reason, but reason *makes* the world so conform. Horkheimer and Adorno's formulation of this crucial point is surprisingly tepid. It is not just that the world is systematized "*in accordance with* the understanding," as they write (64/105, emphasis supplied); whatever counts as the world is *grounded in* the understanding. As the understanding's sole task is to bring the particular under the general in order to fix experience in terms of types – what Kant calls "subsumption" – understanding is "determining judgment," which provides the building blocks for "the system" (63/105). Slightly more technically, subsumption provides a certain form of unity for Kant, i.e. unity in a single state of consciousness of multiple conscious states of object unity. That kind of unity transcends the mere sum of individual conscious states. It is an additional state of consciousness to those it unites, a unity of unities. Without it no general experience can follow.

WHICH KANT, WHOSE KANT?

Horkheimer and Adorno are interested in Kant because his Transcendental Idealism announces itself as the epitome of the Enlightenment. They see Transcendental Idealism as the most comprehensive and controlled statement of enlightenment thinking. But its monumentality is matched by its instability. It buys rational ambit with the currency of the a priori, currency that used to have value in more theological times but is debased when applied to the secular world unless that world is reduced to its formal structuring, to the application of a priori concepts as rules conceived as akin to scientific and logical laws. But the world is not so reducible; there is value in it that is not a product of categorization or of the fixed regularity that categorization brings with it. Kant strides a divide. He makes place for the idea that there is spontaneity of thought, i.e., forms of experience that cannot be reduced in favor of scientistic materialism. Yet the way he avoids the reduction is still beholden to terms set by the natural sciences of his day and, as a consequence, he imports strict conceptions of law into the very domain that he crafts to surmount materialism. It is an impossible balancing act and, once Kant unleashes the idea that reason is only expressed in laws and can treat inclination and nature as foreign domains to be brought to heel, he clears conceptual space for a Sade or a Nietzsche. That is Horkheimer and Adorno's focus and approach.

In pursuing this line, they are concerned with Kant's philosophy as an expression of social and historical forces that they argue are at work in enlightenment. They are willing, that is, to read core features of his theoretical and practical philosophy in the light of *DE*'s general treatment of instrumentalization and myth. This leads to a discussion that may irk experts in Kant's philosophy as being insufficiently subtle and uncharitable. But Horkheimer and Adorno are not interested in nuancing Kant's position to generate more tractable forms of Kantianism. That is a dead end, if their main line in *DE* is correct.

Reason for Kant is an autonomous universal subjective capacity. It alone grounds and, consistent with early modern conceptions of first substance, is self-grounding. It grounds all else *by* grounding itself. Now, what is remarkable about Kant's conception of reason as ground, beyond the point that he seats this in the cognitive subject and not in a world independent of its subjective uptake, is that part of the power to self-ground is to self-limit. Kant's main move here is to limit the claim of reason to know matters about the empirical world. "Pure" reason is able to think anything on condition that thought obeys the laws of logic as Kant understood them. That leaves open room for a great deal of metaphysical speculation about the world that Kant held was undecidable in principle, given the limitation of finite discursive beings to sense. Part of reason's freedom is to recognize the finite situation of discursive cognitive agents and to adjust the scope of permissible forms of reasoning to suit. The result of this self-limitation is the bifurcation of capacities for knowledge into sensibility, on the one hand, and the understanding, on the other. These capacities – what Kant calls "faculties" – are discrete from one another but, crucially, must interact in order to yield knowledge of nature.

As one descends from reason to the faculties associated more proximally to making empirical judgments, there are multiple basic functions relative to cognitive domain, and the complexity of Kant's architectonic increases. But that should not obscure the fact that reason is, via the proxy of its self-limitation, active in all these domains. They are unified in one, overarching reason. Horkheimer and Adorno let this downward force of rational structuration inform much of their critique.

The sovereignty of reason consists in its ultimate power to structure experience conceptually and inferentially. So long as reason meets the demands of its self-critique, the more order and system, the better. Kantian pure reason has an impulse, according to Horkheimer and Adorno, to boundlessly systematize. That impetus radiates through the entirety of human discursive life, from whole theories to everyday perception (64/105). Horkheimer and Adorno, accordingly, will analyze two doctrines central to Kant's epistemology and philosophy of mind as driven by an interest in systematicity and unity, what they sometimes call "unanimity" (*Einstimmigkeit*) (63/104).[2] Both of the doctrines have to do with basic experiential structuration: how concepts and intuitions join in perception and the kind of unity that conjunction presupposes on the part of the cognitive subject, i.e., *schematism* and the *synthetic unity of apperception*.

To establish a baseline, they avert to a basic logical principle (basic, that is, for classical forms of logic), that of non-contradiction (63/104). The principle of non-contradiction says that a proposition and its negation cannot be both true. This is a minimal and entirely formal conceptual constraint, insensitive by its very nature to the content of propositions. While hurriedly made, their point is clear: material nature imposes no limitation on reason for Kant. In fact, the reverse is true for him: Reason imposes limits on nature.

"Nature," it turns out, is a term of art for Kant. It does not mean, as one might expect, "the world, considered apart from discursive access to it." Nature, for Kant, is the sum total of possible experiences, restricted as they are to the a priori laws of the understanding, a priori forms of intuition, and the postulates and axioms derived therefrom. Nature does not supply a contrast with reason for Kant; rather, "nature" is a concept used by him in connection with a limited species of reasoning that belongs to objects of knowledge. That is the main problem Horkheimer and Adorno see with idealism, Transcendental Idealism included.

What Kant terms "experience" (*Erfahrung*) is a result of mental combination, what he calls "synthesis." This provides the first target for Horkheimer and Adorno's criticism. It is not that they hold that Kant is wrong that some human experience depends on synthesis, nor that they hold that synthesis in and of itself brings untoward philosophical consequences. To the contrary, the idea of synthesis as constitutive of experience expresses something they value highly, i.e., the idea that human forms of experience bear within them lability, that they are forms of agency that can change the world, not just take it as given. But they do contest the scope Kant accords synthesis, as well as the basis he seeks for it.

For Kant any knowledge – the objective grasp of reality in judgment – requires synthesis, i.e., the subsumption of singular objective representations under general objective representations. You take various intuitions and unite them in terms of particular concepts and the a priori conceptual functions that undergird them. Kant in his various lectures on logic and anthropology speaks of comparative states of mind short of synthesis that are not, at least not strictly speaking, rulebound. But synthesis in the understanding is a matter of rules for Kant and tends toward applying fixed sets of rules in order to regularize objects and events. It does so spontaneously in that the basic rules are not constrained by, and do not fundamentally regard, the things themselves, i.e., things prior to the work of synthesis. This matters to Horkheimer and Adorno a great deal. Mimesis is concerned with pre-synthetic experience and, as we have discussed, is a basically responsive capacity that takes its creative lead by submitting to the integrity of nature itself. Seating the authority of experience in synthesis, rather than seeing synthesis as a somewhat one-sided subvariant of mimesis, let alone in an a priori form of synthesis, unmoors it from nature. To repeat: Horkheimer and Adorno are not anti-synthesis, but they are anti-unresponsive synthesis. As we shall see in the chapter on the culture industry, they will treat the responsiveness one has to a work of art as a model for the correct regard paid to the claim of nature in human judgment, a position heavily litigated in nineteenth-century German philosophy beginning, ironically, with Kant.

Let's turn now to the main problem with schematism as Horkheimer and Adorno understand it. They wish here to press an ambiguity, as they see it, in Kant's account. Kant's formalism requires an account of how the purely general can combine with the purely specific, i.e., how a priori concepts can even so much as apply to intuitions. The problem is simple to state: what might they have in common that allows for the joining of the two, given that Kant strictly separates the general from the specific?[3] That is a problem, in Horkheimer and Adorno's estimation, that is introduced by Kant's form of dualism, which treats nature prior to thought as ulterior to experience. They do not make the point as explicit as they might, but it is reasonably clear that Horkheimer and Adorno hold the view, initiated in systematic form by Schopenhauer, that the world antecedent to possible thought is formless. That is how, they hold, Kant would have to think of it.

All that said, the idea of schematism is in Kant a repository for something Horkheimer and Adorno cherish: that there is a discrete point at which concepts need to abide by what they describe. If one can, in essence, intervene at that point with the right theory, then some of the more authoritarian aspects of Kant might be mitigated.

We know that *DE* is sensitive to potentially reductive roles of concepts in experience. Conceptual thought is necessary for many human pursuits, but it comes with a cost. To think conceptually (especially in the modern world) is to think generically; one does not regard objects as having singular natures. That is a cost because any set of descriptions rules out other ways objects might be described, other possible ways they might *be* for thought, and conceptual determination may end up screening rather than revealing the object. When general terms further combine in order to increase generality at higher levels of abstraction, this further narrows the range of possibility. In the physical sciences this narrowing is of the essence. Experimental testing, which forms a great deal of the basis for objective knowledge in the modern world, works through repetition, i.e., by replication of results (cf. 65, 98/106–07, 149). If the concepts, then, concatenate into theories, one has a very dense interrelation of repetition in the form of laws.

Transcendental Idealism says that the formal properties of experience are all supplied by the cognitive subject. Kant divides this formal agency into two main sources, along the lines of the two sorts of objective cognitions: (1) formal receptive structures, i.e., the forms of intuition, which are time and space, and (2) formal combinatory structures, i.e., the basic a priori concepts, which he calls "categories." Any intuition must be temporal and, if the intuition is of a purportedly objective thing, property, or event external to the cognizing subject, spatial as well. Intuiting the coffee cup on your desk is being conscious of it apart from yourself and conditioned temporally and spatially: the cup is, to you, *that thing, now, over there*. Experiencing the cup of coffee *as* a cup of coffee involves, additionally, the application of empirical concepts like "cup" and "coffee." But application of empirical concepts for Kant presupposes an application of categories like "unity," "substance and accident," "reality," and "existence and nonexistence." They encapsulate the basic ways discursive beings with intuitions like ours can combine manifolds of intuition under concepts at all.

Now, intuitions are *radically non-general*: they are singular representations. Categories are also formal but are *nothing but general*. So, how does the wholly specific combine with the wholly general in synthesis? Whence the overlap?

This is the problem mentioned above with a bit more specification. In broad stroke, Kant's answer is reasonably clear. Time is the most comprehensive form of intuition; nothing intuited by discursive beings with intuition like ours can be nontemporal. But time can also be thought of conceptually, and that means as a matter of generality. Kant holds that the faculty of imagination has the power to map generality onto specificity, given that it is inherent to imagination to operate with generalization and with specification at the same time. The imagination invents, as it were, the general aspects of what it imagines along with the specifics. Take our coffee cup example. Say you imagine, i.e., visualize, a coffee cup. Your mind is producing an image by creating both the general features of what you visualize and a specific instance that they fit. In this sense there are both conceptual and intuitive aspects to your visualization. That's an empirical operation of imagination, but Kant argues that the imagination has a pure, transcendental form in which this combined work can and must be done for any and all synthesis. This is the ground-zero of Kant's philosophy of mind, his account of how concepts can be at all active in experience.

Horkheimer and Adorno gloss schematism as an instance of *forced* "harmony" between "system and nature" (64/105). There are two things to mark. The first is that the imagination's work in cognition is subject to the dictates of the understanding, and that means to the dictates of rules and, ultimately, to those of reason. Kantian pure reason self-limits to be more responsive to the requirements of the empirical world, but it cannot go far enough because it has divorced itself from the outset from nature as it is in itself. The imagination – precisely the faculty that must lead if one is to think of possibilities other than what is given in terms of conceptual stock – is constrained to model generalities in order to generate the "harmony" of concepts and intuitions. Schematism is, essentially, a yoking of the imagination to the task of ordering. Even perception is affected (65/106–07).

In truth, however, perception is socially structured in terms of modern ideals of repletion and expediency. There are no strict bounds between a priori and a posteriori:

> According to Kant, the homogeneity of the general and the particular is guaranteed by the "schematism of pure understanding," by which he means the unconscious activity of the intellectual mechanism which structures perception in accordance with the understanding. The intelligibility which subjective judgment discovers in any matter is imprinted [*prägt*] on that matter by the intellect as an objective quality before it enters the ego [*Ich*]. Without such a schematism—in short without the intellectual element in perception—no impression [*Eindruck*] would conform to the corresponding concept, no category to the particular example, not to speak of the system toward which everything is directed.
>
> (64/105)

Horkheimer and Adorno then pitch their critique of schematism from the precincts of social theory. They analogize, but just barely, the preformation of perceptions by concepts with the "precensorship" of images in Hollywood films:

> The senses are determined by the conceptual apparatus in advance of perception; the citizen sees the world as made a priori of the stuff from which he himself constructs it. Kant intuitively anticipated what Hollywood has consciously put into practice: images are precensored during production by the same standard of understanding which will later determine their reception by viewers. The perception by which public judgment feels itself confirmed has been shaped by that judgment even before the perception takes place.
>
> (65–6/107)

Note the characteristic move: what are a priori structures for Kant are translated into *unconscious a posteriori* structures for Horkheimer and Adorno. This homologizing move is tricky. As did Freud, Horkheimer and Adorno regard psychodynamics to be unconscious or preconscious, but that does not mean that they are non-natural. True, the processes are antecedent to much conscious activity, but they are not sealed off by their very nature by external, natural causation. Social structures vastly form what antecedent structuration of conscious experience there is. How much Kant can accommodate that thought is a question of some scholarly interest, but Horkheimer and Adorno take it to be an objection to his whole enterprise.

So much for synthesis and schematism. Let's turn now to the second theoretical idea of Kant's that Horkheimer and Adorno find diagnostically important: the synthetic unity of apperception. Apperception is a form of self-consciousness. "Pure" or "original" apperception is the spontaneous act of thinking the thought "I am thinking." Kant holds that that thought must be able to accompany any of my representations in order that they be *mine* in the first place.[4] The *unity* of apperception is, then, the unity of this kind of self-consciousness, i.e., of original apperception.

The synthetic unity of apperception is the fundamental ground for the continuity of experience.[5] The term "continuity" must be strictly construed: not just continuity between different experiences, but also and more fundamentally the continuity within an experience, what makes it the case that synthesis can hold at all. As the introduction of the thought "I am thinking" might indicate, Kant's answer retrofits Descartes. Cartesian epistemology takes its stand with the thinking subject as *res cogitans*. Kant argues that Descartes oversteps in ascribing thinking to a *res*, if by "thing" one means a substance that is knowable by introspection. Nevertheless, Kant never discards the idea that any mental content must have something "extra" to it to make the content *this, my* content. The possibility of the self-ascription of a thought – however that is accomplished – is necessary for there to be a thought at all. The ascription is completely formal; one does not identify even implicitly the thought as that of the empirical you. This "my-ness" is precisely *not* to be understood as a natural property, which is just another way of glossing Kant's insistence that the synthetic unity be "original," i.e., originating, or "spontaneous."

Here as well Horkheimer and Adorno treat the appeal to abstract formality as a phenomenon to be explained socially (68/109–110). The two interlocking dimensions of modern ways to think of subjectivity that Horkheimer and Adorno address in any number of contexts are here in play. The first is Kant's appeal to *formality* as the kind of "I" that binds together experience. The formal I is formal in that it is precisely *not* the actual I of anyone. It is not you in any sense that you would have of yourself as an article of actual experiencing. That is its point. Dire modernity has driven agents so back upon themselves, divorced as they take themselves to be from nature, that any natural specification of them as the selves they are is not enough to confer experiential continuity. Why think of the guarantee of continuity in terms of a summonable piece of consciousness? Why not something unconscious that is not a "thought" in that sense, even a formal one? Why not an embodied state or process? The second aspect has to do with the *fixity* of the self. In order to be I in the relevant Kantian sense, i.e., in order to be the anchor of an integrated line of experience, I must not be a historical being at all. Historical selves are open to contingencies and are not fixed. Whatever a self is, it is not the unchanging substrate of changing experience. Any stability is relative to frame; metaphysically speaking, selves change with their experiences. Modernity, regulated and regularized to the hilt, still sees the fixed self as a requirement, but the way the requirement must be met can only be extremely minimal. The formal I is, in essence, a last-ditch attempt to secure selfhood as a response to a society in which only what is repeatable matters.

In other words, what is basically at work is the impulse to self-preservation, i.e., survival (65, 68/106, 109) under modern conditions. Kant's wish to stabilize a system around emerging modern imperatives, yet avoid their demoralizing force, can only be "ambiguous" (65, 68/106, 109). The utopian need for universality – for true totality – is pitted against the injunction to "calculate" (65, 68/106, 109, 69/110).

MORALITY'S RETREAT FROM NATURE

If nature is divested of its dignity by calculative thinking, self-preservation becomes an end in itself, not a means to greater things. Kant is sensitive to the point but, again, Horkheimer and Adorno find his attempts to address it hobbled by his conception of reason, "the organ of calculation, of planning, it is neutral with regard to ends; its element is coordination" (69/111).

Actually, Kant holds that reason in this, its highest, deployment, is *not* neutral with regard to final ends. What he calls "pure practical reason" takes persons as ends in themselves and deploys that conception of personhood as the basis for ethical action. The key issue here is how Kant bifurcates human nature within human agents relative to their moral vocation and, in particular, how he treats "inclination" (*Aneignung*). Inclinations are dispositions to act that originate in desire and allied natural aspects of people. As such, they are only problematically associated with morality, for Kant conceives of nature as lacking the appropriate power to generate moral norms. Morality involves strict lawfulness. Specifically, moral duties are grounded in a single, overarching principle. The formality issue returns.

As a consequence, for Kant any being that is both rational and sensuous must experience the moral law as a *command*, as an imperative; it is a law imposed *on* the empirical you *by* the rational you. The idea of law as command is joined with the idea of legislating and internalized as reflexive: self-command, duty to oneself, and self-governance. This schema is in essence an internalization of the divine right of kings, in which one rules and is ruled by oneself. Part of you, then, ought to rule over the rest of you if you are being moral.

Inclination and duty do not in all cases diverge of course and, in his better moments, Kant does not think that it is more virtuous to do one's duty when it is against one's inclination than when it is not. The point remains, however, that inclinations are always potentially problematic and, since your inclinations are an ineliminable part of who you are, you will be at least wary of yourself in that regard.

The division between pure rational and empirical self has other impacts as well that cause one to harbor self-enmity or self-doubt. For instance, Kant emphasizes that you can never know that you have acted only out of, and not merely in accordance with, the moral law. That is because you can never rule out that something ulterior to pure reason has surreptitiously determined your act. Because Kantian morality requires acting *only* from duty, even the slightest admixture of empirical inclination ruins everything.

Another sense in which Kant's ethics might be considered formalistic has to do with the claim that the categorical imperative is formal.[6] According to Kant, a maxim – his term for a statement in the form of a rule that recommends a course of action – passes the test and ascends to the realm of moral law if and only if it can be "universalized," i.e., only if the maxim can be willed as binding on all rational agents for all time in any and all situations. The measure for this is whether the maxim so willed could be a strict law, i.e., whether the inclusion of it in a world conceived as having that law would or would not render such a world possible or, slightly differently, whether willing such a maxim would be inconsistent with the very idea of rational willing.

What "possible" means here is heavily litigated – in fact the gloss of the imperative just given is subject to hedging and reformulation at almost every step – but for now let's say that "possible world" means one in which willing according to the law is non-contradictory, where – and here comes another point of construal – "non-contradictory" means "not pragmatically self-undermining." Possible willing, then, would be willing in accordance with what Kant takes to be the basic structure of pure practical reason. So, the complete picture on this standard understanding of the categorical imperative is that any truly moral law can be commanded of all by each without self-undermining. False promising, for example, is supposed to lead to a contradiction. If everyone adopted the maxim of false promising, it would in effect render promising impossible.[7]

But what *is* pragmatic self-undermining? Doesn't that appeal to empirical contexts? Isn't that historically conditioned? Doesn't it spoil the a priori strictness that Kant is after? Horkheimer and Adorno bang this drum repeatedly against Kantian formality and its hegemony of laws. Kantian morality involves the notion of a rule that has substance precisely in abstraction from any of its possible instances; Kantian moral laws do not – indeed cannot, if Kant is right – trace their normativity to concrete historical-social contexts. But if Kant is mistaken and those structures are historical, that puts the lie to the idea that contextless principles can dictate to contexts.

This is, in effect, a moral counterpart to the problem of schematism with which we began. Kant has a problem applying general determinants on the mental side of the equation to the specificities to be determined on the other side. But here the divide is enforced further by the radical difference between transcendental and empirical aspects of the self. Put in social terms, the issue raised is that if we all have pure reason, we should all be united to that (great) measure. The only thing that keeps one from being so is empirical, the inclination to act out of impure reasons. Where does that come from? Society, Horkheimer and Adorno quite reasonably respond (65/90). One simply cannot ground mutual respect in non-materiality (67/92); there is no demonstrable Christian community of souls. The best Kant can do in this regard is to posit transcendentally a Kingdom of Ends.

Society nowadays (and back then) is a place where everyone is in material competition with everyone else. This shows both that formal moral criteria cannot do the job that only social theory can: "The moral teachings of the Enlightenment bear witness to the hopelessness of attempting to replace enfeebled religion by an intellectual motive for enduring within society when material interest no longer suffices" (66–7/108). In a nutshell and put in the Kantian vernacular: pure reason cannot be pure *practical* reason (67/109).

Put in terms of the idea of self-preservation that is central to Horkheimer and Adorno's account of subjective responsiveness, what one has once again is an over-idealization of that relation. What moral respect really does is material; it is a socially effective way for agents to avoid violent interaction or to express their natural predilection to care for others. The dialectical point is that, in evacuating this social imperative into the realm of the ahistorical, transcendental self, what was to be avoided is enhanced. What one has in Kant's attempt to circumvent modernity's rush to scientific forms of materialism and to preserve spontaneity is a faint and formal set of constraints that prove ineffective, all the while giving the impression that they are effective, which is just what reductive forms of materialism demand.

This surreptitiously opens the door to Sade. Sadean erotics do not follow from Kantian ethics doctrinally of course, nor does the categorical imperative authorize the reasons that Sade places in his characters' mouths. It is, rather, that both Kant and Sade presuppose an enlightenment truism: that a formal conception of reasoning *alone* is effective in determining what to do. Such laws are laws at all only insofar as they do not draw their authority from concrete historical-social contexts. The result is that both Kant and Sade put moral inclination to the side, and that is deadly. Sade's ideas are incompatible with Kant's to be sure; they may even appear to be contradictory. But their opposition is in fact to be explained by their being two aspects of a single, overarching, and modern pathology of reason (72/115).

JULIETTE – THE EVIL STEPDAUGHTER

In the generation prior to Kant, the eliminative materialism of Holbach and La Mettrie was a serious philosophical option. Eliminative materialism is the claim that everything is matter or, more precisely, that any explanation can be recast in terms that only make appeal to material processes and entities. Either way that includes all human mental activity: thus, the title of La Mettrie's most famous work, *L'Homme machine* (1748). This is a denial of the ground for the purity of Kantian reason in the supersensible and, to that extent, is anti-Kantian. Still, as in Kant, there is nothing inherently moral about human naturalness or in nature on this picture, and that is what accounts for the overlap of the positions. Bodies and minds are nothing more than automata, complex to be sure, but establishing by virtue of what they are complex is a problem to be solved by experimenting on them, not by armchair philosophizing. Pity, to take one possible source for moral regard that we shall discuss at the end of this chapter, doesn't matter. This breeds excess formality in that anything is subject to mechanistic law and is a candidate for experimentation, inaugurating a topsy-turvy situation in which excessive rationalization generates excess that is extra-rational, that cannot be reincorporated into the rational structure that spawned it. Law strives for ecstatic effects in its effort to cover each and every element of existence, down to the minutiae. That is where Sade belongs.

It is worth mentioning that there is a reaction to materialism that is not Kantian and is important for Horkheimer and Adorno, one that seeks immediate remediation in nature. This is also primarily a French line, what Horkheimer elsewhere calls "irrationalism." Late Romantics like Baudelaire and Rimbaud, symbolists like Mallarmé, vitalists like Bergson and Dilthey, and Dadaists and surrealists belong here. Irrationalism and materialism are strongly interactive, but the materialist sets the terms of engagement. She casts the irrationalist as one who opposes *any* form of reason. Of course, the form of reason with which the materialist is operating, and in terms of which she makes the critique of the irrationalist, is one that claims that the *only* fundamental form of rationality is one that subjects things via testing to natural laws. Whatever is not counts as "superstitious." Any remnant of nature as a source for ethical culture is labeled "taboo" (73/115–16).

Sade applies formality insensitive to natural inclination in order to refashion nature into a domain in which everything is subject to manipulation. Sade's Juliette wants to put fully to work the base materials of modernity in order to uproot any and all sentiment, pity, joy, in short, destroy anything left of the idea of reason-transcending value (81/126–7): "Sade demonstrated empirically what Kant grounded transcendentally: the affinity between knowledge and planning" (69/111). Sade's books are not about pleasure per se, and they are certainly not pleasurable to read (at least not for most readers). They are about the experimentation with and organization of pleasure, its *systematicity*, and pursuing to the utmost the divorce of pleasure from any perceived natural morality (74/117). "Juliette's credo is science" (76/119). One implication of Horkheimer and Adorno's statement that Sade does empirically what Kant has done transcendentally may be that the denizens of Sade's works are not motivated to surmount nature in order to control it. They seek to control it from within.

Donatien Alphonse François, Marquis de Sade (1740–1814) was a member of the *noblesse d'épée* (the oldest rank of French nobility) and a tireless advocate for, and often-foiled practitioner of, unbridled sex. Although he was never convicted of violating French law, he spent long periods of his adult life in prisons or mental institutions. From such institutions – but not only from there – he wrote obsessively and in extreme detail about sex and violence. Rape, incest, bestiality, pedophilia, coprophilia, necrophilia, mutilation, torture, and murder are staged and extolled in his many works.

There are often long passages of discussion. These disputations do not involve knotty questions of whether particular actions constitute rape, torture, or murder; rather, they are arguments for the positive value of rape *as rape*, of torture *as torture*, and of murder *as murder*. The novels *120 Days of Sodom* (1785, unfinished), *Justine* (1791), *Philosophy in the Bedroom* (1795), and *The Story of Juliette* (1797) constitute a remarkably consistent set that offers a unified, comprehensive outlook on their topic.

Juliette's denizens anatomize every action and strive to realize an infinite variation of possible other actions. They aspire in thought and deed to exhaust the universe of carnal possibility. But Sade does not only want to convey a propositional understanding of new possibilities; he wants his characters to imagine themselves into contexts in which things happen according to the principles in play. He demands of them both knowledge and experience.

The program, then, is to establish a form of self by insatiably exploring infinite gradations of using other selves for one's gratification. Such gratification has less to do with animal urges than with proclivities cultivated well beyond the norm. Boundary-pushing is key. The thoughts and actions are calculated precisely to be excessive, to overwrite the norm so resolutely that what is ordinary is destroyed and replaced. This is a philosophy of the extreme, the rational substructure of which ensures the provision of *more*.

When Horkheimer and Adorno write that Sade's motto might have been "no orifice left unused" (69/111), they present that as part of a broader formulation having to do with time as a commodity. In Sade's characters one has a precursor to the entrepreneur (*Unternehmer*) who, when asked what they do, will respond that they make money, and, when asked further as to what good is that, will be nonplussed (84/130). "Time is money," as the old saying goes.

Notwithstanding all of this, Horkheimer and Adorno in the end consider Juliette an imperfect representative of those whose principle it is to make use of others only for purposes of one's own pleasure. That is because part of the pleasure she takes in such activities (and in thinking and talking about them) is reactive:

> For all her rational superiority, Juliette still clings to one superstition. While she recognizes the naivety of sacrilege, in the end it still

> gives her pleasure. But every pleasure betrays an idolization: it is the self-abandonment to an Other. Nature actually does not know pleasure: it does not go beyond satisfaction of needs. All pleasure is social, in the unsublimated affects no less than in the sublimated. It springs from alienation.
>
> (82/128)

Juliette is aware of this tendency in others of her clan and chides them for it (81, 83/127, 129), but she backslides. The point: Pleasure taken in a thought or action on account of its being forbidden depends on implicitly recognizing the power of what forbids.[8] The frisson depends on the sanction.

Given the centrality to Juliette's exploits of the reduction of others' bodies to mere material, one might think that what is on offer in Sade is a perverse return to nature. But the nature that is relevant to Juliette is one that she and her compatriots make. To use Kantian language, they *constitute* it. "Once the objective order of nature has been dismissed as prejudice and myth, nature is no more than a mass of material" (78/122). But that is not nature as Horkheimer and Adorno see it; it is, rather, a deracination of nature. For Sade, quantitative, calculative value has significance over and above what can qualify as nature. All pleasures are notches in one's belt.

NIETZSCHE'S COUP DE GRÂCE

Horkheimer and Adorno present those aspects of Nietzsche that they wish to discuss by braiding them into the discussion of *Juliette*, and it can be difficult to pry Sade and Nietzsche apart on that count. But there are two signposts that permit Horkheimer and Adorno to contrast Sade and Nietzsche even given substantial overlap of some of their views. The first is the rejection of pity as a virtue. The second is the idea of a new form of individuality, encapsulated in the figure of the Overman (*Übermensch*).

Horkheimer and Adorno read Nietzsche retrospectively in the line of both Kant and Sade. This is provocative given Nietzsche's strongly worded, negative assessment of Kant. But they read Nietzsche prospectively as well, seeing German fascism as an enflamed extension of his attempt to rehabilitate noble virtues (89/137).

As the editors of the most authoritative German edition of *DE* and the English translator note, this assessment was a replacement in the 1947 publication of the book. In 1944 Horkheimer and Adorno wrote instead that Nietzsche prefigured "the class society." Both are complicated claims. The first is so because, as Walter Kaufmann emphasized, Nietzsche himself could hardly have been a German fascist, the prototype for which he openly scorned.[9] But that does not of course rule out trying to recruit Nietzsche to fascism *post mortem*, and so he was, not the least by his sister.

The redacted Marxist idea – that Nietzsche be considered a bourgeois advocate for class – is even harder to pin down. Nietzsche did insist on the distinction between ruler and ruled. It is a matter for dispute what sort of naturalism is involved in that division, but it is indisputable that those are not "classes" in the sense of the term political economists use, let alone Marx. But that sense of "class" is clearly what Horkheimer and Adorno mean (thus the redaction). What seems really to have been on their minds in 1944 was the idea that Nietzsche's Overman finds a place in right-libertarian forms of capitalism as the entrepreneur of such self-affirmation that he embodies the anti-democratic impulse of capitalism. He is a modern substitution for the archaic hero. Such knights of industry might be robber barons like the Rockefellers or Mellons or, stepping forward from the Gilded Age into today, Steve Jobs or Elon Musk. It is a figure *DE* associates with the development of fascism.

Sade as a fascist, by contrast, is an easy case. There have been movies made – good ones – about Nazis as Sade-like beings, where what are private vices are transmuted into public virtues (93/142–3). Visconti's *The Damned* (1969) shows just that, its fevered scenes of the Night of the Long Knives close to horror in style. Pier Paolo Pasolini's *Salò* (1975), a film adaptation of *120 Days of Sodom*, covers similar ground with even greater intensity. It *is* a horror movie, almost impossible to sit through so demented and graphic is its violence.

So, to complete the triangle with which we are dealing, what is there of Sade in Nietzsche? The first thing to say is that Nietzsche no doubt had secondhand testimony about Sade and his literary output; everyone did. But he could have had no direct knowledge of the writings, as their publication was prohibited in Europe until the 1950s. Of course, there were copies of the books available if one had the right "connections," but Nietzsche was not interested in that sort of thing. We know exactly what was in his personal library and what he checked out from institutional libraries all the way back to his school days at Pforta, and there is no record he ever read Sade.

Horkheimer and Adorno are not talking about historical influence however. The point is how Sade and Nietzsche stand relative to one another conceptually. Their twin attacks on Christianity – Sade on Roman Catholicism and Nietzsche on Christianity all told – occupy the foreground. The problem of enlightenment is one of unacknowledged myth that is still at work. Prior to the Enlightenment, religion held out that conceptual order mapped directly onto world order, a guarantee ultimately secured by appeal to God's will that is inherited from the Middle Ages: the order of reason and order of things are two sides of the same coin. Early modern rationalism worked freely with this presupposition, then argued about how best to sort out the details. (Horkheimer had a soft spot for occasionalism on this score, as he held that its extravagance underscored problems of the coherence of the two orders.[10]) This all breaks down in Kant, for whom all order is order*ing*, fully on the side of thinking. Preestablished harmony is dead. Kant is a devastation of nothing less than the then-ordinary way to think of what binds knowledge and value in one objective order. On the old picture morals could be considered unproblematically a form of knowledge. Not anymore.

To bring the triangulation of Sade, Kant, and Nietzsche into final focus, consider the concept of pity (*Mitleid*). Kant will have none of it, nor will Sade or Nietzsche. To the ancient stoics *apatheia* was a state reached after laborious meditation on the place of humans in the cosmos. Its ultimate value was therapeutic. To feel is to be perturbed, and it takes a great deal of discipline to free oneself from that. Kant was a great imbiber of Roman stoicism, but he denies pity on transcendental grounds. To pity is to misplace ethical regard. Sade is even more resolute: No object of purpose is to be regarded in terms of any feeling it might arouse, unless that feeling is itself objectified for purposes of consumption. That is the abuser's excitement, now practiced under even more stringent order to void any non-calculative affect. Total disregard of affect except in quantified form – and thus not really affect at all but rather behavior – is what is in order. No one can pity someone they torture and *really* be torturing them. It is rather an exercise of "apathy," with a helping of disdain (75/119) – distanced unfeeling. This is close kin to Nietzsche's "pathos of distance," which may be an emotion of sorts, but it is not the feeling *for others*. It is a distance of regard. For Nietzsche pity is an affront to one's power to choose.

What is at stake in all three attitudes concerning pity is Weber's disenchantment, emptying the world of Christian virtue and, with it under the prevailing historical circumstance, any inherent moral worth (93/142). But for their shared enmity for pity, Nietzsche emerges in an interesting way as importantly dissimilar to Sade and also to whatever Kantian residue there is in Sade.

To Horkheimer and Adorno Nietzsche is something like the Hegelian in-and-for-itself of the Enlightenment, in which a return to myth results from the attempt of enlightenment to push beyond itself (90/138–9). In accordance with this, Nietzsche scripts a specific type of a "more-than-natural" human, a figure for whom the vicissitudes of nature matter in a particular way. Such a being does not sugarcoat the pain of existing but denies it the status of *suffering*, of deprivation.

Horkheimer and Adorno's suggestion that Nietzsche sums up modern philosophy is drawn from Nietzsche himself, who holds that the excessive valorization of the scientific conception of truth that is typical of modern thought hits a wall at the very point it seems to win the day.[11] Truth whittled down to being subject to empirical testing is not truth enough to undergird full-blooded forms of life. Enlightenment is really an "idol" (*Götze*), a false form of what it banishes from the world. If scientific truth is meant to propitiate nature, there can be no such hope. Empirical truth is useful no doubt, but it is not the be-all and end-all.

The deficiency in Nietzsche's views, in Horkheimer and Adorno's estimation, lies in his conception of the Overman. It trades in the idea that true rebellion is lofty while crime is base (79 & n.43/123 & n.43). One might consider this an advance on Sade: The Overman is not a reactive, pseudo-iconoclast. Running about and committing crimes out of the sheer will to break the law is too bound up with the authority of those very laws to count for much. Nietzsche holds that freedom consists in the will to create *new values*, not merely despoil the old ones. While Horkheimer and Adorno allow the point, they are not convinced that it sees Nietzsche out of the thicket of deformed enlightenment. Juliette's refusal to see the lowly as pernicious is a salutary refusal of transcendence. Nietzsche falls prey to the idea that one could reclaim nature by a heroic act of individual will (92/140–1), and that is a variant on Kant. That closes the triangle.

PUNISHING THE RETURN OF NATURE: THE STATUS OF WOMEN

The dichotomy introduced by Sade between sex and love, in which sex is increasingly pleasurable without love and in which loving sex is either a compromise or an impossibility, permits a brief excursus within the excursus to address the status of women in enlightenment (86–8/133–6).

The conceptual background for this short but dense passage can be provided by the writings of Johann Jakob Bachofen, the nineteenth-century Swiss legal scholar and philologist. His 1861 book *Mother-Right* argued that matriarchy preceded patriarchy in the evolution of human culture.[12] He associated this era in development with Neolithic establishment of agricultural communities, chthonic mystery rights, and the worship of Demeter. In this period a much more direct and submissive attitude toward nature was central, with woman occupying the primary social roles. The power to bear children, essential to the continuation of kinship and tribe, takes precedence.

According to Bachofen, this is followed by patriarchy, which advances through two stages. (There is also a stage prior to matriarchy, a hunter-gatherer, "free love" phase organized around the worship of Aphrodite.) The two periods will be familiar to readers of Nietzsche's *The Birth of Tragedy*: Dionysian and Apollonian. The Dionysian is a relatively brief phase of patriarchy in its infancy, in which there are the beginnings of a separation from nature. Here the directness of the mother-right must be achieved via special rituals in which the nascent individualism that comes to characterize full-blown patriarchy is set aside. The Apollonian stage is fully patriarchal. With it begins civilization. The overlap with Nietzsche is no coincidence. Bachofen taught for a time at Basel, where Nietzsche (twenty years later) had an academic appointment. Nietzsche read Bachofen, and they shared intellectual debts.

In its own time *Mother-Right* was a famous (or infamous) book. In the 1920s, Bachofen's work was much discussed again, due to the publication of a selection from his work edited by the fascist philosopher and Kant expert Alfred Baeumler, who more than any other intellectual argued for the relevance of Nietzsche to Nazism. Benjamin, who read deeply on the topic of mythology (not only Bachofen, but also Ludwig Klages) was aware of its potential for fascist appropriation, but tried to read it against the grain, as did Fromm. Bachofen is never mentioned by name in *DE*, but *Mother-Right* was "in the air" and is clearly in the background of these passages. Without that background in mind, the central claims of the passages can appear undermotivated.

Women – whom Horkheimer and Adorno, looking toward their last chapter, analogize to the position of Jews in Europe – are living reminders of the old order of myth and made to suffer for it. The figure of woman, that is, expresses the closeness with nature that had to be socially repressed in order that civilization emerge. The oppression of women arises because of the continued importance to female solidarity of the "old ways" of "enthusiasm." This suite of claims is based in an account of Freudian projection to which we turn in earnest in discussing antisemitism, but the controlling idea can be stated without that resource fully in view. Women are singled out for hatred by those who hate what they themselves have become, having had to give up their naturalness in order to be civilized, i.e., the naturalness that women possess. And given that modern society requires civilization, possessing this near relation to nature must appear antisocial and in need of strict control. On the one hand, women are put on pedestals in order to be idealized as men would have them, i.e., stripped of their real power and compartmentalized. On the other, there is Sade and the sexual objectification of women as erotic machines.

These days, pairing women and nature may not seem exactly like cutting-edge feminism. That would depend of course on what one means by "nature" and how one does the aligning. But, in any case, those days were not these days. So, maybe some slack can be cut. Moreover, the analogy of the status of women to that of Jews will be put under pressure, for at least one kind of modern antisemitism will turn genocidal and seek on principle the radical "negation" of those emissaries of forgotten nature. But that is a topic for Chapter 6.

FURTHER READING

O'Connor 2005 and 2012 contain excellent discussions of the relation of Kant to Critical Theory. Chapters 2 and 3 of Bernstein 2001 discuss instrumentality, identity thinking, and determination in relation to Kant's ethics.

Most contemporary Kant scholars would find Horkheimer and Adorno's criticisms groundless. Horkheimer and Adorno would no doubt reply that that is not surprising, since modern interpretations of Kant are themselves products of reified society. Closer to the mark for them are earlier reactions to Kant's rigorism in the first wave of reception to his work. Hamann 2007, Jacobi, 2004, II.1.261–331, Herder 2002, Schiller 1983, Schelling 1989 and 1993, Schlegel 1991, Novalis 1997, and Hegel 1988a and 1988b.

For a sustained argument that Kant is a source for capitalist exploitation, which is in close proximity to early Critical Theory, see Sohn-Rethel 2020.

Sade's books form the basis for a significant amount of work in French art and philosophy, but detailed knowledge of Sade is almost altogether lacking in the anglophone and Germanophone worlds. Grove Press brought out a fair amount of his work in English translation in the 1960s. *Juliette* (Sade 1969) is a companion to *Justine* (Sade 1966b), whose heroine is the converse, i.e., a virtuous woman despoiled. It was brought out in two editions with a change in subtitle for the second, which presents it alongside *Juliette*. The slightly earlier *120 Days of Sodom* (Sade 1966a) is the summit (or nadir) of his particular genius, and the dialogue *Philosophy in the Bedroom* (also available in Sade 1966b) contains material of interest.

NOTES

1 Kant 2005, 54.
2 The English translation gives "self-consistence." That is not inaccurate, given the very next sentence, which states that the principle of contradiction (i.e., the law of non-contradiction) is what is at stake. But *einstimmig* is also a musical term meaning "in unison." The overriding idea here is monophony, that the system be of one voice, not that the theory does not contain contradictories. Given Adorno's musical background and penchant for allusion, one cannot rule out this connotation.
3 For readers trained in Anglo-American analytic philosophy, a more familiar version of the difficulty is stated in Davidson 1984: 183–98. Davidson there argues against what he calls a "third dogma of empiricism," an addition to and criticism of W. V. O. Quine's earlier critique of what he, Quine, took to be the two dogmas of empiricism. Quine 1953: 20–46. Succinctly, the problem is that what one wants from what is given for conceptualization is that it both is pre-propositional and justifies belief. But standing as a justification requires having propositional structure, which is precisely what is denied to whatever is prior to belief. The conclusion Davidson draws, which he considered an extension of Quine's original point, is that only beliefs can justify beliefs.
4 Kant B131–2.
5 Kant B131–2.
6 Much of Horkheimer and Adorno's treatment of Kant's moral philosophy is a modern, industrial-age updating of Hegel's criticisms of the same. On the issue of formality, see Hegel 2019: 246–52, 347–56.
7 Kant 2012: 15 and 1996: 605–16.
8 The case is reminiscent of Augustine's pears. See Augustine 2009: 28–9 [II. iv.9].
9 See Kaufmann 2013.
10 In particular the work of the Flemish metaphysician Arnold Geulincx (1624–69), of whom Beckett was also fond.
11 Nietzsche 1999: 75 [§ 15].
12 Bachofen 1967 contains selections from this massive work.

5
CULTURE AND COMMODIFICATION

When Horkheimer and Adorno arrived in Los Angeles from New York in 1941, they found in place a vibrant German-speaking community that included the writers Bertolt Brecht, Leon Feuchtwanger, and Heinrich and Thomas Mann. The composers Hanns Eisler, Erich Korngold, Ernst Krenek, and Arnold Schoenberg were also in residence, as were the film directors Fritz Lang, Max Ophüls, and Billy Wilder. They were the newcomers. The film industry had already attracted several of its actors, directors, and composers from Central Europe: Michael Curtiz, William Dieterle, Marlene Dietrich, Peter Lorre, Ernst Lubitsch, F. W. Murnau, Max Steiner, Josef von Sternberg, Erich von Stroheim, and William Wyler. Taken as a whole, this Germanophone community was Hollywood-centered, its parties as posh as were the houses at which they were held. Movie stars and millionaires were by no means rarities.

Left-wing artists were not, however, the only Germans in town. A West Coast Nazi mouthpiece, the German-American

Volksbund, flourished in LA, and the German consulate was active in inviting fascist artists like Leni Riefenstahl to town. Her recently-completed *Olympia* went unscreened during her visit due to protests, but Walt Disney did entertain her, a fact that negatively impressed Horkheimer and Adorno. There were Nazi rallies in Los Angeles until the United States entered the war, and they were no small affairs.[1] 1940s Los Angeles may have been a "Weimar on the Pacific,"[2] but it was a transplanted Weimar, shadowed still by what had forced it to be the transplant it was.

Horkheimer and Adorno knew some actors, like Charlie Chaplin, well enough to be invited for cocktails and were well-placed in the German intelligentsia, but they were not true insiders. This position – neither inside nor outside the Hollywood crowd – served them well in writing the chapter on what they call "the culture industry." Adorno was the lead author, and he flashes his outsider credentials freely. The writing is condescending, cynical, and coruscating. Southern California is presented as phony through and through, a sham paradise manicured to seem natural to the untrained eye. One can take the impression from his personal philosophical document of his time in Los Angeles, *Minima Moralia*, that Adorno had drawn himself into his own recalcitrance, into a reactivity that had a readymade home in the splendid isolation of the displaced European aesthete. Lukács said that the Frankfurt theorists lived in the "Grand Hotel Abyss," from which they could declaim in comfort the degeneration of modern culture without doing anything about it.[3] Substitute "beach" for "hotel" and one takes the point.

DE was not the first time Horkheimer and Adorno committed their thoughts about American popular culture to paper. Adorno had been employed for three years in New York by the Princeton Radio Research Project, the remit of which was to study the impact of mass media – mostly radio – on US public opinion. (The Project was one of the first studies to deploy the idea of public opinion.) Adorno was hired to research the broadcast of live and recorded music, and his 1938 essay "The Fetish Character in Music and the Regression of Listening" and the *Essay on Wagner* (composed between fall 1937 and spring 1938, but not published until 1952) document his evolving views on mass art. Nor does the culture industry chapter constitute the end of his thinking on the subject. During its composition, he co-authored with Eisler the book *Composing for the Films*, which addresses the uses and misuses of non-diegetic music, and contributed to *The Authoritarian Personality*, the first monograph in the *Studies in Prejudice* series edited by Horkheimer. As if that were not enough, he was also at work on drafts for his *Philosophy of New Music* and on *Minima Moralia*. It was a period of intense work for him, and the culture industry chapter must be read as a part of the whole of that activity.

The idea of a critique of mass culture was not in itself novel. Mass culture had existed in Europe since the mid-nineteenth century, and the artistic credentials of new media was the focus of heated debate. Baudelaire's skeptical encounter with photography is an early case in point. Siegfried Kracauer's essays were forerunners, and several of Benjamin's essays from the 1930s provided inspiration and direction. What is distinctive about Horkheimer and Adorno's approach to mass art is its institutional bearing. Recall that one of the main tasks of the Institute for Social Research in its prewar period was to understand why the economic oppression of workers under capitalism was insufficient for socialist revolution. Historical materialism at its most pristine had made a structural prediction: capitalism would collapse under its own weight. This amounted to saying that capitalism would be shown through its practice to be incoherent. But that did not happen. Marx lived to see two rounds of failed revolutions, and much of his work was given over to policing conceptions of communism in order to get better results. By the time the early critical theorists are writing, they had before them the February and October revolutions in Russia and the failed European revolutions of 1918–1919. Those latest revolutions did not generate enough in the way of solidarity to form common cause against either capitalism or fascism, the latter of which was now, in 1944, alarming to say the least. So, the question was presented: how has capitalism managed not only to withstand potential global revolution but also to strengthen its hand? What is it that keeps workers in their place? Horkheimer and Adorno's answer is: culture.

One can divide the chapter on the culture industry into seven sections, corresponding to the unnumbered page breaks in the

1947 version of the manuscript and marked as such in your English translation. They are devoted *seriatim* to the following themes: (1) the definition of mass culture, (2) the concept of style, (3) the concept of amusement, (4) the relation between chance and instrumentality, (5) cultural tragedy, (6) the form of emptiness typical of mass art, and (7) advertising's commodification of language.

MASS CULTURE

Horkheimer and Adorno deploy a number of terms to refer to the form of culture they wish to discuss: "mass culture" (*Massenkultur*) (95/145), "mass society" (*Massengesellschaft*) (96/147), "cultural monopoly" (*Kulturmonopol*) (96/147), the "cultural corporation" (*Kulturkonzern*) (104/156, translation emended), the "entertainment business" (*Amüsierbetrieb*) (108/161), the "pleasure industry" (*Vergnügungsindustrie*) (116/171), and most famously, the "culture industry" (*Kulturindustrie*) (95 et seq./145 et seq.).

Mass culture is the broadest category and the place to start. One might understand the concept as working along three dimensions. It designates, first, a culture or set of cultural *objects* designed to be produced in great quantities with broad distribution. Movies – the primary concern of the culture industry chapter – are almost always such objects. Photographic film was what all commercial movies were made of until the advent of digital media, and photographic images are as a general matter easily and quickly reproduced with little loss in representational accuracy. They can be shown at many different venues and to many people subject to the capacity of the venue in question. Second, the term "mass culture" refers to the *experience* of such objects by many people gathered together. At the time of the writing of *DE* one went out to watch a movie; seeing a film meant going to a theater. Some of these movie theaters were quite lavish, built to compete with opera houses, and part of the attraction was to see and be seen by the "right people." Experiencing a film as part of a crowd is still a draw, even though the pleasure palaces are no more. Part of the reason to see a film screened at a theater rather than streamed or played from disc at home is to have the experience of others experiencing the film with one, from which one can take the sense that one's own individual reactions are part of those of a greater whole. Film has always been sensitive to this, even as a matter of form. Contemporary to the writing of *DE*, one could find communal visual and aural immersion in Disney's *Fantasia* (1940), the first commercial film with stereo sound. Third, the cultural object may reflect *values and practices* of a population at large, those of the everyday person. Such an artifact belongs to mass culture because it is attuned to being readily accepted by society as expressive of its average self-understanding – i.e., by the masses. In order that such acceptance follows, the objects tend to be standardized.

Consider Riefenstahl's *Triumph of the Will* (1935). It operates at – indeed, celebrates – the union of all three of these dimensions. It is a film of the 1934 Nazi Party Congress, held over four days at Nuremberg, attended by upwards of three-quarters of a million people. The rally was choreographed in order to have the film made; the rally and film are one. No political rally is merely an accumulation of people; it is meant to instill in those people an experience of being part of a throng, an undifferentiated whole. Nothing could be more suited to fascist purposes than to orchestrate such an experience. To say that Riefenstahl's filming of the Congress accentuates that experience is a radical understatement. What was (and still is) awesome and awful about the film is its power to recreate the sense of being there, and that is all one could want from propaganda. *Triumph* was, well, a triumph, widely screened across Germany. It translated the experience of being part of a mass consciousness to a mass, by means of mass-produced and mass-distributed art.

Horkheimer and Adorno place emphasis on all three of these dimensions, as well as on their interactivity. What is surprising perhaps – especially given Adorno's background in musicology and composition – is their disinterest in the formal features of filmmaking. Not only is there no discussion of shot composition, Horkheimer and Adorno also do not discuss form at the more general level that often impressed the early theorists of film, e.g., its intrinsic realism (i.e., that what was photographed had to have been present before the camera), the nature of light as an artistic medium (i.e., that film is standardly seen by projecting light-images on a screen), or representational issues involved in cutting (i.e., montage versus mis-en-scène editing). One might think even social analysis of film benefits from close attention to film construction. Sergei Eisenstein, Rudolf Arnheim, Béla Balázs, and Kracauer certainly thought so. Maybe Horkheimer and Adorno's final judgment that commercial films were silted with fake details caused them to think that more precise analysis was unnecessary. But that is not a good excuse.

One bit of formal analysis – if one can call it that – that does get over the transom is Benjamin's signature idea that "mechanical reproducibility" is indicative of late-modern mass culture. All the art Horkheimer and Adorno consider in the chapter lacks what Benjamin called "aura" (100/152).[4] More precisely, they hold both that mass art lacks aura and that mass art is commodity. But the conjunction of those two propositions does not entail that all art that lacks aura is commodity art. Lacking aura is conceptually distinct from being a commodity – there was loss of aura prior to capitalism – although being a commodity is one form of lacking aura. Aura is a formal property of art, but only in a loose sense. Aesthetic form is usually a matter of perceptual form. But aura is not a perceptual property, although of course one must perceive those things that have or lack aura in order to encounter them as having or lacking it.

Aura is a *value* that the appearance of a thing has in virtue of that thing's uniqueness. The thing stands apart from other objects in terms of the amount of originality it shows. Benjamin speculates that this apartness originates in the religious significance of totems and other cult objects. Such objects are often kept out of daily life and especially commercial relations. Only the adept may see or handle them, and even where viewing is more general, strict protocols are followed as to their showing. These are objects that call upon the presence of the deity, for instance, the Eucharist in Roman Catholicism or an Orthodox icon. The stock example of a secularization of this sort of thing, which travels a bit more freely in the world at large, is the classically beautiful work. Vermeer's *View of Delft* is like no other; it is *this-and-only-this*.

Aura is radically intransitive and nonrepresentational. To the extent that art can be reproduced it loses aura. Outside the cultic context, artworks could always be copied to some extent, and Benjamin tracks the increase in the technique of reproduction from stamping to printmaking to etching. But both the number of copies and the verisimilitude of copy to original were limited by the technology. Photography and film change all that. The very means by which an original is generated in the photographic arts is mechanical. While it does not follow from just that that the means of reproduction of the original must be mechanical, in the case of the photographic arts as they are commonly practiced, that is so. There are knotty questions concerning precisely what constitutes the original in the photographic process, but the fact that knotty questions remain is good evidence for Benjamin's thesis. It can be difficult to tell what is an original painting and what is a copy, but that is not a matter of principle. The original/copy dichotomy is well established – causality is authority – on account of aura.

In photography, the dichotomy becomes unstable – causality is not authority, for any print is in principle as good as any other. This is already apparent in printmaking technologies: woodcuts, engravings, etchings, lithographs, silkscreened images, etc. But those are still handwork items that require the intercession of the "artistic touch." As such, they convey a certain vulnerability. Benjamin stresses machine reproduction, i.e., reiteration in a copy that does not wear thin the authority of its causal source. Sure, it is better to see a Friedlander print in a museum than it is to have it on a postcard, and there is caché in having a numbered print of one. But, again, that it is a numbered print makes the point; the limit to a number of prints has to do with clawing back a sense of aura from a possible massive number of reproductions, each more or less the same as the others. That is why the slight slip in the first translation into English of the title of Benjamin's essay matters – i.e., from "reproducibility" (*Reproduzierbarkeit*) to "reproduction." Benjamin's point is that being-reproduced is written into the very nature of such images. They exist to be copied and, if one thinks that all prints are copies, all one ever sees are copies, not originals. Accordingly, what Benjamin calls "exhibition" trumps aura. No longer cult items limited to a select audience, artworks inhabit the public sphere on terms dictated by mass appeal. Reproducibility – the capacity for reproduction – is the key idea because one sees *in* the photograph or the film that it only ever existed in order to be repeated.

Benjamin held that some art of substance might be without aura. Such art would be expressly political; in essence, it would accept its status as only being in the public sphere and would speak directly to public matters. Lotta Lenya reports that, when asked by actors how to read their lines, Brecht told them to read them as if they were reading the newspaper. It's a sly comment typical of Brecht. Most who hear the story think he meant for the actors to read it deadpan, and that may be part of what he was saying. But that is not the famous *Verfremdungseffekt* or, at least, not the whole of it. He must have meant also to read the lines with the urgency of the horrors of today, as that is what newspapers contain. Moreover, that they, newspapers, are the source for most of such "current events" is also horrifying. He meant: say the lines *like that*. There is no reason to think the great Lenya did not appreciate all of it.[5]

Adorno is much less sanguine about such directness, if directness it is. He and Horkheimer do not rule out photographs or films being art, but in order for them to be art they would have to critically take into account their reproducibility. That is, they would have to be about the loss of aura, i.e., be in a broad sense ironic.

If this line of thought is right, these artifacts are "products" not merely in the anodyne sense that they are produced by agents, but are so in the more restricted sense that they are *product*, i.e., the result of labor organized according to capitalist economic practices. Given the Marxist understanding of what product is – items whose character it is to have as little character as necessary so that they flow freely in the current of money – these cultural objects will tend toward standardization. Their standardization increases their fungibility and makes them more potentially profitable. Because such products are ideological – they exist to give the impression, and give it systematically, that their purchase and use is freeing – they cannot be just numerically different instantiations of the qualitatively identical thing. They have to have specious appeal.

This is where the concept of *genre* comes in for Horkheimer and Adorno. We will turn to the question of generics in art in the next section. For now, it is enough to take the point that Horkheimer and Adorno hold that the culture industry produces highly standardized works not because people freely choose that such works be produced, but because people's tastes, expectations, and demands are *already* shaped by the culture industry (97/147–8). It is not as if one is just dropped into a cultural context from without, equipped with an unsullied critical apparatus that decides freely what one desires. Rather, aesthetic desires are themselves products of widespread conformism, and the conformism in question is not just a matter of what is represented or expressed in the products.

Imparting conformism is part of what being a commodity entails, and commodities make no secret of the fact: The "unified standard" is a matter of "conspicuous production" (97/147–8).[6] But the standardization of product and consumer must be to a degree covert; you may want to conform, but that is because it is not apparent to you that to conform is to be unfree. This means that undoing the conformism is a tall order – a matter of social ontology, not just consciousness raising – since one would have to make plain and change conceptions of the very nature of cultural products. One can make as many films as one likes about disadvantaged and marginalized peoples, but if the films cannot challenge more basically the ontology at work, they not only fail to resist the culture industry, they will exemplify it. They will do so by giving the impression that the business of serious cultural critique is being done when all that has really been achieved is garnering critical prestige for the industry. This is what keeps Horkheimer and Adorno up at night, not obviously fraudulent art but art that gives the false impression of depth.

Because they diagnose the standardization to centrally involve reproducibility and, thus, technology, it is important at the outset to flag that it is not technology as such that is at fault. Rather, it is an understanding of the value of technology for culture, which is a specification of an understanding that we have already discussed, i.e., the modern conception of it as an instrument through which to dominate nature (95/145). The main driver of that conception is capitalism and its reductive understanding of economic value. Recall the double reduction. There is a tendency to reduce any and all social value to economic value. That is conjoined with a reduction of economic value to the sort of value capitalism accords to products. All social value is economic, all economic value is commodity value; therefore, all social value is commodity value. This is where appeals to reification find their home: commodity-form is like a Kantian category. That is just an analogy of course. The point is that thinking of things generally as having value as commodities is to think of them in such a manner *in advance and without notice*. It is the economic expression which, as we saw, is a matter of rating determinate judgment to be experientially primary, thereby downplaying the cognitive importance of difference. This is a plea for imagination, for remaining cognizant of the difference between what is and what might be.[7] Nature is nothing but the domain of "judgables," according to the idealist, and what is nowadays blithely called "normativity" is a seed ground for the mass deception referred to in the chapter's subtitle. The art that confronted Horkheimer and Adorno in California was right-off-the-shelf normative.

The culture industry chapter does not treat in any detail the sort of art that might resist being a commodity. One has to go to other of Adorno's and Horkheimer's works for such discussion.[8] *DE* focuses on art that is so subsumed into commerce that it is drained of any and all critical tendency: pulp novels, magazines, comic strips, record albums, radio broadcasts, cartoon shorts, and (more speculatively) television.[9] But it is Hollywood movies that are most on their minds. These are products of a thoroughly vertically integrated corporate structure. Major studios owned the acting and directing talent, production facilities, means of distribution, and in many cases, the theaters at which the films were shown.

STYLE, SCHEMA, CLICHÉ

Style is an aesthetic concept, but it is not limited to art. Broadly construed, style pertains to how one comports oneself as subject to public judgment. This has to do with grooming, gesture, and how one speaks and writes. When Buffon said that "style is the man" (*le style est l'homme même*), he was talking about literary style, but the point generalizes.[10] One would hardly have needed to mention to Buffon that style depends on convention. More precisely, style is invention within convention. Buffon's *bon mot* is, then, compatible with Boileau's contention that "he who knows no limits, never learned to write" (*Qui on ne sait se borner, ne sut jamais écrire*).[11]

Horkheimer and Adorno's discussion of style in relation to the culture industry deploys a distinction between style and stylization (101 & n.1/153 & n.1). Adapting to purpose Stendhal's dictum that "beauty is only the *promise* of happiness," they write that "in every work of art, style is a promise" (103/155). Horkheimer and Adorno do not italicize "promise," as does Stendhal, but they might have done, for that is where the stress must fall. Key to a work having real style is that its uniqueness is not offered in completeness. The effect of style working with convention is that the convention in terms of which the audience will receive the work is both appealed to and challenged in the appeal. The promise in question is an open-handed offer to make the connection between individuality and generality. Recognizing style requires style.

Nowadays the word "style" floats free from such subtleties. Turn to the style section of any major newspaper and you will find fashion advice, rich people in dream houses, luxury travel destinations, and the latest remedies for balding. It's common enough to see style "put on," as something you can buy. The usual concern is with trends; internet influencers are the new style makers. But being up to date is not the only kind of stylishness. Dressing like a Victorian says something about who a person is. They want, above all else, to be noticed as stylishly out of style.

The manufacturing of style – that it too is subject to mechanical reproducibility (100/152) – is a main concern of the chapter. Here one is forced to follow Horkheimer and Adorno and make a distinction between nominal and true style: "[T]he style of the culture industry [...] is at the same time the negation of style" (102/154). Making the distinction in this way – i.e., in terms of dialectical negation – requires one to reflect on the conceptual dependency of nominal on true style, to mark how being merely stylized is dependent on its more substantial correlate. Style, which works at the edge of convention in order to generate invention, is rendered inert by stylization, which tips the balance too far in the

CULTURE AND COMMODIFICATION 141

direction of convention and then makes it appear as if something unconventional were in play. Horkheimer and Adorno immediately connect this claim to what they take to be the basic structure:

> The reconciliation of general and particular, of rules and the specific demands of the subject, through which alone style takes on substance, is nullified by the absence of tension between the poles: "the extremes which touch" have turned into a murky identity [*sind in trübe Identität übergegangen*] in which the general can replace the particular and vice versa
>
> (102/154) (translation modified)

Stylized style is a "caricature (*Zerrbild*) of style" (103/154). It reveals something about genuine style, but only if one sees the vitiation of the latter by the former. Otherwise, it is entertainment parading about as more than it is.

This is perhaps the point at which to consider a common misunderstanding about *DE*. Horkheimer and Adorno have no brief against entertainment as such. What they fear is: (1) that entertainment takes the place of *all* art and (2) that in order to do this entertainment produces ersatz art that dresses itself up as serious. *DE* mentions the filmmaker Orson Welles in this connection, who "is forgiven all his offences against the usages of the craft because, as calculated rudeness, they confirm the validity of the system all the more zealously" (102/153). Welles's *War of the Worlds* radio broadcast was known to Adorno from the Princeton Radio Research Project, but the reference here must be to *Citizen Kane*, which RKO released in 1941, and perhaps also to *The Magnificent Ambersons*, which followed the next year. The word "genius" is thrown around lightly nowadays, but Welles certainly was one. He was young (26 years old at the time of the making of *Citizen Kane*), brash, and brilliant. He was what the studios wanted dearly, a homegrown American filmmaker who could rival the European imports for substance and outstrip them in technique. In short, he could make art out of big-budget movies.

To Horkheimer and Adorno the fact that RKO could absorb his anti-authoritarian credentials meant the studios *owned* those credentials and, thus, could make it seem at least sometimes as if their product were more than a commodity. And *Citizen Kane* is more than a commodity. Yet the full thought is better borne out by *Ambersons*. Welles submitted two theatrical cuts at audience pre-screenings. The response was muted. He did not reserve final cut in his contract and was otherwise distracted; so, the studio removed over forty minutes of footage, recut scenes, truncated the score, and otherwise rearranged material, especially the conclusion of the film. The cut portions were unceremoniously destroyed in order to make more room in studio vaults for other films. The best one can do to glean any idea of what might have been is to view stills from outtakes. The point of the example is that Welles's imprimatur as *enfant terrible* could only go so far, i.e., as far as marketability dictated. His rudeness was real, and that reality was certainly part of the calculation of the studio but, in the end, it too was only a commodity, good only so long as it did not impede profitability.

Stylization simulates style by substituting "detail" for true individuality (98–9/149–50). Horkheimer and Adorno are not here saying that attention to detail in the creation or experience of a work is not very important. The ontological and epistemological framework within which they develop their ideas on the culture industry dictates that generalities not bury specificities. To the extent that a detail is a specificity, it should be what claims aesthetic attention. They instead are claiming that the culture industry hijacks specificities and makes them into bearers of the generic. The German word here, *Detail*, is a loan word from French (*détail*), which means "a small portion of something," but also something "ornamental" or "something fit out for sale." All these senses must be heard here. Details are generic specificities that, in being generic, are superficial and spruced-up for commerce. They give the work the appearance of newness, like minor variations of plot in BBC murder mysteries or hooks in pop songs. But detail may be posher, less conspicuous. One gets the sense that this is what Horkheimer and Adorno think about the famed "Lubitsch touch" (125/182, English in original). It is not that they begrudge Lubitsch true style. That style, however, has been coopted as *a* style. And that means that it is no longer *his* style at all.

What seemed magical to Kant about imagination is now revealed – the capacity to prearrange particulars so that they conform to conceptualization in advance (98/149). The culture industry – and commodity culture more generally – is a proper schematism. It supplies the unconscious with scripted modes of reception that, although they cannot strictly qualify as a priori, are experienced subliminally. Kant's fidelity to enlightenment yoked him to faith in neutral, abstract mental operations in which concepts and intuitions are readied for one another. For Horkheimer and Adorno, schematism is a matter of unconscious, already socialized construction. Generic fungibility is the capitalist version of Kantian concept-neutrality.

FUN

Culture works not only with intellectual materials but also with affect, and the affect with which commodity works is "fun" (English in original), a "medicinal bath (*Stahlbad*) that the entertainment industry never ceases to prescribe" (112/166). Fun, enjoyment, amusement, entertainment – the ideas are more or less synonymous – substitute for the transcendent element of the experience of art; this is the form of uplift native to products of the culture industry. Yet affect is never separate from its social production; fun is anchored in liberalism and its economic expression, capitalism.

European art retained a degree of autonomy from advancing commercialism thanks to the residuum of the patronage system of the past (105/157). This was especially so in countries like Germany that were late to industrialism. The United States was not late to industrialism; its ever-increasing technical prowess, with markets to match, meant that its cultural institutions were baptized into capitalism. Think of Carnegie libraries and the founding of private universities in the late nineteenth century by captains of industry: Chicago, Duke, Stanford, Vanderbilt, etc. European dependence on US industry after the First World War came ready-fitted with openness to this new commercial culture and, as a result, fun existed in Europe. The United States set the pace.

Capitalism is a form of life in the United States so unquestioned as to its authority as to be invisible (106/157). Culture industry art is calculated to reinforce this unknowingness. It only ever so slightly idealizes the conditions of its making in its formal arrangement and content. What such art engages is not imagination, at least not any exercise of it that might extend beyond convention. It is, rather, the replication of affect. It is not merely that works rouse the same affects. It is that being-replicated becomes the primary aesthetic property of works and carries its own affective charge. The affect has repeatability baked into it: sameness as "ever-sameness" (*Immergleichheit*) (106/159).[12]

Such works are aesthetically undemanding, but, as mentioned above, the problem is not precisely the divide between "light" and "serious" art. Serious art is bourgeois art, which relies for its seriousness on excluding the ludic, working-class *cum* peasant entertainment (107/160). That is to say that light art should not be burdened with being an outlet for bourgeoise soul searching. Light art *as such* does not really exist in the culture industry, for its necessary contrast, serious art, also does not. So-called serious art is also commodified. Horkheimer and Adorno point here to the adoration of musical prodigies, star conductors, and nights at the opera.

The real issue is how the art of the culture industry functions ideologically through its works, high or low. It does so by making people pliable, willing to accept amusement as transcendence and to return to the working world without pressing new demands on it (107, 109/160, 162). The need for relief from the grind of capitalist labor is great, due to the arduous form of boredom it incurs, but the movie or hit song is only a respite, not a release. It offers the same standardized experience with a bit of gloss or, as Horkheimer and Adorno put it, with the color of the actual workplace bled out of it (109/162). To say that "off-duty workers experience nothing but after-images of the work process itself" (109/162) is to say that their reactions in the cinema are as regularized as those in the workplace, as well as to say that the content of what they watch may be escapist, but is not for that an escape. Precisely not.

One might think of melodramas, romances, and crime mysteries, but Horkheimer and Adorno emphasize comedy in this regard.[13] The comedy with which Horkheimer and Adorno were familiar in Weimar Germany could be quite satirical and critical. Surrealism and Dada incorporate comedy and, whatever one thinks of their potential to induce social change, they cannot be called complaisant. The comedy that Horkheimer and Adorno are discussing is closer to the LA scene and more conventional: narrative film and cartoons.

One would not want to dismiss out of hand that American film comedy might rival European sources for critical potential. An example would be physical comedy in silent film at the high-end, something as multilayered as Chaplin, Buster Keaton, or Harold Lloyd. Horkheimer and Adorno cite Chaplin, the Marx Brothers, and the Betty Boop cartoons as critical mass art.

For the sake of contrast, consider what they say about Chaplin and the Disney cartoon figure Donald Duck. The most telling mention of Chaplin alludes to *The Great Dictator* (1940).[14] What impresses Horkheimer and Adorno about the film is the power of its last shots to show up hollow antifascist rhetoric in the United States (119/175). But the film's most memorable scene suits their purpose better. There Chaplin, playing the Hitler-double Adenoid Hynkel, dances *pas de deux* with an inflatable globe to strains of the prelude from Wagner's *Lohengrin*. *Dictator* was Chaplin's first sound film, and the aesthetic baseline for the scene is a return to his silent film origins, for which his Tramp is iconic.[15] This immediately places before the viewer an extended allusion to the visual pathos characteristic of those early films and turns to political commentary. Hitler was not funny; it is the fact that he is the precise opposite of funny that makes the scene a comic classic.

Chaplin, Keaton, and Lloyd were absolute masters of the long-form physical gag, which often pitted the protagonist against basic forces of nature – a comic sublime. The Marx Brothers, on the other hand, came out of vaudeville, and their humor consisted in verbal pyrotechnics: puns, double-entendres, sexual suggestions, nonsense in the form of sense looping back upon itself endlessly. Harpo may have been silent, but his is a very different form of silence than the silence of silent films.

Donald Duck is another story. His wisecracking and bucking of authority are always shown to be physically punished; the violence done to him is the prompt for the laughter (110/164). In so laughing, the audience unknowingly takes the position of its oppressor. One laughs when one is told.

Consider laugh tracks to US and British sitcoms. They may have been deployed to give home viewers the sense of being in a movie theater with other patrons or of seeing a broadcast live with a studio audience. But the laugh track was initially a technical accommodation to compensate for the static effect of single-camera shooting. Soon the laugh track became normative, however, signaling what is funny enough to laugh at, how hard to laugh, even what sort of laugh to give. The industry-speak for this was "sweetening." This ludic additive was dropped in the late 1980s, not entirely because shows had adopted more advanced camera techniques nor on account of its tiresomeness, but because it was no longer required to cue a correct response. The comedy in essence comes with a set of instructions that are meant to generate a repeatable, predictable, and habituated response. Audiences will want more of the same in order to laugh "correctly." Of course, none of this is strictly speaking a standing order of existence for people. The point is that this is what transcendence amounts to in consumer comedy: to so identify with authority that one forgets oneself in it to the point of self-punishment, indeed to the point of enjoying both it and the self-punishment (111/165).

So fun is far from free. It circulates as a kind of currency, through which generic entertainments provide generic respite from generic work, due to an enforced equivalence between the various modes of experience – work, personal relations, media, cars, etc. You might say that this is "soft" power; after all, no one is making anyone see *Titanic* or listen to Taylor Swift (or to Adorno's scourge, Toscanini). But that does not mean that the source of influence is not power proper. Part of its power is to isolate subjects from one another, monads in a mere simulation of social activity (112/166), in order to reintegrate them as the sort of subject that capitalism requires: competitive pseudo-individualists who lack in solidarity. As mentioned, even high-end art is affected. The modern novel is the realm of interiorized consciousness, which is at the same time a refuge from and creation of the social conditions that make the culture industry possible. Adorno found positive valuations of this sort of subjectivity in philosophy suspect. Whatever one thinks about his contention that Kierkegaard was haut-bourgeois, one can detach from it the main idea. While the culture industry cannot completely extinguish the human need for creativity, it can recast and control this need by providing a picture according to which art is serious on account of its asocial, subjective focus. One might consider the recent hunger for memoir in such a light.

CHANCE

When Horkheimer and Adorno discuss the use of "chance" (*Zufall*) in the culture industry, they are not interested in randomness, and when they discuss "fortune" (*Glück*), it is not destiny that is on their minds. They are concerned, rather, with the use of statistics and probability calculations to gauge and predict audience response. Both are deployed in order to better craft cultural products that suit such responses.

The discussion is a holdover from Adorno's days with the Princeton Project. Art ought not to be preadapted to audience expectation. Part of what makes art critical is that the audience can gainfully compare the world of the artwork with the everyday world. One's experience of an artwork of substance unfolds in that comparative form. It is not that works need present discrete, alternative visions of reality in their content, i.e., tell stories of how the world might be better. Adorno in particular is very skeptical of that, as he takes it to serve acceptance of the status quo. It is, rather, that works challenge the imagination through formal innovation. That gives no prescription as to how to change the world, but it does depart enough from conventional uses of imagination to better engage openness to alternatives to the status quo more generally. Almost all films, novels, and music reinforce by design what is customary. Advance screenings, pre-release press, top-ten lists, all of these things and more help art producers accede to what is already liked. "Likes" are now a category of measurement of product and, on the internet, which is rife with all manner of such quantification, they matter. They prompt decision.

Chance is a phantom. There is really very little of it, very few things that could break through the mass production and consumption of art. The use of quantitative measures to assure "quality control" in films and broadcast music is not the only thing in question here. Take the myth – and thus the presence of mythic thinking in the enlightenment-fueled culture industry – delivered to the audience that the stuff of which entertainment is made is "just like them." Nowadays the operative term is "relatable" (cf. 116/171). The problem is that the culture industry actually works within a broader social system in which everyone is the same, yet distinction accrues only to the few. Distinction is arbitrary, not based on any substantial difference between individuals. What makes this seem rational is that culture consumers accept chance as what makes for distinction. This seems non-arbitrary because distribution of value is perceived to be a matter of averaged result. Fortune is not blind happenstance; it is the result of a plan meant to keep machinations obscure (117/172–3). One identifies, then, not with an individual portrayed in a movie as an individual, but rather with the everyman type one also instantiates, the idealized result of a probability calculation. Your identity is second-hand. You don't want to be lucky you; you want to be the lucky *one*. If one takes lotteries and gambling tables to be the proper lens through which to view the distribution of goods, that might seem rational. Capitalism may not be entirely a crapshoot, but the point is that the difference between a game of dice and being an individual who can see himself as a movie star is a matter of degree, not difference. Both depend on perceiving an overall rationality in random outcomes spread over time as a measurable field. You don't think that *you* can be a billionaire, but there is a slim percentage chance of something approaching that for someone vaguely *like you* (112/165–6, 125/182).

Horkheimer and Adorno conclude the section on chance by circling back to connect (1) the ever-sameness of what is shown and the ever-sameness of its showing with (2) mechanical reproducibility in art (118–9/174–5). They make the point in terms of beauty. A beautiful thing is supposed to surmount the merely real; it has aura. One may cite matters of sensible form when assessing beauty, but it is what makes those formal relations hold in the first place that is at issue, not just their legibility. Nowadays, however, "[b]eauty is whatever the camera reproduces" (*Schön ist, was immer die Kamera reproduziert*) (119/174). The full thought is that whatever the camera reproduces – whether that thing is beautiful or not – is made beautiful in the reproduction. Even ugly things can be beautified by photographing them. Reproduction in and of itself can beautify because transcendent value is reduced to being ready for reproduction. The world is presented as a harmonized whole by virtue of its automatic representation.

TRAGEDY PAYS

Classical tragedy involves the downfall of someone great on account of an error in judgment.[16] There can be no stinting on either the greatness or the downfall; both must be near-absolute. The designation "tragic" has broadened over time to the point that works typically counted as tragic – e.g., *Macbeth*, *Andromache*, *Faust* – would not qualify under the more restrictive ancient formulation. The reasons for this are perhaps best given by commentators like Herder, Hegel, and Nietzsche: the bourgeois conception of individuality is simply too trivial. Falls from an office chair – even from the throne of Denmark – are not enough.

Tragedy depicts radical suffering that strikes at the root of one's existence. Modern life may have fainter versions of that, commensurate with the decline in aristocratic figures, but they exemplify suffering nonetheless. Art must continue to address this. A question arises, then, as to how the culture industry accommodates suffering in its products. It does so along two dimensions. The first has to do with acknowledging suffering in a form that the culture industry can sell and control. No matter how much fun and chance it can promulgate, it is unrealistic not to offer a mirror to the public that reflects back to it some form of its suffering, even if that form is engineered to be unobtrusive. That tragedy has already become more moderate even in substantial, bourgeois art helps. Melodrama has incrementally taken the place of tragedy. Here Horkheimer and Adorno point to the heroine with a heart of gold (121–2/178), whose purity of intent is untouched by the "misfortune" (*Unglück*) she suffers and whose form of resistance is her upstanding personal integrity. There were many such figures in the films of the 1920s, 1930s, and 1940s. Second, and also eased into place by the decline in tragic heroism, is a more frontal attempt to incorporate tragedy into consumerism by extending a defense mechanism we have already discussed: the prestige product, targeting a bourgeois audience. The effect of depth – the caché of the classic – is sturdy enough to bear a greater measure of suffering and to do so at historical distance. There are precursors to this in the operetta, a form that interested Kracauer greatly. *Anna Karenina* (1935, dir. C. Brown), which starred an Adorno favorite, Greta Garbo, would qualify. Beginning in the late 1940s, film studios turned resolutely to such fare – adaptations of Shakespeare took off and have never looked back.

The ultimate purpose of mass art-grade tragedy, then, is no different than style, fun, and change: to return the spectator to the unquestioned everyday. That the section on tragedy follows the one on chance is no accident. To suffer a mis*fortune* is the key idea, and the idea of fortune undergirding it is that of a bad statistical outcome. To suffer at the hands of chance is to be in the wrong place at the wrong time. It has nothing to do with you as *you*; moreover, it is not really tragic.

PURPOSELESSNESS WITH A PURPOSE

Kant writes in *The Critique of the Power of Judgment* that beautiful things appear in one's judgment of them as beautiful as if they were made for sheer contemplation and nothing else: They are "purposive without a purpose."[17] Horkheimer and Adorno reverse the formula or, rather, claim that mass art has done so. In it there is only "purposelessness for purposes" (127–8/185). Instead of works whose aesthetic value lies in transcending any pragmatic aim, one has works whose value is aimlessly pragmatic.

The inversion hinges on a distinction between extrinsic and intrinsic purposes. Commercialized art has purpose. If Horkheimer and Adorno are right, it serves to seamlessly reintegrate the audience into a life that it takes for granted as, for all its shortcomings, good as it gets. But that is an aim of society at large under liberalism/capitalism, not an aim specific to each artwork. The purpose controls the work from without, making the work subserve a prearranged goal. By contrast, an intrinsic purpose is one a work has as the particular work it is. One can of course argue about how pure such purposes are, how truly intrinsic to the work they might be. The main idea, however, is that there is some core element of the work that organizes it from within. Typically, this has been assigned to the intent of the artist or to formal features of the artwork, however one understands them. But even if one is wary of these notions, one might accept that the work has native to it a power to slip free from the dictates of society at large, perhaps on account of the subversive unconscious processes it expresses. To say, then, that the art of the culture industry is purposeless with a purpose is to say that, speaking of intrinsic purpose, it has very little of it because, speaking of extrinsic purpose, it has quite a lot.

"The purposelessness of the great modern work of art is sustained by the anonymity of the market" (127/184). Even art that outpaces the status quo in ways that can critically engage the imagination, break out of the fast yet easy schematism of the commercial, is – and this is the important point to remember, *has always been* – a matter of social oversight. The patronage system, even as it gave way in the nineteenth century to capitalist commercialism, allowed for a margin within which imagination could work. Whether patronage was ignored, tolerated, calculated, or simply unaware of this allowance doesn't matter. The point is that the Kantian idea of disinterested engagement as a hallmark of aesthetic experience was always an allowance, one that Kant idealized uncritically. What the lack of regard of the art market to radical art "shows" (127/184, English in original) is both that all art has its price and that today most art *is simply* its price.

The consumer-side equivalent of the averaged-out hero here is the "heroizing of the averaged-out" (*die Heroisierung der Durchschnittlichen*) (126/183). We have seen versions of the idea at work in other sections of the chapter. The artist is now confronted brutally with what she has always sensed was true: she operates with freedom in the period of bourgeois art, but that freedom was always on loan. Now payment comes due. This is the "social liquidation of art" (127/185).[18] Its commodification becomes unrestricted.

As for the audience, its character as average also has a phony form of standing out from the crowd: to be "in the know." The

New is replaced in the culture industry by the More: more content, more access, more chances to experience. To be special as an audience member is simply to be everywhere at once, to have seen and heard it all (128/185–6). One feels inadequate at having to admit one has not seen the latest show, whatever that might be. Here radio leads. It is "free" in the sense that one does not pay for the programming (advertising does that); so, the commercial character of what is being transacted is not so much hidden as it is smoothed over. In what turns out to be a prophetic flourish near the close of this section, Horkheimer and Adorno opine that "if the technology had its way the film would already be delivered to the apartment on the model of the radio" (130/189). They mention television as the next development of the idea, visual radio to their imaginations. Streaming internet content on multiple platforms to personal screens, some as small as your wrist, jumps to mind nowadays.

COMMODIFICATION OF LANGUAGE

The culture industry chapter closes with a consideration of mass art's ability to cause the audience to reproduce and amplify its effects linguistically. This is pressing on account of the contesting roles of expression and representation in language: language is the most powerful human means of communicating information, but it is also where one can find one's voice, i.e., can inhabit a rich, idiosyncratic form of experience. To the extent that cultural products undermine such expressivity, they compromise individuality.

Horkheimer and Adorno's basic claim does not surprise: the culture industry skews the balance between expressive and informational aspects of language in the direction of information. How one speaks bows to what one speaks.

One might not be very impressed by the observation. People speak mostly to communicate of course, and much of what they communicate is information. One might even hold that that is what language is for – i.e., that it develops so that information can be more easily shared – although linguists like Chomsky would contest that claim. The conveyance of content is not all there is to it of course – there is poetry, there is romance – but when it comes to charting the relative priority given in language to the communication of fact over personal nuance, it is reasonable to favor the former over the latter.

Unsurprisingly, therefore, there is a tendency in the philosophy of language to treat expressivity as independent of informational (or propositional) content and, further, as something added onto base linguistic meaning. Thinking of expression as "personal nuance," as we put it, seems to assume that expressivity relates to the perspective from which one presents meaning and not with meaning itself. But there is an important tradition in philosophy of language – one that does not emerge from philosophical logic, as did much philosophy of language in the early twentieth century, but rather out of historical linguistics in the early nineteenth century – that treats linguistic expression and representation as strongly interactive. The emphasis in this line of thought is on *utterance*, on spoken language, with special attention paid to claims that in speaking one is manifesting the spontaneity of linguistic production. This spontaneity can be recessive – when simple informational exchange is the order – but it is never completely absent. A further claim is that when that spontaneity is most present in speech, speech stretches convention, and what may seem like non-semantic properties of language move forward. The musicality of poetry is often discussed in this regard. The main thinkers in this line are Rousseau, J. G. Hamann, J. G. Herder, Friedrich Schlegel, Wilhelm von Humboldt, and Fritz Mauthner.

Horkheimer and Adorno's conception of language works with this tradition in a form presented to them – again – by Benjamin, who developed a hermetic speculative historical scheme to ground this conception of the relation of expression to representation. To review: for Benjamin, language is at its most primeval a one-to-one relation between utterance and thing. In retrospect, one might hold this relation to be referential, but the idea that one is pointing out the thing by means of a linguistic item must be understood at this primary level as more than a matter of simple designation. It is an attempt to mold sound to thing. Because in human language sonics implies phonics, the fundamental idea in the Idealist-Romantic philosophy of language is that this aboriginal naming involves onomatopoeia, a speculation at least as old as Plato's *Cratylus*. Benjamin does not take precisely this route.

He leaves more open the question of what it is in language that best achieves the one-to-one relation. The controlling thought is that in naming something – or more generally, in any use of language (since Benjamin treats concepts as names gone rogue) – one is calling on a thing to matter, "sounding it out," so to speak. Doing this is expressive because it carries with it the spark of creation and uniqueness. What is important for Benjamin is that such names are strictly non-substitutable; they are one-offs, i.e., are singular. Modernity's embrace of technology escalates generality to the point that meaning seems not only generic but also without expression: Meaning is pure information, disembodied and, to that extent, more conceptually apt.

That is the background to Horkheimer and Adorno's obscure reference to the "magic word" and its decline as "demythologizing" (133/192). Consider an example from poetry. Language is the more contentful the more it preserves specificity of utterance. Take these lines from Geoffrey Hill's *Mercian Hymn* XV:

> Tutting, he wrenched at a snarled root of dear crab-
> apple. It rose against him. In brief cavort he was
> Cernunnos, the branched god, lightly concussed. (1–3)

Why "wrenched," not "grabbed?" "Brief cavort," not "short step?" "Tutting, he wrenched" rather than "he wrenched, tutting?" Why does any of that matter? The dull but more or less correct answer is that it sounds better the way he wrote it. But *why* does it sound better? Because the sounds of words and metrics of phrases bear such an intimate relation to what they say; the sounding is the saying. For Benjamin, Adorno, and Horkheimer, Hill has named something.

An entire language of such names would be highly inefficient, if it would constitute a language at all; we are talking here of parataxis, of terms with no semantic relation to one another. But the point of the speculation is to stress that expressive function and meaning coincide. Words are supposed to *count* for something. They make sense to the extent to which a speaker stands behind them; to speak is to lay claim, to question, to challenge, etc. Linguistic generality is powerful, as it increases shareability at a certain level of content, the informational level. But generality always tempts genericity; there is always the concern that generality will compound to the point that what is said is divested of expression. It becomes whatever it is that people say. Heidegger called this *Gerede* (idle talk) but cautioned about getting moralistic about it.[19]

The culture industry includes among its capacities talking about itself. As a matter of fact, it mostly talks about itself. It comprises advertising, less direct modes of marketing, licensing agreements, blogs, etc. Consider what is by now a pedestrian form of this: product placement. At the express end of the scale are films in which a manufacturer's product is front and center. The high-water mark of this was perhaps dressing Audrey Hepburn, an actor of transcending beauty on whom clothes took near-Platonic form. *Charade* (1963, dir. S. Donen) has earned laurels as the best Hitchcock film not directed by Hitchcock, but it might as well be remembered for each and every outfit Hepburn wore in it (Givenchy, by the way). More often companies buy rights to have their products feature incidentally in films: cars, clothes, liquor, almost anything one can think of that might be identified at a glance.

But what does it take to identify at a glance? Your mind has to be alive to branding; recognizing a brand has to be as automatic as seeing a color. Ads provide just such exposure. Film becomes an extension of advertising, just as advertising can be seen as an extension of film. Hitchcock was a master of this, drumming up business for *Psycho* by advertising that there would be medical personnel available at theaters if one were overcome by fear. The *Star Wars* "franchise" – the operative term now, since a blockbuster film is only as potent as is its spawning of sequels and prequels – was perhaps the first with a coordinated media assault via toys, lunch boxes, costumes, and the like.

In such a habitat, words are easily traded, isolated markers drained of anything but picking out their referents arbitrarily. We are now in the realm of modern theories of reference. Horkheimer and Adorno deploy a distinction that has come to be crucial to philosophy of language, between designation and meaning (133/192). The motto is that meaning determines reference, i.e., that because names (or nouns more generally) are arbitrary tags, descriptive content or some other relation to what is meant is required to secure reference. Horkheimer and Adorno's thought is that words designate arbitrarily, but meaning has become too generic to supply the needed specificity (134/193).

If communication is as shallow as Horkheimer and Adorno take it to have become in mass media, it is easy to slide back and forth between expressions. All that you say is at least potentially what is said – what an anonymous *one* says. Fascism is well aware of this and utilizes film and radio to normalize violence: the violence *of* the words is not *in* the words (135/195). And it is as all-American as apple pie too. It was not for nothing that Hitchcock chose as a protagonist in the espionage thriller *North by Northwest* (1959) an adman, Roger Thornhill (Cary Grant). One of the first things we see him do is dispossess people waiting in front of him in line for a cab by lying to them. Later, when he lights Eve Kendall's (Eva Marie Saint) cigarette on an overnight train bound for Chicago, his matchbook reveals his monogram, ROT. It's an inside joke, the adman as a rotter.[20]

AND NOW?

No portion of *DE* has received as much attention as has the culture industry chapter. Many of its concerns are still with us, but the extent to which that matters is controversial. The Europe from which Horkheimer and Adorno had been exiled had already been touched by US popular culture. But firsthand experience of the original must have been disorienting. In a way, New York was a buffer for them. California was not until the 1960s synonymous with the American *Zeitgeist*, but what they encountered there was the advanced edge of that, a combination of consumerism, gimcrack self-assurance, and naïve optimism. Hollywood studios called themselves "dream factories" and, in a way, Horkheimer and Adorno agree.

The utter negativity of their discussion of the culture industry is informed by sensitivity to consumerism. The United States is a country whose history has been relatively isolated from the avant-garde. When Americans wanted that, they expatriated themselves to Europe. What was lost about the Lost Generation was found in Paris: escape from provincialism and conformity. The United States had not had a war fought on its soil since 1865, to the great benefit of its industrialization. California had become in many ways the heart of the country, and it seemed only natural for it to set the beat for culture in the form of mass media.

While Adorno showed some interest in nineteenth-century American art, art prior to the advances of late capitalism in the United States – he had written a libretto for an opera based on *Tom Sawyer* in the early 1930s – what struck him and Horkheimer about California was its sense of what was new. What most attracted them about the country always had a large measure of what made them feel most foreign there and was something both felt in a personal register. Adorno was more than happy to present *Minima Moralia* under that guise. California was a massive domain of alienation, stemming in large part from the felt lack of alienation of its native inhabitants.

There have been two main criticisms of Horkheimer and Adorno's position on the culture industry. The first is to deny that they are right to follow Lukács in holding that commodity form has substituted more or less completely for the idea of an object in general. It is not that critics have not seen some truth in the claim, but it is a matter of degree, and Horkheimer and Adorno have overestimated that. This criticism has been leveled from within Critical Theory,[21] but it was also a common reaction of sociologists to early Critical Theory after the 1970s. A second objection assumes that commercialism is rampant in the arts but asks why that is so bad. In a way, this is a more direct approach, denying that reification is, or is any longer, a problem.

1980s poststructuralism challenged views like Horkheimer and Adorno's, which took the avant-garde as the be-all and end-all. Dialectical argument, which looks to the negation of any apparently stable view as a condition for both destabilizing it and, thus, understanding it more completely, came to be replaced by deconstruction, which dissolved negativity into sheer multivalence. There was nothing to be negative about because there was no positivity either; even the positive/negative binary overdetermines semantic terms. With this came a knowingness about commodity.

Sure, commodities are everywhere, but even a child is aware of that and, if we are aware of that, we can't be subject to the sorts of ideological distortion that Horkheimer and Adorno fear. The proper philosophical regard to the phenomena of any cultural product or form is to reconceive it as existing in an ever-changing and pliable semantic network with which one can "play" (*jouer*).[22]

The first thing to note in response to this second objection is that, as we discussed, Horkheimer and Adorno never claim that we are unaware of the overarching presence of commodities in culture. For them, the fact that we are aware of this and are still unaware of its effects is one of the strongest indications of how pernicious those effects are. The correct description of the state of play for them is that we are aware that there is a culture industry, but we believe both that it does not control our general engagement with objects and that we have sufficient resources in subjectivity to not be defined by it. In other words, when it comes to what makes you *you*, you control the industry. Horkheimer and Adorno hold that neither is true. It is not the case that the world in general escapes the form of thinking that crystallizes in commodities. You may revel in the Grand Tetons as an untouchable wilderness not to be despoiled at any cost. But you are looking at them, at least derivatively, as not being subject to being despoiled at any *cost*. You are acknowledging, in a way, the terms of commodity, i.e., that the threat is precisely that many would hang a dollar sign over those mountains. Moreover, that you believe that you might be completely inoculated against a pervasive nefarious social structure is reason for concern. Part of the advanced nature of social structures like late capitalism is that they anesthetize prior to attack.

As we have stressed, *DE* is not a philosophical treatise nor does it propound a theory. It is meant to provoke, and one of its techniques is exaggeration. Horkheimer and Adorno exaggerate in that they are saying more than you would expect, going beyond the bounds of where you might think a thought should end, more than you are ready to hear. Perhaps they are saying more than they started out intending to say when they first put pen to paper. Perhaps the most cautious thing to say, then, is that Horkheimer and Adorno raise flags about what they take to be the diminution of human experience via the very medium that used to try to assure its elevation: art. They see this not as an isolated matter, but as the deliverance of more general social trends in late modernity. The scope of their claim may be over-the-top, but is the phenomenon not present at all? This lands one back in the first objection, but perhaps Horkheimer and Adorno could accept that even commodification has limits.

Let's close by looking briefly at two contexts in which the chapter remains vital. Much culture nowadays is available to one digitally. Sure, you can go to the Gerhard Richter collection at the National Gallery in Berlin or catch Andrew Cyrille playing at NuBlu, but the access most people have and want to have to art is via the internet. If you do go to see live country, pop, rock, or hip-hop, you'll have to contend with a forest of cellphones anyway, recording the performance for later internet posting. And that will condition the performance as well, since the performer will know that the performance will not only be distributed well beyond the precincts of the club, but will be so in perpetuity. How many chances would you take as a musician under those circumstances?

Now, there are very few sites on the internet that one can visit without encountering advertising. YouTube videos, unless one buys a premium subscription, are interrupted by commercials, there are pop-ups galore on Amazon, and those are just two examples of a global phenomenon. Public access to the internet began in the mid-1990s and was very quickly capitalized. eBay, which started out as a mom-and-pop venue geared to selling curios, is now mostly populated by professional sellers. Influencers do what they do to create consumer desire as a form of insider knowledge, and rockumentaries are designed to give a specious sense of being backstage in order to increase Spotify hits and downloads. A new development is in AI-generated bots that simulate interaction, via holograms, with dead loved ones, the so-called "death-tech" industry. It is hard to canvas in short form the depredations on hand: the short-circuiting of grief, that you might have to rent or renew them, that you might not be able to cancel them (i.e., that they might "stalk" you), their openness to advertisement, never mind that your "conversations" might be tracked by third parties. From Horkheimer and Adorno's perspective, this is all depressingly predictable. Constant exposure to this form of entertainment imperceptibly teaches one that this is what culture *is*. The more "content" one ingests, the less content one gets.

A second example hits closer to home. We are both professors of philosophy and, thus, academics. Being an academic is not the same thing as being a scholar, which is not the same thing as being an intellectual, which is not the same thing as being a philosopher. But being an academic is the form that houses all of those things nowadays, and academics is a business. Universities in the United States may be nonprofit entities as a legal matter, but they exist in large part to make money, mostly from athletics, government funding, and the licensing of scientific research. Humanities and the social sciences deal with culture, not the cold hard cash of technology. How much of the world in which they operate is formed nonetheless by industrial conceptions of products? A great deal. We are not talking about the obvious layer of administrative work that goes on at the departmental and college level, although that has certainly increased with the piling up of assistant and associate deans. Nor is the subject one's teaching, which for most of us always has a service component having to do with staffing required distribution courses. (US undergraduate degrees, unlike those in Europe and elsewhere, combine roughly two years of general studies with two years of more specialized work.) It is, rather, our own research and writing that is interesting to think of in terms of the culture industry.

As it happens, the market dictates that govern both universities and external sources for research funding have turned scholarship firmly toward the standard dried good. Academic papers take their turn on the circuit of conferences and colloquia, at which one's peers have a go at them, raising objections to this and that, to which one dutifully replies, the result of which is an essay written by a committee. Fellowships are doled out on the basis of trend and demography, sabbatical applications granted or denied on the basis of whether one has secured outside funding, rankings of journals and presses in which one publishes and citation indices have replaced substantive evaluation of work. Is scholarship under siege by forces that make it subservient to quantitative measurement? Is making a difficult text such as *DE* more accessible not making it less itself, less obstinate than it is intended to be? You might very well ask such questions.

FURTHER READING

Hammer 2015 concerns the importance of art to Adorno's conception of modernity. Hulatt 2016 discusses the relation of art to truth in Adorno. Weber Nicholsen 1997 traces the importance of the idea of exact experience through Adorno's conception of aesthetic objects. Schwartz 2005 investigates the interaction of Critical Theory and the theory and practice of the visual arts in twentieth-century Germany.

Adorno 2006 is a reconstructed text of the unpublished *Current of Music*, a draft of Adorno's planned book about his work on the Princeton Project. Adorno and Eisler 2007 (rev. ed. in Adorno 1970, 15:7–155) is important for understanding Adorno's thoughts on the interplay of serious art and entertainment. Paddison 1998 is excellent in all aspects of Adorno's philosophy of music. Bernstein 1992 and Menke 1998 place Adorno's aesthetics in the postmodern context.

The main works in aesthetics important to the formation of the concept of mass culture are Kracauer 1995 and 2002 and Benjamin 1969, 217–52. Koch 2000 is an excellent overview of Kracauer's work. For recommendations on secondary work on Benjamin, see the suggested further readings section following Chapter 1.

For Adorno's thoughts on mass media after his return to Germany, especially on television, see Adorno 1954 and 1998, 49–70. An outstanding discussion of Adorno's views on the visual media, as well as those of Kracauer and Benjamin, is Hansen 2012.

Leslie 2002 is a lively discussion of the social import of Hollywood animation from a roughly Critical Theory perspective. Saunders 1996 treats the importance of Hollywood films to Weimar culture.

The passages on chance have as their background the emergence of probability as the dominant form of rationality in modern Europe. There is a sizeable literature on point, see, e.g., Daston 1988, Hacking 1975 and 1990, and Foucault 2003, 2009, and 2010.

NOTES

1 See Ross 2017 for a comprehensive assessment of fascism in Los Angeles.
2 Bahr 2007; see also Friedrich 1986.
3 Lukács 1974: 22. It is not often noted that Lukács's charge repeats one he had already made against Schopenhauer. See Lukács 2021: 243.
4 Benjamin 1968: 166–95.
5 It is too bad that most American audiences only know Lenya through her role as the Smersh agent Rosa Klebb in the second of the James Bond movies, *From Russia with Love*. This is especially unfortunate because the film is homophobic, casting as perverse and evil her character's lesbianism.
6 Original in English, a play on the sociologist Thorstein Veblen's concept of conspicuous consumption, i.e., buying things to display one's wealth and good taste. See Veblen 2007.
7 More specifically, the imagination operates with possibility that diverges from actuality. The reason for the qualification is that on certain modern logical conceptions of possibility, if a thing is, it is also possible that it is (since it is).
8 For instance, Horkheimer 1995: 273–90.
9 Horkheimer and Adorno mention jazz several times as music that reinforces rote reaction. Its use of syncopation in particular is picked out as problematic. Adorno wrote several short pieces on jazz over his career, all of which have come under a great deal of criticism. We cannot do the subject justice here and, to be fair, it is a bit of a worn topic anyway. It is possible, however, to make some summary points. First, Adorno's prewar experience of jazz was limited to white American and European appropriations of Black music. That means, second, he was not in a position to construct a dialectical context in terms of which to understand the music. Third, he seems to have thought that this was so because jazz, in essence, had no history of its own, i.e., no working out of musical ideas that was not reliant on European art music. Fourth, that was his limitation, not the music's. Fifth, the remedy is obvious: do not make the mistake that the European context is the only one that has a history over which dialectical musical understanding can work. Sixth, Adorno worked in offices only a few blocks away from Harlem jazz clubs. Perhaps he visited some. In any event, he lived long enough to have heard Bop, Hard Bop, Cool, modal, and free jazz if he cared to lend an ear. The first and second Miles Davis quintets, the Coltrane quartet, and the Coleman quartet and double quartet stand at the summit of the history of jazz, all active in the late 1950s and early 1960s. So, he really has no excuse. Ironically, given what he thinks about the trajectory of Schoenberg's music (atonal period excellent; twelve-tone period retrogressive), he should have preferred Cecil Taylor over *Moses und Aron*. Robinson 1994 is a judicious assessment.
10 Buffon 1844: 1.30.
11 Boileau 1966: 158.
12 A neologism found in other of Adorno's works.

13 It is hard to shake the impression that this emphasis was brought on not only by the examples of Chaplin and others present in the Hollywood of the time, but also Henri Bergson's idea that comedy was critical because it (typically, in displays of physical comedy) juxtaposed the inflexibility of the protagonist with the flexibility of reality (112/166; cf. Bergson 1912). Inflexibility is unnatural and the laughter contains the critique—it takes the side of flexibility. This is the precise opposite of the structure that Horkheimer and Adorno find in commercialized comedy. For Adorno's further reflections on Chaplin, see Adorno 1996/1970: 10.1: 362–6.

14 Chaplin was the subject of intense philosophical admiration in the intellectual circles that mattered to Horkheimer and Adorno. Lukács, Benjamin, and Balázs wrote important essays on his early films.

15 *Modern Times* (1936, dir. C. Chaplin) contains important – indeed crucial – sound elements, most notably the factory director's voice and the nonsense song that closes the film. The incursion of the song is of special philosophical interest and suggests a form of linguistic freedom that suits Benjamin's account of language well. It is strange that Horkheimer and Adorno do not focus on *Modern Times*, especially perhaps the greatest comic scene ever set to film, the assembly line breakdown. It captures just about all that they want to say, at least at first pass.

16 Aristotle 1965: 1449b21–8.

17 Kant 2000: 111 [§ 15]; Horkheimer and Adorno use the formulation at 69/96.

18 As in the cognate English, the German *Liquidation* can mean both destruction and selling an asset. Both meanings are in play here.

19 Heidegger 1962: ¶ 35.

20 It is actually a triple inside joke. It is generally accepted that the middle initial "O" is a reference to David O. Selznick, the studio head. Eve asks Roger what the O stands for and Roger responds "nothing." Is it then a letter that stands for no middle name? Did Roger just put it there because monograms with three letters are stylish? Or is it the numeral zero? If the former, a failure of reference; if the latter, reference but to a nullity. No commentator seems to notice that the orthography of the monogram is complicated. The O is set in larger style than the other letters, which would, formally speaking, make it the initial for Roger's last name, not his middle initial. That may make one see the O as not a letter at all. Its shape is coffin-like: yet another layer. There is a lesson for Odysseus here.

21 See Honneth 2008.

22 There is a slightly naughty connotation of the French verb (in certain contexts), made explicit by Barthes 1975. There he groups texts into those for *plaisir* and those for *jouissance*, the latter meaning "bliss" but also "orgasm." It is a nod to Bataille.

6

CONJECTURES ON ANTISEMITISM

The chapter on antisemitism, the last in *DE*, was also the last composed. Its section VII was written by Horkheimer alone and is absent from the 1944 mimeograph version of the book that circulated narrowly.

Antisemitism as such was not a central concern of the Institute prior to its arrival in the United States. The attention given to the status of Jews in Europe was directed toward questions of class. Even when fascism was discussed, Judaism did not present as a problem of stand-alone systematic persecution. It was, rather, an issue of how Jews would assimilate if advanced capitalism subsumed those financial sectors in which they had traditionally been permitted to work. You might say: exactly, that there were *permitted* sectors and, by implication, prohibited sectors, expresses antisemitism. You would be right of course, but the Frankfurt theorists did not at first see things this way.

That changed in exile, but the change was not immediate, nor was it complete. Writing in 1939, Horkheimer still endorses the economic analysis when it comes to the European situation of the Jews.[1]

Two stages of the Institute's empirical research – the first funded by the Jewish Labor Committee, the second by the American Jewish Committee – focused on prejudice specifically in the United States, with particular attention to demagogues in mass media. The second resulted in the five-volume series *Studies in Prejudice*, published in 1949–50 with Horkheimer as series co-editor. Two books in that series, Leo Löwenthal and Norbert Guterman's *Prophets of Deceit* and the Adorno co-edited and co-authored *The Authoritarian Personality*, are of particular relevance, even though they were published after *DE*.

Löwenthal and Guterman's study found that demagoguery was strongly resistant to counterevidence. No matter how far one went to debunk charismatic authoritarians, people still believed in them. This led Löwenthal and Guterman to conclude that unconscious factors were at work, in particular, paranoid projection. We shall see that Horkheimer and Adorno take a similar tack with regard to the relation between antisemitism and fascism.

The Authoritarian Personality was concerned with profiling the sorts of persons attracted to authoritarian figures by utilizing questionnaires and personality tests. It is perhaps most famous for its "F-scale," which assigned a value for susceptibility to fascism (thus the "F") based on the intersection of several character traits. It also had an "AS-scale" for antisemitism. The profiling in either case was not very telling. The questions asked were stacked with bias. And, even if they had not been, any results would have been mere manifestations of antisemitism – points to plot on the coordinates of authoritarian thinking. They did not go after root causes.

But the economic approach did not entirely subside in favor of social-psychological exposition. This is unsurprising. As we have seen, Critical Theory is happy to work with psychoanalytic theories when dealing with cultural phenomena, including political economy. Also adjacent to Horkheimer's and Adorno's writings on antisemitism and authoritarianism were deepening economic analyses of the rise of fascism and its relationship to both capitalism and socialism. As antisemitism in Germany became even more alarming under fascism, it stands to reason that this work would impact thinking about the phenomenon of antisemitism generally. There developed two competing lines of interpretation, both of which held fascism to develop out of what was termed "monopoly capitalism."[2]

In order that capitalism persist in the face of diminishing returns, as predicted in Marxist interpretations of it, monopoly capitalism stabilizes ownership of surplus value by consolidating wealth in state-sanctioned monopolies. Both Friedrich Pollock and Franz Neumann – the main representatives of the approaches in contention – argued that state intervention in capitalist markets was needed to promote market stability under these conditions. And both Pollock and Neumann argued that, in the end, capitalism would have to be superseded in order that democracy prevail. Moreover, they both held that this would in fact happen. But that is where their agreement ends.

Pollock borrowed the term "state capitalism" – terminology in use on both the political left and right of the times – to refer to what he considered to be a new form of capitalism, the successor to monopoly capitalism. State capitalism is principally a political, not an economic phenomenon. It can take two forms: democratic and totalitarian. *Democratic state capitalism* features a state-administered economy, but one that is still answerable to the needs and desires of a general public, who had the freedom to elect government representatives. Pollock was, to be fair, circumspect about the retention of liberal democracy in such a practice and favored a social democratic resolution. Oligarchy, which can be expected to flourish in such a climate, would have to be controlled. But, ideally at least, that could be done. The view of capitalism implicit in *DE* may be indebted to this notion, which might help explain why its authors seem to see no natural successor to this formation. The tensions that might have brought a traditional Marxist observer to anticipate change have quite simply been brought successfully under control by the government. That brings us to the second type, *totalitarian state capitalism*. Its main representative is fascism. Here one does not need to be coy and speak of a possible conceptual space for democracy in state capitalism. One knows that totalitarian capitalism is possible because it is actual. Nazi

Germany was a control economy in which industries were not nationalized but were doled out to oligarchs pledged at least nominally to the *Führerprinzip*.³ In it the stable democratic ideals of individual freedom and equality have no traction. Resistance from within – especially as Marx conceived it – was a near impossibility. Sometimes Pollock seems to hold that democratic state capitalism is the only bulwark against fascism; other times he is less open to that idea.

Neumann objected to Pollock's approach root and branch. "State capitalism" for Neumann is in effect a pseudo-concept and a dangerous one at that. There is no successor form of capitalism to monopoly capitalism. Fascism is monopoly capitalism in its necessary, final form. There is no democratic form of this last gasp. Neumann called this last, but not new, form of monopoly capitalism *totalitarian monopoly capitalism*. It can appear that all that is at stake here is Marxist hairsplitting, but the disagreement between Pollock and Neumann cuts deeper than that. Both are, like Horkheimer and Adorno, wary of putting all their cards on the table while in the United States, capitalist as it is. But if you are a Marxist political theorist any successor version to capitalism will have to develop out of contradictions in capitalism's final stages. Neumann thought that Pollock had betrayed that idea, as he, Neumann, could find no dialectical analysis at all in the arguments for state capitalism. The idea that there could be both totalitarian and democratic versions of it tokened that. Socialism is the only viable successor to capitalism.⁴

That is more traditionally Marxist. Neumann held that the antagonisms that form the basis for socialist change could compete in fact with fascist propaganda for the allegiance of workers. In other words, ideological processes could still operate dialectically. They could in the end produce a critique of the standing order. Nazi control of ideology was too unstable to compete with the daily effects of material historical conditions on the worker. Chapter 4 of his *Behemoth* addresses the intertwining of German racial theory and antisemitism, and provides a distinction between totalitarian and non-totalitarian forms of antisemitism. Antisemitism for Neumann is ultimately a question of economic ideology. Blaming the Jew is misdirection, a way to take attention away from capitalist exploitation. It concentrates and leverages populist prejudice, which would be otherwise too vague and diffuse to be socially cohesive, and piggybacks it on worker anger. Even the Nazis only used antisemitism as a tool to rid the Reich of democratic residue. If an antisemite is one who wholeheartedly and as a matter of reflex believes that all Jews are subhuman and to be killed immediately, most Germans and perhaps many Nazis weren't antisemitic according to Neumann.[5]

There is disagreement among commentators about whether Horkheimer and Adorno sided with Pollock or with Neumann. Their view of late capitalism as predominantly static and crisis-free points in the direction of Pollock. *DE* was dedicated to him, after all. But either way the result was a series of redactions and then eliminations of telltale terms related to this debate, terms like "monopoly" (redacted in both the 1944 and 1947 versions of the manuscript) and "rackets" (also eliminated in both). As we have noted before, Horkheimer and Adorno were themselves wary of being Marxists in the land of anti-Marxism, and they were never Marxists of a standard sort. Perhaps they merely wished to stay clear of the internecine dispute. Or perhaps it is a sign that, in fact, they disagreed with Pollock, who used those two terms copiously.[6]

Whatever the reason, leaving all of this out of *DE* renders more indeterminate what one nowadays one might most expect from a chapter on antisemitism, i.e., a discussion of its relation to fascism as a political conception and an actuality. This is not only pertinent to understanding Nazism. Whether one agrees with Pollock or Neumann (or neither) will greatly affect what one will say about US politics both then and now. If Neumann is right, then the United States is a monopoly capitalist economy tending toward totalitarianism. Fascism in the United States, then, is very much a live issue. If one agrees with Pollock, there may be a stable and somewhat democratic form of oligarchy, but oligarchs being oligarchs, authoritarianism is also not off the table. In any event, this plays in well with the work on authoritarianism, mentioned above, that Adorno and others were to undertake a bit later.

What results in the text due to these multiple unsettled currents of thought is untidy and difficult for the reader to manage. Before getting into the details of Horkheimer and Adorno's interpretation of antisemitism, it is good to have a relatively terse statement of its main line.

Due to the variety of allegiances – suppressed in the text or otherwise – Horkheimer and Adorno are thrown back on the philosophical anthropology that drives their discussion of the interactivity of myth and enlightenment. That template is overlaid onto the phenomenon of antisemitism. It is clear that they consider their interpretation of antisemitism to be the culmination of the overarching presentation of the book. It is supposed to unify *DE* by showing myth and enlightenment feeding off of one another at the very limit of their relationship. Here, then is a rough sketch of that overarching structure in retrospect. First, they build out the philosophical anthropology in terms of what they take to be the core contemporary philosophical alternatives: Kant, Sade, and Nietzsche. That is the subject matter of the first chapter of *DE* and its two excursuses. They then canvas a Weberian twist to those alternatives in the chapter on the culture industry: art under the sign of bureaucracy. Now they turn more resolutely to Freud. Commercial relations underwriting antisemitism are still mixed in with extending the interactivity of myth and reason, but the main categories here are those of *sacrifice*, the "discontent" (*Unbehagen*) occasioned by civilization, i.e., the internalization of law, and a resulting projection onto a scapegoat.

Jews cannot live up to the taboo on mimesis that they originally put in place. Civilization requires that one renounces the "old ways" of responsiveness to nature in its own terms and embraces a more observational and transactional regard of nature as something to manipulate. This break with mimesis is accomplished by means of iconoclasm and a shift from image to word, in particular to the power of language to generalize in the form of statements of laws.

Jews set this process in motion; they are the great civilizers. Yet they seek to evade its consequences. This amounts to "hypocrisy," which provides the fascist with the terms with which to contrast himself with the Jew. The Jew is the self-undermining one, the one who is a nullity to the non-Jew. He is made to pay the price of alienation that he has wrought just because he seeks escape from it. The observant Jew attempts to escape by absenting himself from general society. But even the assimilated Jew who is mindful of "civil society" – a category Horkheimer especially considers important – is placed in this bind. For the antisemite will view assimilation as a priori impossible. For him the Jew is a member of an "anti-race" (*Gegenrasse*); any attempt by the Jew to be German is a contradiction in terms.

All the failures of civilization are in this way summed up in the figure of the Jew – so the antisemite thinks. Antisemitism is, according to Horkheimer and Adorno's narrative, mimetic backlash. Nazis murder Jews in order to enforce the only kind of "assimilation" possible from the point of view of the antisemite: annihilation. The Shoah is a behemoth of pathological mimesis.

That is the interpretation in its essentials. Now, one thing to be on alert for as we step through its details is the extent to which the description of Jewish cultural impact is merely Horkheimer and Adorno's periphrasis of what the antisemite thinks. One of the main concerns that has hounded this chapter of *DE* is the degree to which it blames Jews, not of course for the Holocaust, but for setting in motion, and even realizing, the conditions that make genocide possible. As Horkheimer and Adorno both had Jewish heritage, this can get into heated debates about so-called "Jewish self-hatred," a very controversial topic, especially given how readymade it is for antisemitic appropriation.

SACRIFICE

As we saw in our discussion of Horkheimer and Adorno's treatment of the *Odyssey*, the practice of sacrifice is transactional and, thus, categorial, but it typically strikes the balance overall in favor of mimesis. Sacrifice is adaptive to nature in that it gives back what nature first provides, appeasing nature in its own terms, life for life. But what is returned to nature, even where sacrifice is at its most basic, is altered and made slightly abstract. The offering is a surrogate or token, i.e., sacrifice becomes symbolic (146/207–08). What can count as a surrogate is elastic to an extent. Ritual tattooing of an image of a feared or desired animal or the drawing of a figure on a cave wall might serve.

The role of biblical figures in Horkheimer and Adorno's genealogy of antisemitism is best captured by the account of the giving of the Law to Moses. There is a kind of sacrifice going on here as well, implicit but all the more determinative for that. Here the substitution is linguistically expressed: the divine ordinance meant to bind the Israelites. At this point in reading *DE* we know what is to become of language in modernity; it is the vehicle of generalization run amok. So, our ears prick when the terms of a covenant between humans and the divine are put down in language, as they are in the Ten Commandments. A fatal step has been taken, albeit on Horkheimer and Adorno's reckoning a necessary one as well. For the attempt is to create out of mimesis-heavy obeisance a substitute that will tend toward the non-mimetic. In other words, it is an attempt to appease nature (in the form of the creator, God) via a modality that distances one from that very nature.

This is an inherently universalizing moment. The one God proclaims to the head of a nation a code that binds all of its people, inscribing the code on tablets by the touch of His finger. There is only one Law, i.e., it is part of the Law that there is no other. The monotheism is essential to the moment. This is a being so overarching in its power that no divisions of divinity are permitted, a being so powerful and commanding that *it does not deign to appear in nature* no matter what sacrificial transaction is in play. Horkheimer and Adorno contend that this is the birth of the idea of the sovereign subject that affects so much of modernity.

The god of the Books of Moses has people problems: Adam and Eve, Cain and Abel, those left to drown in the Great Flood, Sodom and Gomorrah, and one could go on. He is done showing people things; it is time to say them. But matters are complicated. This is the post-Babel world in which tongues have proliferated and the divine spark of language has been spent. What language could still have the power of sacrifice? The answer: language issuing from God to Moses. The status of graphic representation of divinity is central here. The key Commandments are the first two: the proscriptions against worshipping any god other than the one God and against crafting visual representations, i.e., idols ("graven images") or images ("likenesses"). The ban is total: no idols or images of anything that exists on earth, sea, or sky, including gods or God.[7] The Law drastically reshapes the terms governing sacrifice by prohibiting images and substituting for them a determinate and universal ordinance. There is no ground for haggling over the concession, nor is there elbow room for interpretation about what the Law means. Images and icons are banned because transient. They change over time, whereas God doesn't. There are images of other gods, and that is blasphemous on the presupposition that there is only one God. And even if the images were restricted to images of God, no one can carve or model a figure after God, since after the Fall God is not something that one can see. The one God is immutable and all, and so is the Law.

This move to language is defining, a move toward generality in thought at the expense of mimesis and image. The iconoclasm extends even to the articles of language that are permitted. Direct reference to God is strictly controlled, if not forbidden. The name of God in Biblical Hebrew is akin to a proper name or an all-encompassing essence, not a description such as "the Lord" or the compound given by God to Moses.[8] God's name is proper only to Him, perhaps even proper only in His "mouth."[9] Human utterance of the name – transliterated as "YHWH" or, with vowels supplied, "Yahweh" – is very restricted. Those who feel so proscribed often refer to the name indirectly as "Tetragrammaton."[10] We point these matters out here merely to underline the care taken within Judaism to avoid anything linguistic that tends toward the kind of directness an image might have when it comes to God.

Sacrifice and its transformation by Law set the mainspring for enlightenment, i.e., increased ambit for instrumental control with a coordinate increased alienation of subject from nature. The unconscious becomes the sole domain in which nature can have its say. But the unconscious is the realm of the repressed and, according to Horkheimer and Adorno's genealogy, that means of repressed nature.

THE JEW AS THE OTHER

In late-modern European philosophy the word "Other" is given a special sense. It designates an individual or group that one perceives as different enough to provide oneself a contrastive sense of self. The idea has a Hegelian provenance, but Horkheimer and Adorno add to it a Freudian twist. The connection between the implicit acknowledgment and explicit aggression tracks latent and manifest content. The key concept here is *projection* as Freud deploys the concept in *Totem and Taboo* (162–63 & n.3/227 & n.3).

Projection is the attribution to another person or thing of a property, usually a mental property, that is actually one's own. For Freud, this is a matter of individual psychology. Horkheimer and Adorno extend this idea to group agency. The activity is not marked as such by the projecting agent; it is part of its point that one who projects not recognize the projection for what it is. Recognized projection is no projection at all.

What is the mechanism of projection? Freud held that everyone harbors an ambivalence to others, especially to those close to one.[11] One hates whom one loves, but admitting this is socially unacceptable and, at the same time, retaining it in one's personality is unbearable. One hates oneself for hating the one whom one is not allowed to hate. Self-hatred is a powerful, destabilizing psychological state. When it is present, one tries to relieve the pressure it imposes on one by projecting the hated qualities onto another, socially acceptable object. Projection both *distances* oneself from another and *shifts the burden* from oneself onto another. Those most readily projected upon will be those about whom one already has ambivalent feelings, in many cases based on false beliefs.

Jews have been such a group in Europe from late-medieval times to the present, onto whom Christians and their secular descendants have transferred their own alienation from nature and guilt. That there are many distinct European Jewish communities, sometimes very different, not to mention many different ways to find those communities meaningful, is not an issue for such projection. It simplifies its objects in order to discharge its task, and one way to simplify is to essentialize.

The third essay in *Totem and Taboo* expands the role of projection, arguing that primordial, magical thinking involves a comparatively unbounded projection of psychic forces onto nature – animism, panpsychism – due both to a wish to control and to the mind's inflated sense of its own importance. The latter idea is pure Nietzsche, but note as well the proximity of the schema as a whole to Kant, who held that nature is structured antecedently by discursive mental operations. In this vein, Horkheimer and Adorno write that projection is present in any perception "in a sense." Perception is "an extension of the readiness for combat with which higher species reacted actively or passively to movements, regardless of the intention of the object" (154/217). The idea here seems to be that perceptual states are limpid, anticipating pre-inferentially what will happen next. You see an object move and project onto it, as if seeing ahead of time where it moves next. Horkheimer and Adorno hold antisemitism to be based on "false" projection, i.e., projection that does not merely anticipate nature but recasts it so radically that its objects no longer have any independence from the presuppositions that inform the perception of them. The impulse charging the projection is faulty, repressed, and models nature as foreign in the extreme (154–56/217–20).

Unlike normal projection, false projection does not permit a return of the self to itself by virtue of projected encounters with objects. When you perceive something, you anticipate ways it might later be proximate to its present stage. The object will often to a fair degree conform to these anticipations due to their source in banked past experiences of like perceptual situations. When it does not, adjustments will be entered into the anticipatory stock of concepts going forward. Either way, the projection allows feedback from the world to the self. Indeed, that is the point of projecting in perception.

False projection anticipates the object in severely alienated terms, which ensures that the object will *not* routinely conform to expectation, with the result that the self is left traveling a one-way street that sets nature against itself in anticipation (156–57/219–20). Such projection is false, then, in that, while projective, it is not truly projection (156/219); the feedback loop is broken. Moreover, because there is no validation from nature flowing back to the subject of what was anticipated, there is no possibility of reflection (*Reflexion*), no chance that what one receives back from nature can be combined to increase cognitive stock or be put to the test of countervailing evidence (156/219–20). Even disconfirmation allows for reflection and reorganization of cognitive stock. But the lack of expected fit in false projection is not mere disconfirmation of an anticipation, as the anticipation is not well-formed in the first place. All that is delivered back to the subject is *blank resistance*. The subject starts out with an anticipation that is null and receives nullity as a response. Horkheimer and Adorno go on to argue that this is *paranoid* in structure, a point to which we return below.

Antisemitism is, then, self-hatred projected onto Jews, who are cast as *both* the authors of the move away from adaptive mimesis, and thereby from nature, *and* as those who exempt themselves from what they have wrought, i.e., the developed, calculative forms of that movement. The exemption takes the form of non-assimilation to a purportedly universal society, whose new "nature" is a proliferation of images, rules, and anonymous economic exchanges. The exemption becomes a form of resistance to be begrudged and envied. This could be keeping kosher, going to synagogue, observing high holidays – in short anything that is "observant" and, therefore, separate from civil society at large. The Jew is the Other because both natural and unnatural, mimetic and non-mimetic.

Moreover, that the Messiah has yet to come, as well as the power that that thought exerts on the reservation of the Jew to a Christianized civil society, means that the basis for happiness, final reconciliation, and making the world whole, gives a form of hope to the Jew that the antisemite lacks. He resents the Jew for what he cannot have: a world in which the Messiah has not yet come and, so, a world that awaits better days. The Jew becomes a Romantic figure, for whom *noch nicht* is a cherished and private possession. The antisemite, by contrast, is stuck with a world that a savior has already visited and, despite that, a world that confronts him as alien.

Horkheimer and Adorno draw attention to the way physiognomy plays a role in such prejudice. The nose becomes the *principium individuationis* (Schopenhauer's term for the power of Will to individualize beings) (151/213–14). Large noses are both natural and unnatural – natural because noses, unnatural because outsized for function. The signification of Jews by bodily features – which is of course a complete falsehood – expresses this. To say that you are your nose may be synecdoche, but it is an attempt to represent figuratively, i.e., without abstraction. It is also stereotyping and, to that extent, deploys categories and is supremely modern.

Christianity is a transformation of certain strands of Judaism that existed in the first century CE, and the terms of transformation further distance Law from material nature. "Judaism was hardly separable from national life, from collective self-preservation. The reshaping of the heathen ritual of sacrifice not only took place in worship and in the mind but determined the form of labor process" (146/187). The reformation of sacrifice into Law structured *work*, and this transformed sacrifice into rational agency as praxis, overseen by priests, who have sole authority over Law and who exercise that power overtly, forging a new relation to nature. Christianity breaks from Judaism by rendering nature in terms of "spirit," doing so in increasingly human terms. It attempts to more fully clothe power in mind, not material circumstance. It "repudiated self-preservation by the ultimate sacrifice, that of the man-god" (146/187) and thereby rendered material life sinful. If in Judaism God represents nature at its source, in Christianity God-the-source becomes human and so does nature:

> The progress beyond Judaism is paid for with the assertion that the mortal Jesus was God. The harm is done precisely by the reflective moment in Christianity, the spiritualization of magic [*Vergeistigung der Magie*]. A spiritual essence is attributed to something which mind identifies as natural. Mind consists precisely in demonstrating the contradiction inherent in such pretensions of the finite. [...] It is that which makes Christianity a religion, and, in a sense, the only one: an intellectual link to something intellectually suspect, a special sphere of culture.
>
> (145–46/207)

The main idea is, again, Hegelian. For Hegel Spirit is the process by which humans realize that what is divine is human, and religion (what he designates Revealed Religion) makes this truth comprehensible in images and stories. "God as Spirit is the principle *opposed to* nature" (145–46/207, translation emended, emphasis supplied).

Pace Hegel, Horkheimer and Adorno insist that this transformation is incomplete, indeed, incompletable, if what one means by completeness is that Christianity effaces the need for non-spiritualized nature, i.e., the object of mimetic thought. Instead – and perhaps this was the purpose of the transposition – one gets a skepticism. The idea that nonhuman nature – and non-intellectual nature in humans – could be completely intellectualized is itself intellectually incomprehensible.

Horkheimer and Adorno offer the doctrine of transubstantiation (*Wandlung*) for consideration in this connection (145–46/207). It is a passing reference; so, its significance needs to be brought out. According to Roman Catholicism, there is a real change in the ontological status of bread to body and of wine to blood in the Eucharist. That is a holdover from prior conceptions of sacrifice. Nowadays, in a world in which enlightenment conceptuality has secured a complete victory over nature, that is no longer credible. A sacrificial substitution (that tries to reestablish the corporeality of sacrifice) must appear to be superstitious to the enlightened Christian. So, one graduates to the nature of the Eucharist in Protestantism, to the doctrine of consubstantiation. The wafer really is bread, but is also really Christ's body. The surrogacy of bread for body and wine for blood is more abstract and formal than in Catholicism. Christians:

> repressed that knowledge and with bad conscience convinced themselves of salvation by the worldly ruin of those who refused to make the murky sacrifice of reason [*das trübe Opfer der Vernunft*]. That is the religious origin of anti-Semitism. [...] Anti-Semitism is supposed to confirm that the ritual of faith and history is justified by sacrificing those who deny its justice.
>
> (147/209)

The idea of sacrifice thereby is set on its head. To the antisemite the Jew is offered up as a hypocritical archaic figure, one who desires to exempt himself from what he set in motion by remaining at an earlier point in its development, the modern unmodern, a scapegoat (*Sündenbock*) to pay for the sins of modernity (142/203). But such a sacrifice is ineffective, for its terms have been "forgotten": "The Jew, burdened with his tormentors' guilt, mocked as their lord, they nail to the cross, endlessly repeat[s] a sacrifice in whose power they are unable to believe" (138/198). The Jew cannot truly assimilate to European culture to the satisfaction of that culture;

even assimilated Jews are viewed as opting out of the burden they have imposed on all by preserving a private dimension of kinship that defines itself as more intimately connected to the original law. ("Assimilated" is an adjective loaded nowadays with political and social ambivalence within Jewish thought, but Horkheimer and Adorno use the word freely.) This alleged exceptionalism preforms the Jew for the antisemite's projection. Given that the Jew, according to the antisemite, is an incomplete sufferer, he is a proper object for transferred guilt.

Horkheimer and Adorno are playing with fire here. Is it truly their contention that Jews, in historical fact, have exempted themselves from the very thing they set in motion? And would this exemption not be appropriate grounds for negative reaction to Jews as a people, were it true that they so exempted themselves? Or are they simply reconstructing the origin of antisemitism's self-conception? Is this a replay of Marx's essay "On the Jewish Question," which raises such questions absent the florid anthropological/theological speculation?

Consider what they write about the figure of the Wandering Jew (141/201–02). The character comes from medieval European folklore, a Jew of various names who, after taunting Jesus on the way to crucifixion, is cursed by God to wander the earth until the end of time. In the eighteenth and nineteenth centuries he becomes a pan-European literary figure, prominent especially in German and Scandinavian literature. The most famous depictions are Wagner's *The Flying Dutchman* (1843) – based on a story by Heine in which the Dutchman is set by analogy to the Wandering Jew – and the "The Unhappy One," a section of Kierkegaard's *Either—Or* (also 1843), where, under the guise of Ahasuerus, he is grouped with Don Juan and Faust as ethical wantons. Horkheimer and Adorno emphasize in this connection claims that Jews are by nature migrants, who live only abstractly and marginally in general society. Modern European sociality has become increasingly economic, which is to say capitalistic. Jews are involved with the technical, formal features of that sphere, the movement of currency.

False stereotypes abound, for instance, the Jew as swindler or "haggler" (*Schacherer*) (141/202). Take Shylock from *The Merchant of Venice*, whom Shakespeare has bargain for "a pound of man's flesh" in case of default of debt.[12] Shylock is a moneylender by profession, yet what he exacts as penalty for forfeiture is not in kind, i.e., not in currency, but in a measure of the debtor's body. The archaic idea of sacrificial flesh is at hand. The result is a premodern specification of what is sacrificed, flesh, joined to a modern specification of how much, a *quantum* of sacrificed flesh. The Jew again turns up as a figure at once premodern and modern, as one who deals in the abstracta of the modern world but, when it comes down to it, takes payment in the old ways. He both renounces and does not renounce the modern turn to commodification.[13]

The identification of the position of the Jew with the depredations of capitalism – specifically with moneylending and, more broadly, dealing in currency – is controlling. Debt was always a central part of capitalism and of much economic organization before that,[14] but the premodern Christian proscription against lending at interest, along with the desire not to personally collect rents and taxes, left such occupations primarily to Jews. The precapitalist idea that making money from money is sinful, or at least extremely undesirable, leeches into the capitalist context. The same tension we have seen before is in play: the Jew is the Other to whom is allotted the tasks that would disfigure one, notwithstanding that those very tasks all but define one. The Jew is blamed for the alienating effect of rapid exchange through financial middlemen, innovations the Jew was in a historical position to make on account of the Christian having put him there in the first place.

Let's take stock. The composite claim is that prejudicial stereotypes of Jews are projections of antisemitic self-hatred, a hatred stemming from an alienation from nature and the ensuing powerlessness that drives enlightenment, which Horkheimer and Adorno go so far as to label a "trauma" (144/205). The trauma in question is reconfigured and dissembled in the exterior pose of the "productive creator," the entrepreneur. But, as noted at the outset of this discussion, critical theorists did not think of capitalism, or of its house philosophy, liberalism, as insulated against fascist tendencies. One might well think, accordingly, that these points pertain to fascism as well.[15]

LIBERAL AND NATIONALIST ANTISEMITISM

Horkheimer and Adorno distinguish between liberal and nationalist (*völkische*) antisemitism. For the liberal antisemite, "the Jews, free of national or racial features, form a group through religious belief and tradition and nothing else" (137/197). This is "[d]iametrically opposed to" fascism, for which "the Jews are not a minority but the *anti-race* (*Gegenrasse*), the negative principle as such; on their extermination the world depends" (137/197, emphasis added). Nationalist antisemitism, the predecessor view to fascism, "wants to disregard religion," "claims to be concerned with purity of race and nation," and feeds "unchanneled longing [...] into racial-nationalist rebellion" (144/206, translation emended).

Longing (*Sehnsucht*) is a central Romantic idea in literature and philosophy, indicating an intense striving for an object that is in principle unattainable; as some of the Romantics put it, both the striving and its object are "infinite." This unattainable point is often a deeply past origin, the striving for which confronts one with a remote future in which one might become closer to that origin (145/206), here the point at which we were sundered from nature. This is projection writ very large; nature is to be reenchanted. The resulting nature is – it is important to mark – a *result*; it is not "raw" nature. It is an attempt to find in nature an affinity to freedom.

The nation can spell what is longed for, the aboriginal unity of a people (*Volk*). That is the definitive turn of antisemitism toward racism, toward a racialized conception of an allegedly pure community. Horkheimer and Adorno mention Wagner's *Parzival* as a reflection of and on such purity.

"Race" is far from a natural category. It is "*regression* to nature, to mere violence, to the hidebound [*verstockte*] particularism which, in the existing order, constituted precisely the universal" (138/198–9, translation emended, emphasis supplied). Nationalistic racism identifies race as mattering because of a fear that what is exceptional will compromise the community and, with it, a path back to nature. The power of the concept of race to unite a people consists in its power to exclude Others as those who cannot be parts of the universal: Others, that is, are failed universals.

The liberal antisemite is comparatively mild, if one judges him in terms of his potential for physical violence. Part of that is because liberal antisemitism is subsumed under the larger project of capitalism and, finally, under that of controlling a nature that no longer matters in itself. But more broadly, liberalism is a doctrine tooled to manage conflict between individual agents whose essential characteristic is personal freedom. Personal freedom, in turn, consists in the pursuit or ability to pursue one's interests as one sees them, consistent with like pursuit on the part of others. If one is Hobbesian such brokered concern is what liberal sociality consists in. If one takes Locke and Mill on board, that will be enlarged by natural rights or affirmative duties of tolerance to others. Enflamed antisemitism – antisemitism violent enough and broad enough to be socially determinative – will be contrary to liberalism. That is not because liberals cannot be antisemites; natural right is a vague concept and tolerance is hardly affirmation. It is, rather, because liberal democrats are capitalists. Virulent antisemitism is bad for business, inefficient in contexts where market relations are determinative. Antisemitic rage does not incentivize coordination of self-interest. Liberal antisemitism is a private affair.

Horkheimer and Adorno bring this assessment in line with their general genealogical account of antisemitism. Liberalism takes the state to be free in that it is a realm of law. That presupposes that the basic correct social order has been identified and is in place. A set ideal of universal political order, best for everyone, is in play, and conformity to that order is essential. "Deficient adaptation" reneges on the whole liberal project; any exception spoils a universal claim (138/198). Freeriding is a particularly sore point, because liberalism owes its very existence to *each and all* shouldering the burden of trading their freedom to do as they like for security. To refuse to adapt is to thwart the universal in that sense too:

> The universal, that which fits into the context of social utility, is regarded as natural. But anything natural which has not been absorbed

> into utility by passing through the cleansing channels of conceptual order [...] whatever is not quite assimilated [...] is felt as intrusive and arouses a compulsive aversion.
>
> (147–48/209)

The aversion is *compulsive* because generalization has become routine by this point; liberalism is a teaching of complacency. It is *aversion* because, to repeat, a single instance of nonconformity spoils a universal claim.

Universalization as a default mode of thinking of society must be a deficient conception of society as a totality for Horkheimer and Adorno. Thinking of discursive order as merely subsumption instead of as being organically structured distorts the conception of wholeness key to Critical Theory's approach. This leads, in turn, to a truncation of thought, a phenomenon that we have already seen at work in the commodification of culture:

> The less social reality kept pace with educated [*gebildete*] consciousness, the more that consciousness itself succumbed to a process of reification. Culture was entirely commoditized, disseminated as information which did not permeate those who acquired it. Thought becomes short-winded, confines itself to apprehending isolated facts. Intellectual connections are rejected as an inconvenient and useless exertion. The developmental moment in thought, its whole generic and intensive dimension, is forgotten and leveled down to what is immediately present, to the extensive.
>
> (163/227–8)

Jews must adapt to the given terms. Non-adaptation threatens completeness: "Anti-Semitism always starts with an appeal to complete the task. Anti-Semitism and totality have always been profoundly connected" (141/202). What is sought is a false totality, a completeness of hierarchically arranged laws, a pyramid of greater and lesser abstractness, but always of abstractness. But as we have already seen, the figure of the Jew is set up as the "fall guy," to take a concept from film noir. She can never meet the demand, and that is because she has been set up so as not to be able to meet it. That is her whole reason for being to the antisemite.

Liberal antisemitism is a matter of bourgeois "self-assertion": assimilation on all fronts of individuality, subordinating race to something as instrumental as counting, i.e., to demography. The antisemitism remains, but its force is to obfuscate a deeper structure of oppression – the exploitation of workers. While the liberal antisemite's Jew offers a handy, alternative source of blame for capitalist immiseration, the comparative mildness of the antisemitism allows it to circulate freely, almost neutrally. The liberal is free at the margins – at home, at parties, at the country club – to express his fake individuality by letting more pointed antisemitism reveal itself in conversation, in lapses of "good taste" or in the "off-color" joke. If one were a fellow traveler, one might even think that, if that is all that antisemitism is any longer, the problem of antisemitism is more or less taken care of to everyone's satisfaction, even the Jew's (142/202–03). But that is only because antisemitism has been recruited where it can do its real work in the hustle-bustle of modern life, where normality often masks cruelty.

FASCISM, PARANOIA, AND ABSOLUTE EVILS

Fascism is the flower of the nationalistic branch of this genealogical tree of antisemitism. Horkheimer and Adorno extend the account of projection to encompass fascism by turning more resolutely to psychoanalytic theories of paranoia.[16] The starting point is that, unlike liberalism, fascism requires antisemitism to play a role in stabilizing its sense of unity in the community; market rationality and consumerism are not enough. To that extent fascist antisemitism is irrational by the lights of modern economic rationality. This does not mean that Nazis cannot cite reasons internal to their beliefs for action, nor does it mean that fascist antisemitism does not do economic duty and is not reformed to an extent by calculative rationality. What it means is that philosophically explicating fascist antisemitism has to appeal to unconscious causes for what are on the surface irrational beliefs and actions. Given Horkheimer and Adorno's speculative anthropology, that means tracking repressed nature at work at both the individual and community levels.

For Freud, projection of *persecution* typifies paranoia, a form of neurosis in which the subject is fixated on the homoerotic stage of sexual development.[17] Ordinarily, according to Freud, homoeroticism is a transitory stage, positioned between autoeroticism and object-love (i.e., taking another, not oneself, as the primary locus of sexual attraction), in which one experiences sexual attraction to another but does so in autoerotic terms. That is to say that homoeroticism is mimetic; one seeks a love-object who has the same type of genitalia as one has. This process is not in itself pathological.[18] Nascent homoeroticism is sublimated into social benevolence, deep friendship, even altruism. Continuing in Freud's voice, as a child one loves another in one's own terms quite literally. One desires a same-sex other because she or he mirrors one's own sex in virtue of having a vagina or penis. As an adolescent one internalizes that homoeroticism is socially unacceptable. Blocked, however, it results in an ungrounded suspicion that one is being persecuted and, consequently, in a hatred of the perceived persecutor. Unconsciously one recasts the Other as what one finds threatening about oneself, the social unacceptability of same-sex erotic thoughts and actions. One persecutes oneself because one has interpolated the persecutions of others and externalizes them as persecutions of a select Other. Other-love engenders Other-hate, and does so out of self-hate.

Horkheimer and Adorno put Freud's account of paranoia to work on a very broad canvas, in order to add heft to their account of the wages of increased instrumentalism in modern society, which is then turned to situate fascism, and with it, fascist antisemitism, alongside liberalism. Fascism, for all its irrationality, is not an outlier. It is a crucial part of a comprehensive account of the possibilities of modernity. They hold, for example, that the psychodynamics of paranoia as Freud understands them are latent in modern epistemology: "Paranoia is the shadow of cognition [*Erkenntnis*]" (161/225). They expect the reader to pick up immediately the implications of the word here translated as "cognition." *Erkenntnis* for Kant is empirical knowledge. For the Marburg neo-Kantians – who, we have seen, were always a negative touchstone for early Critical Theory – the meaning is narrower still: "scientific knowledge." Reduction of thought to cognition (see 163/227–8) in these restricted senses, or even an overvaluation of thought of this sort, has paranoia as its "shadow" because paranoia is one possible form that a normal and natural capacity, i.e., projection, can take.

For the Kantian, what Horkheimer and Adorno here call projection is an unconscious imaginative exercise necessary for any synthesis that can have objective reference (154 & n.2/218 & n.2). One can discern this aspect in Kant especially in contexts in which he discusses states of mind that fall short of explicit conception, such as in his aesthetic theory. The statement that paranoia is the shadow of cognition indicates that what becomes enflamed in cases of paranoia is always involved in perception. The projection is characteristic of all thinking that features abstraction through the subsumption of particulars under concepts. In fascism, however, the shadow no longer trails but leads. And when it leads, paranoia is projection without a check in reality. One no longer takes cues from nature in order to anticipate what comes next. Instead, one freely projects onto nature prejudices that can have no real referents. And that is exactly what sort of object fascist paranoia seeks, a *nullity*. The suitable object for projection of this content has been set by more traditional forms of antisemitism. On this basis Horkheimer and Adorno claim that fascists conceive of Jews as "the negative principle as such" (137/197). They wed a Freudian idea, i.e., pathological projection, with a Hegelian way of approaching the issue: "The process is one of the liquidation instead of sublation, of formal instead of determinate negation" (170/236).

As we discussed in Chapter 1, Hegel views irreconcilable tension in the core concepts as the engine for conceptual change. The sharpening of tension between core elements of a concept and then release of that tension in a new understanding of the concept typifies progress for him. Especially in the French reception of Hegel, one set of such tensions is held to be emblematic of how this process works: the struggle for recognition between Lord (*Herr*) and Bondsman (*Knecht*) set out in his *Phenomenology of Spirit*.[19] Hegel details how humans gain confidence by dominating, first, nonhuman nature, and then each other. The word Hegel uses for "confident" is the same word as is translated in English-language editions of the book as "self-conscious" (*selbstbewusst*). The ordinary German can have either meaning, and there is a connection between them in everyday speech as well: one who is self-aware is on better footing with regard to their self-conviction. Hegel also intends both meanings and their connection. The Lord's outlook on the world purchases what integration it enjoys by treating the things it encounters as opportunities for its control. Recall the first-pass discussion of Otherness earlier in this chapter. To control something is to make it bend to your will and that, in turn, increases your sense of your own solidity as a person over and against other things. You prove your power by overcoming resistance. The dialectical point Hegel is driving at – and one that becomes most apparent to the one who is on the receiving end of the control – is that integrating yourself by treating others as nugatory – as if they are there solely to be mastered – is in fact a form of dependency of the controller on the controlled. For the Lord to be free by his own lights he must be (unwittingly) unfree. That is the tension at stake.

Now, a primitive form of this negation, i.e., of treating a thing as insubstantial, is simple consumption. You see the tasty apple on the tree; you want the apple; you pick the apple; you eat the apple. The apple is so completely *for you* that there is no discounting your desire in terms of its continued existence. You "negate" (*vernichten*) in that you deprive it of its very existence. But in Hegel's estimation, if you are to get anywhere securing a viable, ongoing sense of self in this manner, objects that rate low in terms of their resistance to your actions won't do. What is needed is that you confront increasingly more challenging objects, ones that better resist your attempts to negate them. The most challenging object in this regard is another human being, another person whose self-consciousness/self-confidence is also on the line. Because both parties in such an encounter are trying to secure their substantiality at the expense of the other, resistance will be stiff, "to the death," as Hegel puts it.[20] There are two possible results, only the second of which is in the long run progressive. (1) One of the parties dies; the prevailing party does not really prevail, however, given that one cannot exercise mastery over an Other who no longer exists. (2) One party submits and agrees to servitude and, thereby, provides an ongoing sense of mastery to the prevailing party. The point is that the best outcome for the subordinating party is not annihilation of the Other; it is continuing subordination of the Other.

But the relation of the fascist to the Jew is one of "liquidation instead of sublation, of formal instead of determinate negation" because the fascist regresses to the *most basic* form of control just outlined, but does so in connection with the *most advanced* object. "Sublation" translates the German *Aufhebung*, a term of art in Hegel with three interlocking meanings: to elevate, to supersede, and to annul. Hegel is keen to exploit them all: a new conception supplants its predecessor(s), annulling the predecessor as controlling, yet preserving in retrospect the importance of the predecessor to the development of the current conception. To say that there is no sublation in the fascist's view of the Jew, then, is to say that, that there is none of that; there is no dialectical rationality to it. Fascist projection is simply destructive. And – to complete the thought – that is precisely what "formal negation" means for Hegel ("formal" is almost always a term of deprecation for him). The fascist negates the Jew in a fashion that can lead nowhere.

Fascism is regressive then in both the psychoanalytic and Hegelian senses. The fascist's paranoia stems from fixation at a prior stage of what would otherwise be normal psychosexual development. The effect is stultification, a locked-in state of mind. This explains Horkheimer and Adorno's comment that "fascists, who are absolute evil, brand Jews as absolute evil." The point is about projection, but it is also about dialectics. That which is absolute is free from limitation. By definition no finite being, process, or structure qualifies – including fascists and Jews. The trick to unraveling the wording is that "absolute" is being used to characterize a finite structure that, by its own reckoning, is infinite. That is how fascists think. The fascist is absolute evil in that his thinking is completely and utterly wound up in itself, unresponsive to reasons offered by others not caught up in the paranoia. Casting of the Jew as absolute evil is a projection of just the sort of object that suits this deficient absoluteness, one that requires no acknowledgment even of its continued existence, because the Jew is substantially nothing at all (139–40/200).

HORKHEIMER'S SECTION VII

By the time Horkheimer and Adorno's book was readied for republication in 1947, the war was over and knowledge of the death camps was widespread. Germany had been reverted back to its 1938 boundaries, been divided into four occupation zones, and denazification had been handed over to German authorities. Most Germans who were polled still thought that fascism was a good idea poorly executed. Horkheimer composed the final section of the antisemitism chapter with all of that in mind.

It is very hard to follow. More than any other part of *DE*, a book full of allusion and foreshortened arguments, section VII is a crosshatching of contentious statements, which draws on the rest of the book freely but without explicit reference. These are not merely Horkheimer's afterthoughts, added as a coda to the rest of the chapter and book. It is meant to be a summation of the chapter and of the book as a whole, and that puts even more pressure on its coherent presentation. One gets the impression that he is writing here more than in any other place in the book for the Institute's insiders, whom he assumes to be already clear on the issues.

Especially challenging for the reader is how this section intersects with the rest of the antisemitism chapter. Three years have passed since the writing of those portions of the book, and Horkheimer and Adorno seem not very concerned about ironing out the tensions that chronology introduces. We shall see that there are times when Horkheimer seems to depart from the more general analysis given to antisemitism in the rest of the chapter, and this is especially complicated by the fact that he sometimes does this when drawing on those other parts of the chapter. He does not exercise enough care in identifying clearly which claims from prior sections are still relevant and which are being modified. Specifically, he sometimes runs together without signposts Weimar liberalism, the emergence of Nazism, its stabilization in the wartime period, and the situations in postwar Germany and the United States.

Problems arise immediately. The section opens with a declaration. "[T]here are no longer any anti-Semites. The last were liberals who wanted to express antiliberal opinions" (165/230). This seems to continue a train of thought introduced at the end of the preceding section, i.e., the hope that antisemitism might be overcome and "the Jew [seen as] [...] a human being" by checking the mass projection of the ills of modern society onto others (165/230). The agency for this overcoming in the 1944 manuscript is liberalism. It is too bad that mention was redacted for later publication.

What is Horkheimer saying here? What attitude does he take to the proposition expressed in the first sentence of the quote: "There are no longer any anti-Semites?" We will have to impose a structure on his presentation right from the start and follow its implications for the rest of this chapter. There are three possibilities at least, and we can't rule out that Horkheimer knows this and wants ambiguity left alone here. In any event, the three possibilities are:

1. He is utilizing *oratio obliqua* to put the words expressing that proposition in the mouth of the antisemite or perhaps someone oblivious to antisemitism, a proposition one suspects him to contest in what follows.
2. He is speaking in his own voice, but ironically. One would expect either a continuation of ironic statement, with the intent of more intensively involving the reader in efforts to share the irony. Or one would expect a piercing of the irony at some point, with a more direct statement regarding the truth or falsity of the proposition.
3. He is speaking in his own voice declaratively. He endorses the proposition, either flatly or with conditions.

Consider the first two possibilities. One might think that the jump from aspiration to fact – from the hope of overcoming antisemitism in the prior section to its actual overcoming in this section – provides a clue that the sentence in question is meant ironically, is *oratio obliqua* put in the mouth of the antisemite, or both.[21] Surely antisemitism cannot have disappeared with the end of the war! If one takes the statement to refer to the postwar situation in Germany, Europe more broadly or, for that matter, the United States, widespread prejudice against Jews did not perish with the defeat of the Nazis. Horkheimer and Adorno have already allowed that those who espouse liberalism can be antisemites. Recall popular anti-Jewish sentiment in the United Kingdom in 1947 during battles between British and Zionist forces in what was then Mandate Palestine, or temple bombings in the United States over the last sixty years. And that is not to mention the presence in the United States and United Kingdom, liberal democracies both, of fascist political groups like the National

Front or British National Party. Holocaust denial is still a staple of the hard-right in these countries. So, fascism persists. Example: Franco ruled Spain until his death in 1975. Complication: Salazar, who held power in Portugal from 1933 to 1968 and was a fascist, did not include antisemitism in his understanding of fascism, on the grounds that antisemitism was anti-Catholic.

But it is a consideration of (3) above – the apparently least likely of the three possibilities – that requires one to plumb the rest of section VII for content. It may not be what Horkheimer intended, but considering that possibility brings the most out of the section.

What could it mean to say that there are no more antisemites, when it is obvious that there is still prejudice against Jews in several quarters? The most plausible way to make sense of that assertion is to qualify what the term "antisemite" means. In other words, it is worth considering whether Horkheimer is pivoting, at least in terms of emphasis, toward considering "antisemitism" as a term of art, which pertains to only some prejudice against Jews. Perhaps he intends a *restricted* sense of the term. If this is so, perhaps the claim that antisemitism no longer exists need not conflict with the fact that what is normally, i.e., *non-restrictively*, considered antisemitism obviously does exist.[22]

We have two specifications on the table for main forms of mid-twentieth-century antisemitism: liberal and fascist. We know that Horkheimer and Adorno take liberal fascism to have beached itself on the country club reef. Antisemitism does public work in liberal democracies so long as capitalism needs it to. Capitalism marshaled the "ambient" antisemitism of European and US culture in order to obfuscate, through scapegoating, the immiseration of worker oppression. That is no longer required. Capitalism can do the job via other apparatus, specifically the culture industry. Anti-Jewish prejudice persists, but if one reserves the term "antisemitism" for active and necessary public political or social use of the prejudice against Jews, then there is no more liberal antisemitism. It is in this sense that the second proposition in the quote above becomes true: the liberals were the last antisemites.

That leaves us with the fascists. Can one run the same line with them? Possibly. Fascism looks to antisemitism to create a sense of integrity in the (non-Jewish) people by severe contrast with the vilified Jew. The function of antisemitism is nation-building, not economics. The two nations that tried that are defunct, Nazi Germany and Italy under Mussolini. Racialized antisemitism was always important for Hitler. Early on, Mussolini dismissed antisemitism as trivial and stupid but, ever the opportunist, by 1938 he had embraced the racial laws.

How much did the average German embrace antisemitism leading up to and during the war? The answer Horkheimer gives is that express antisemitism was important prior to the establishment of fascism as the state politics of Germany because it cleared away the liberalism of the Weimar Republic. Once there was a Third Reich, the average German saw antisemitism as a plank in the greater Party platform. It required allegiance, but no longer had priority. Horkheimer sees the postwar situation as a further demotion of antisemitism in authoritarian thinking:

> Anti-semitic views always reflected stereotyped thinking. Today only that thinking is left. People still vote, but only between totalities. The anti-Semitic psychology has largely been replaced by mere acceptance of the whole fascist ticket, which is an inventory of the slogans of belligerent big business
>
> (166/231)

and

> The ticket acts as a gearwheel in this process. Anything in the old psychological mechanism which was compulsive, unfree, and irrational is precisely adjusted to it. The reactionary ticket which includes anti-Semitism is suited to the destructive-conventional syndrome. It is not so much that such people react originally against the Jews as that their drive-structure has developed a tendency toward persecution which the ticket then furnishes with an adequate object.
>
> (171/236)

These two passages, ostensibly about the same historical moment, display the tension that informs Horkheimer's thinking. The first detaches fascism from antisemitism and suggests that what survives as ideological is thinking in terms of stereotypes, slogans, and views prearranged for one by the "fascist ticket" (171–72/237–8). The second passage also refers to "ticket thinking" but allows that antisemitism still plays a supporting role. The first passage seems to refer to the postwar situation (e.g., "today"), the second to wartime Germany. But Horkheimer – to put it mildly – does not signal this.

There is certainly prejudice among postwar Germans against Jews, and surely there were (and are) fascists too. But could prejudice do the job of making a people? Perhaps no longer. If that is what "antisemitism" in the limited meaning is, i.e., not just prejudice or even systematic prejudice against Jews, but socially and politically effective prejudice against Jews, perhaps in that limited and special sense antisemitism might be a thing of the past. Recall the initial characterization of the stakes of antisemitism with which the chapter begins:

> Anti-Semitism today is for some a question affecting human destiny and for others a mere pretext. For the fascists the Jews are the anti-race [*Gegenrasse*], the negative principle as such; on their eradication [*Ausrottung*] the world's happiness depends. Diametrically opposed to this is the thesis that the Jews, free of national and racial features, form a group through religious belief and tradition and nothing else. Jewish traits relate to Eastern Jews [*Ostjuden*], and only to those not yet assimilated. Both doctrines are true and false at the same time.
>
> (137/197, translation emended)

What this line of interpretation of Horkheimer's remarks in this section suggests is that the power of the myths that surround the figure of the Jew has receded past the point at which the myths no longer are expedient, no longer get results. That is so even given the ruthless murdering ordered as a "solution."

What is the final word on what was for Horkheimer the "present age"?[23] Fascism is typically thought of as archaizing. It gathers what strength it has by idealizing a pure point in the past, after which there has been a significant decline to a state of decadence. The hopes of a fascist: If only one could burn through the decay and reestablish the radiant origin! Given this backward-facing imaginarium, it is easy to forget that fascism is also supremely modern. This point is certainly not lost on Horkheimer and Adorno. Marinetti's Futurism and Pound and Lewis's Vorticism are but two examples of modern art movements that embraced and were embraced by fascism. Albert Speer, who designed the *Zeppelinfeld* stadium that formed the backdrop to much of *Triumph of the Will*, built heavy-handed simplifications of Vitruvius, but what makes them so flat is his attempt to be relevant to modernism. In more capable hands fascism could be impeccably modern, as it was in the period in which Le Corbusier designed with kindred ideas in mind.

The modernity most associated with German fascism marries the cold efficiency of capital with the heated brutality of suitable myth. Combining ruthless efficiency with barbarism is not unique to the Nazis, but the death camps are so overwhelming that it is hard – impermissible even – to think of the Shoah as just one of any number of genocides. The combination of vileness and calculation, the *administration* of mass murder, is fascist antisemitism run to the brink.

The IG Farben man was detached, non-vitriolic, embedded in a bureaucracy he needn't think about. His violence not only can, but must, be expressed statistically. But it operates in tandem with forms of social control that can have extreme consequences. No one who sits at a desk at corporate headquarters and requisitions Zyklon B is just a functionary. He may appear to be, but in reality he is part of an infernal machine, along with the guard at Treblinka cramming men, women, and children into the chambers.[24]

Horkheimer ends the chapter and the book on a muted note of optimism: "Enlightenment itself, having mastered itself and assumed its own power, could break through the limits of enlightenment" (172/238). He alludes to Kant's characterization of enlightenment as "freedom from self-imposed immaturity," with the difference that in *DE* enlightenment is not only what must do the freeing, but that from which one must be freed. Enlightenment must free itself from a version of itself, from an understanding of itself that is unenlightened. The fascist ticket has failed. What is left to critique is the liberal ticket. Might fascism make a return? It is open on Horkheimer's analysis that it might. This is especially so if one does not appreciate its overlap with capitalism (e.g., "Trumpers" in the United States, the RN in France, the AfD in Germany).

FURTHER READING

Rensmann 2017 is the most comprehensive treatment of the issue of Critical Theory's engagement with antisemitism. Jacobs 2015 is also a good discussion of themes of antisemitism in connection with Critical Theory (especially valuable is its chapter two) as are the relevant portions of Rabinbach 1997 (it omits from consideration § VII of the antisemitism chapter). Diner's essay in Benhabib, Bonß, and McCole 1993 is a worthwhile conspectus of Horkheimer's views on antisemitism. Pulzer 1988 and Lawrence Rose 1992 are valuable resources on the rise of antisemitism in Austria and Germany. Namli, Svenungsson, and Vincent 2014 and Stoetzler 2023 are collections of papers on relevant background.

Bauman 1989 is very close to *DE* in its approach to antisemitism, as well as to the first section of Arendt 1951. For readers with German, Claussen 1987 and Diner 1988 can be recommended. Postone 1980 is a complex consideration of the relation of Critical Theory to the antisemitism of National Socialism.

Benjamin's views on the epistemological and ontological status of symbolism and allegory are divided between his two dissertations, Benjamin 2004ff.: 1.116–200 and 2019. Morgan and Gordon 2007 contain valuable historical discussion.

NOTES

1. Bronner and Kellner 1989: 77–94 / Horkheimer 1985a: 4.308–31. For his views in the postwar context, see Horkheimer 1974a: 101–18, 119–23 / Horkheimer 1985a: 8.160–74, 156–9.
2. Lenin 1970 coined the term.
3. Pollock 1982.
4. Neumann 1944. Jay 1980 points out that there is an increase in seriousness between the 1942 and 1944 editions of the book on the issue of antisemitism but, as he also points out, Neumann's final position is more or less the same.

5 Neumann 1944: 120–22. Neumann's views on the matter seem to have evolved within a short period. See his letter of 14 Aug. 1940 to Horkheimer, cited in Rabinbach 2000: 53 n.18 for the sake of comparison.
6 For a lively account of the dispute and its impact on *DE*, see Schmidt 2016.
7 Ex. 20:4–6; Deut. 5:7. The first mention of idols as problematic is perhaps Gen. 4:26. For an argument that conceptions of ideology are rooted in the prohibition against idolatry, see Halbertal and Margalit 1998: 164–65.
8 Exod. 3:14 ("I Am that I Am") [KJV]; cf. 145/186 ("the iron word, I am" (translation emended)). What that biblical passage means is subject to dispute. Alter 2004: 321 & n. translates "I-Will-Be-Who-I-Will-Be," capturing both the elements of volition and of eternality. The King James version is "I am all existence; existence is all I am," which looks like a sentence, not a name or an essence.
9 Perhaps the reason God does not give his name to Moses is that, as Robert Alter points out, in so doing he might suggest that there were other proper names of other gods. In any event, the question is raised of the utter difference between creatures and their creator – the supreme being is not supreme as a matter of mere rank order but a stark difference in kind. Using the divine name to successfully refer is to claim *acquaintance* with its referent. If that entails something like taking the measure of the referent by such use or identifying its essence thereby, that would be profane and sinful.
10 The text of the Commandments does not apply obviously to linguistic utterance, although the Commandment forbidding taking God's name "in vain" might be argued to cover the case. As a historical matter, it is settled that this name was spoken rather freely by the Israelites at first but became more restricted until, after the destruction of the Second Temple, it became prohibited. Writing the name is also controversial, even in a foreign language. Even the Tetragrammaton, once written, may not be disposed of except under strict conditions. If the medium on which the name is to be inscribed is likely to be disposed of, this argues for proscribing writing it on that medium. Certeau 1988 argues that the word in question is not meant to be referential; it is the graphic trace of *deus absconditus*, indicating absence of the possibility of reference.
11 Freud 1953ff.: 12.97–108 [1912].
12 I.iii.144–51, 165–69. Shakespeare's attitude toward Shylock is complex of course: "if you prick us, do we not bleed?" III.i.64.
13 Less familiar to most, but more present to Horkheimer's and Adorno's minds, is the dwarf Mime from Wagner's *Siegfried* (147/188), a character not explicitly Jewish (he descends from the figure Reginn in the Norse sagas and eddas), but who nonetheless embodies false stereotypes ascribed to Jews. It is still a matter for debate whether Wagner intended Mime (and other characters in his operas) to signify Jewishness and, if he did so, whether that impugns the work's aesthetic value. Adorno answered in the positive to both. See Adorno 2009/1970: 13.7–148.
14 See Graeber 2012 for a critical overview.

15 Note what one might call a dialectical interaction of the antisemite's Jew with the figure of Odysseus encountered in chapter two of *DE* (see 54/93: "Odysseus already bears features of the Jew [...]"). Odysseus, after all, also is "homeless" in a sense. His ace in the hole is wiliness, which allows him qualified mastery over nature through bargaining and sacrifice. One might raise the question, then, of whether the Jew and Odysseus are bookended figures, Odysseus standing at the outset of enlightenment (although already having emerged as enlightened to a degree) and the Jew at its end or, as the subtitle to the chapter says, "at its limit." See Porter 2010 for sympathetic thoughts along this line. One might even suggest that the antisemite's Jew is a modern Odysseus, an Odysseus finally caught by the monsters of the present day and held by them to pay (cf. Leopold Bloom in Joyce's *Ulysses*). A nice bit of symmetry, but imperfect. Odysseus, after all, has a home to which to return; that is what draws him on. That is true even if his status as his home is under siege. And, in the end, he does reclaim what is his. The antisemite's Jew, by contrast, is bereft of a homeland. As the antisemite would have it, the Jew has ever been and ever will be homeless. Of course, if the idea is that the Jews are *inherently* rootless, that they *never* had a homeland, that is false. There are various biblical passages describing (albeit sometimes pretty vaguely) the geographical extent of the lands promised to the Hebrews. See Gen. 12:1; 15:18–21; 26:3; 28:13. Moreover, there were two Israelite kingdoms in the Levant from *c.* 1000 to 722 BCE, Israel and Judah. Even if one wished to be technical about the point and contend that Judaism did not coalesce as a religion and ethnic identity until the Second Temple (true), the lineage is there.

16 The idea that fascism could be approached through psychoanalysis was not new. Wilhelm Reich had argued that the turn to fascism instead of communism in Germany was due to sexual repression in the Weimar period and, closer to Horkheimer and Adorno, Fromm had speculated that the turn to fascism was a reaction to the overwhelming threat posed to autonomy by science and mass society. See Wilhelm Reich 1980 and Fromm 1976.

17 Freud 1953ff.: 7.133–203, 12.1–82.

18 This is also Freud's understanding of narcissism. See 1953ff: 14.67–102.

19 Hegel 2019: 108–16. The most important point of reception was Alexandre Kojève's lectures on Hegel, delivered at the École pratique des hautes études in Paris from 1933 to 1939. In the audience was a who's who of twentieth-century French literature and philosophy: Raymond Aron, Georges Bataille, André Breton, Jacques Lacan, Maurice Merleau-Ponty, and Jean-Paul Sartre. Notes and transcripts of some of these lectures were published after the Second World War, a selection of which are available in English translation as Kojève 1980.

20 Hegel 2019, 111–12.

21 The ironic or indirect speech alternative is consonant with contemporaneous statements elsewhere of Horkheimer's. See 1946: 1–10/1985a: 5.364–72, in which he clearly allows for the real and continuing presence of antisemitism in Germany and in the United States and goes on to specify various

strands of antisemitism with regard to social psychology and politics. See also Horkheimer 1945: 1–10/1985a: 5.373–6. Adorno revisits the question in 1962, stressing especially the ongoing nature of the phenomenon and its connection to mass media. 2025/1970: 20.1.360–83. Both essays are compatible with (and cite) *DE*'s broader approach and with the more empirical work of the Institute in the 1940s.

22 The term "antisemitism" was coined by the nineteenth-century Hebraicist Moritz Steinschneider (1816–1907), who used it to characterize the views of Ernest Renan (in *La Vie Jésus* (1863)). Several of Renan's contentions crop up in section VII without attribution.

23 See Kierkegaard 2009: 68–112 for the concept.

24 Farben ran a factory for the production of synthetic rubber just outside Auschwitz. It used slave labor – mostly Jews – provided from a satellite camp, Monowitz. Primo Levi and Elie Wiesel survived that camp.

7

THE RECEPTION OF *DIALECTIC OF ENLIGHTENMENT*

DE has been received and interpreted in a wide variety of intellectual contexts, ranging from technical discussions regarding the nature of Critical Theory to political, aesthetic, and philosophical debates regarding modernity, late capitalism, and social criticism. Some readers dismiss it as too speculative, disjointed, or one-sided in its focus on the ills of commodification and instrumentalization. Yet others find it a treasure trove, a work that towers not only above all else in the writings of the Frankfurt School but over much modern social thought more generally.

The aim of this chapter is to mark and discuss some of the central stations in this complex reception history. It will start by revisiting the ambivalent readings offered by representatives of second- and third-generation Critical Theory, especially those of Habermas. We then move on to questions, central to more recent reception after the turn of the millennium, of subjectivity, social

DOI: 10.4324/9781003195047-8

critique, and politics. We will, finally, consider *DE* in light of the theoretical, political, and existential challenge of the climate/environmental crisis. In all these cases, we present readings of *DE* that highlight its continued intellectual power.

LATER GENERATIONS OF CRITICAL THEORY

Since the late 1970s it has been common to distinguish between first- and second-generation Critical Theory, and observers of this tradition now also recognize a third, and even a fourth, generation. In addition to Horkheimer and Adorno, the first generation consists of figures such as Fromm, Kirchheimer, Löwenthal, Marcuse, Neumann, and Pollock. The work of the first generation centers around the project of interdisciplinary materialism, attempting from a roughly Marxist angle to uncover and criticize impediments to social and political progress. This early phase culminates with *DE*, although work of the first generation continues into the 1960s with Adorno and Marcuse as the standard bearers. The second generation centers on the work of Jürgen Habermas – as well as Seyla Benhabib, Axel Honneth, Albrecht Wellmer, and others – who with his Kantian-pragmatist philosophy of communicative reason breaks with many of the guiding assumptions of the first generation. At the same time, he continues to support the first generation's commitment to providing a framework for conducting rational social critique with a view to uncovering regressive as well as progressive tendencies in liberal, mainly Western societies, such as that of (West) Germany in the post-Second World War period. The work of the third and fourth generations – Rainer Forst, Rahel Jaeggi, Christoph Menke, and others – which is engaged as well with critically receiving earlier generations' contributions, deserves to be discussed in the context of understanding the reception of *DE* in this tradition. However, due to limitations of space, we restrict the discussion of *DE*'s fate within the history of Critical Theory to Habermas's important and influential response.

DE is the writing that for Habermas more than any other work marks the culmination of first-generation Critical Theory; so it seems worthwhile to begin by asking how it was taken up in the post-Second World War generation to which Habermas belongs. While in the 1950s available only in the Querido edition and not within easy reach in Germany, in the 1960s it was widely read by German intellectuals and academics on the left interested in radical forms of social critique. By 1955, though, when he became Adorno's research assistant and an associate of the Institute of Social Research, Habermas would certainly have read it.[1] Habermas, however, was equally interested in Lukács, Heidegger, Schelling, Hegel, and the Young Hegelians, including of course Marx. Indeed, like many in his own environment at the time, Habermas was at the outset predominantly influenced by Marx, though without having much sympathy for objectivist interpretations that would postulate a necessary historical development toward freedom.

In view of his later turn toward Kantianism and liberalism, it is worth noting that Habermas may at the time have been more inclined toward traditional Marxism than were either Adorno or Horkheimer. Considering him too left wing for the Institute of Social Research, Horkheimer even went as far as to prevent Habermas from taking his *Habilitation* in Frankfurt. Instead, Habermas took up a post as *Privatdozent* in Marburg and, in 1962, was appointed as a professor of philosophy at Heidelberg, effectively leaving the Institute. In 1964, however, he succeeded Max Horkheimer as professor of philosophy and sociology at the University of Frankfurt.

Despite Horkheimer and Adorno's increasing worry that the despair expressed in their co-written book could nourish extreme forms of political activism to which they neither morally nor politically could subscribe, together with Marcuse's *Eros and Civilization* and *One-Dimensional Man*, *DE* had a significant impact on the many radical groups of students and intellectuals of the 1960s. Reading it they found a critique not only of positivism, commodification, standardization, and mass culture, but also of fascism and authoritarianism, the forces to which so many of their parents had succumbed and against which they struggled.

Although Habermas supported many of the radical student movements that sprung up in response to the war in Vietnam and pleaded for social reform, he could not accept the student movement's more voluntaristic elements and did not, ultimately, see them as representing anything like genuine historical agency in the Marxian sense. In particular, he worried about the students' tendency to reject liberal democratic norms in favor of direct action.

It is not surprising then to find that liberal democratic commitments started moving to the foreground of Habermas's burgeoning theoretical edifice around this time. While Marx had viewed societal rationalization exclusively in terms of labor, Habermas now added "interaction" (*Interaktion*), a sphere of linguistic communication in which agents orient themselves with regard to one another rationally in order to achieve "mutual agreement" (*Verständigung*). As opposed to the pessimistic conclusions drawn by Horkheimer and Adorno's exclusive emphasis on formal and instrumental reason, Habermas hoped to launch a new research program oriented toward criticizing what he called systematically distorted communication. His plan was to develop an account of social rationality that could model greater transparency and accountability even in highly bureaucratized and market-driven societies, in which incentives are generated by mechanisms that typically are withdrawn from political and rational will-formation. Unlike the orientation toward self-preservation which marks Horkheimer and Adorno's understanding of humanity, Habermas attributed to communicative action *as such* the anticipation of a more humane existence of freedom and dignity. With reference to communicative action of the kind he had discussed in his 1962 study *The Structural Transformation of the Public Sphere* – reasonable debate among citizens who, at least as an ideal, consider each other as free and equal beings – the ideal of an enlightened society could be conjoined with a robust commitment to active, participatory democracy. For the sake of contrast, note that a few years later Adorno was working on what is perhaps his most pessimistic work, *Aesthetic Theory*, in which resistance to the "occluded" (*verfinsterte*) condition of post-Auschwitz, late-capitalist society is deemed to be the prerogative of advanced, modernist art in conjunction with negative dialectics.

In the 1981 two-volume *The Theory of Communicative Action* Habermas presents the fully developed version of this view. In the spirit of *DE*'s account of rationalization it features an analysis of how modern societies risk having markets and bureaucracies "colonize" the communicatively structured "lifeworld" (*Lebenswelt*). As a counterweight to colonization stands the sphere of communicative action in which agents commit themselves to ideally free and rational argumentation among equals. Such encounters involve claims whose justification is open to every participant of the dialogue to scrutinize, accept, reject, or discuss further.

The Theory of Communicative Action does not just contain an account of the system/lifeworld dualism and of communicative action, it also presents a host of extended critical readings of the modern classics of social theory; Marx, Durkheim, Weber, and Horkheimer and Adorno. Habermas interprets *DE* as a totalizing and finally incoherent critique of reason which fails to justify Critical Theory. All it ultimately achieves, he claims, is falsely to suggest that we are condemned to fatalism and despair. The legacy of the historical Enlightenment, to which Horkheimer and Adorno wanted to belong, is betrayed.

Habermas begins his reconstruction of *DE* with the idea that reason must be understood anthropologically and naturalistically as a function of the instinctually structured imperative of self-preservation. It is in this sense "subjective." While aiming to represent the world by imposing a conceptual order on the given and act by subjecting herself to instrumental imperatives, a conscious agent is essentially oriented toward the establishment of domination over nature. One might argue that both representation and action, so described, harbor certain normative commitments. In accordance with norms of what counts as evidence, the effort to represent seeks to be as closely in touch as possible with reality. Likewise, instrumental imperatives command rational agents who have aims to provide the means for securing them.

Habermas, however, sees in this model a "normative deficit." In his Nietzscheanizing reading, once the abilities associated with rational behavior are as thoroughly naturalized as they are in the *DE*, the freedom required to subject oneself rationally to norms goes missing. While humans inevitably strive to maximize certain goods (epistemic or otherwise), according to Horkheimer and Adorno, we are ultimately being "pushed" or "forced" to do so by the brute mechanism of human nature.[2]

According to Habermas, this lands the authors of *DE* in a performative contradiction. On the one hand, they purport – in a Kantian spirit, one might add – to have reason criticize itself. On the other hand, their totalizing critique of reason undercuts the possibility of such a self-critique. As he puts it:

> this description of the self-destruction of the critical capacity is paradoxical, because in the moment of description it still has to make use of the critique that has been declared dead. It denounces the Enlightenment's becoming totalitarian with its own tools.[3]

While more traditional ideology critique served enlightenment thinking by questioning the validity of typically unacknowledged assumptions of great scale, informing both theory and practice more generally, Horkheimer and Adorno indulge in a global skepticism that makes their project incoherent.

Part of the enlightenment legacy, according to Habermas, is that reason has been embodied and cultivated in modern science, universalistic ideas of justice and morality, and autonomous art and art criticism. Horkheimer and Adorno, in his reading, view all these expressions of reason as mutilated by reason's transformation into mere power. Science has degenerated into being a service-provider tailored toward technical utility, thereby forfeiting any claim it might have had to provide knowledge and human insight. Stacked up against the false authority of science, morality and law have lost their normative standards and, in their place, one is left with merely instrumental shells of them. Art has been fused with entertainment and become a commodity like everything else. Its claim to contain self-reflective, critical, or utopian content is a relic of its former self.

Habermas's colonization theorem – that markets and bureaucracies have *in some cases* substituted communicative rationality in the lifeworld for instrumental imperatives – marks this. But he holds Horkheimer and Adorno's claims to be radically overstated: the cultural conditions of late modernity simply are not this bleak.

As the final part of his criticism of *DE*, Habermas claims that its authors, and especially Adorno, end up appealing to an "irrational" capacity, that of mimesis, which, on his reading, is a speechless form of imitative responsiveness to the Other (viz. nature) that, like the late-Heidegger's "mindfulness" (*Andenken*), "intentionally retrogresses to mere gesticulation."[4] In view of its own self-created *aporiai*, Horkheimer and Adorno's critique of reason ends in mysticism. According to Habermas the only real counter to this melancholy conclusion, to this extreme, self-defeating skepticism, involves a complete and utter change in paradigm. One must shift from the "philosophy of consciousness" to which Horkheimer and Adorno allegedly subscribe, which theorizes the problem of reason in terms of the subject-object relation, to the philosophy of language and intersubjective communication, which theorizes the problem in terms of communicative relations between subjects understood as rationally oriented reason-givers.

Habermas's criticisms changed the intellectual environment in which Critical Theory existed. Leaving aesthetics, culture, subjectivity, and a general preoccupation with the destructive effects of an unreflective implementation of instrumental reason behind, Habermas flung open the door to the significantly more sanguine discourses on language, pragmatics, justice, and social progress. However, as many subsequent commentators have pointed out, there are serious questions surrounding his reading of *DE*, and much can be said in defense of Horkheimer and Adorno's position.

At a general level one might argue that dismissing the dark tone and despair of the *DE*, while perhaps necessary in order to better locate existing progressive trends, comes at a price. The undeniable moral seriousness with which Horkheimer and Adorno confronted fascism, totalitarianism, and the conformism of certain features of liberal democracy can hardly be said to have been out of place. Habermas's theory may encourage us to call for more discourse and more democracy; yet it provides no direct critique of the so-called subsystems of purposive-rational action, markets, and bureaucracies, only of their colonizing *effects*. Compared with the critical bite of *DE*, the pragmatic neo-Kantianism of Habermas's mature writings, with its formal reconstructions and presuppositions concerning idealized speech, can seem toothless, hardly the theoretical tool with which to approach the challenges and traumas of the twenty-first century: climate crisis, massive social inequity, war, international terrorism, untrammeled neoliberal globalization, fascism, and various widespread psychological disorders. Even if *DE* does not transpose easily for purposes of contemporary debate, its unstinting tone may seem worth revisiting. Perhaps that intransigence is even its purpose, the form of resistance it offers, or so we have suggested.

Still, the particulars of Habermas's criticism deserve consideration. Take the problem of intersubjectivity. Horkheimer and Adorno employ the traditional language of subject-object duality, steeped as they are in German Idealism. However, they are primarily neo-Hegelians; accordingly, they cannot be dismissive *tout court* of what Habermas calls intersubjectivity – the relationships of mutuality and responsiveness between subjects in formal and informal social contexts. In his book on Husserl, *Against Epistemology*, Adorno insists along Hegelian lines that there can be no "I" without a "we," no capacity for normatively structured intentional life without networks of mutual recognition:

> "My" ego is in truth already an abstraction and anything but the original experience that Husserl claims it is. [...] "Intersubjectivity" is posited along in it, – only not as a arbitrary pure possibility, but rather as the real condition for being I, without which the limitation to "my" ego cannot be understood[5]

For Habermas, beyond just a formal acknowledgment of rational agential capacities, the theorizing of these networks seems often to leave limited room for thinking more concretely about subjectivity. This is one reason Horkheimer and Adorno continue to deploy this vocabulary. An agent for them is much more than a mere locus of validity claims, and they hold that philosophy should be able to address subjectivity in all its fullness. Another reason they keep in place the subject-object dyad is that – to be sure, for contingent historical reasons – we happen to think of ourselves as independent individuals facing a world mainly of entities to be objectified and instrumentalized. One of the great ambitions behind *DE* was precisely to provide a sense of how we came to be *those* beings, *those* subjects. To eviscerate that process by calling simply for a theoretical change of paradigm makes little sense. It is a shortcut that leads at best back to where one started.

Horkheimer and Adorno do present a thoroughgoing critique of reason, the coherent formulation of which poses great challenges. But one thing is abundantly clear: they do not accept Habermas's Cartesian-Kantian notion that radical critique presupposes an ahistorical, rationally indisputable foundation, which Habermas claims to find in his account of the universal presuppositions of rational argumentation and which he sometimes calls "quasi-transcendental." As we have stressed, their critique of reason is dialectical: by observing the operation of reason in its various *historical* configurations, they point to its ambitions and shortcomings, its structure and structuration.

One of the advantages of dialectical approaches is that they can deal with the issue of cognitive limitation in a way not open to transcendental argumentation. Transcendental argumentation, even in Habermas's weak, pragmatic version, regresses on the conditions necessary for the possibility of a target phenomenon. That in turn implies that it is impossible to think otherwise about what ultimately conditions the phenomenon in question. But impossibility is tricky; it is amazing how possible it is to think of what one once thought impossible if one varies background assumptions. That, at least, is Hegel's teaching. For Habermas the limit of conceptual thought is a frontier not to be crossed, because it is conceptually impossible to do so. For the dialectical philosopher, the frontiers can shift and so can the idea of what is beyond them. Horkheimer and Adorno's conception of dialectic is, as we have emphasized, not closed. Unlike in Hegel, there is no complete system of possible transitions, no complete accounting of limitations. That means that they are open as a matter of principle to treating things that reason cannot reach as real, e.g., as unconscious, affective, and somatic. Reason's critique and self-limitation does not entail its all-inclusiveness.

Is there a "normative deficit" in Horkheimer and Adorno's account? To be sure, while they do go far in naturalizing our theoretical and practical capacities, they do not relinquish the notion that we are *agents*, beings who must commit ourselves to the rational implications of what we take to be the best evidence and the most promising justifications. The imperative of self-preservation weighs heavily on us (to the extent, indeed, that they are willing to see "thought as an instrument of power" (92/141)), but, as discussed earlier, we are not robots; there must be more to how we successfully interpret each other than the attribution of causal properties and relations along determinist lines. In fact, Horkheimer and Adorno – perhaps because of their philosophical background in neo-Kantian humanism – do not attend very much to the threat of reductionism of the kind that Habermas seems to attribute to them. Their naturalism is inclusive; it accepts the existence of "second nature," of the mind as a site of rational thinking. Instincts and, in advanced societies, ideologies, do impact behavior and even, as they argue, to a large extent shape the commitments we consider to be rational. But there is always the possibility of saying no – of resisting the forces that shape us. Without that, there could be no Critical Theory – and, more than that, no coherent account of *critical* agency. While we are natural beings all the way down, our way of being natural includes rationality.

It is worth noting in this context that Horkheimer and Adorno see truth not primarily as a metaphysical relation between a truth-bearer (proposition, statement, sentence) and a fact (or state of affairs, or world). Rather, truth is something to which we, given standards of warranted assertibility (and stipulation of rationality), must, when asserted, be able to assent to rationally. (In contemporary anglophone philosophy, this would be called an epistemic conception of truth.) For someone to be able to hold a proposition true (and to thereby make a truth-claim), it is necessary that they know *why* it counts as true. Some orientation toward evidence, even if idealized, is required. As they argue,

> it is in the nature of truth that one is involved in it as an active subject. People may hear propositions which in themselves are true; but they experience their truth only by thinking as they hear and by continuing to think.
>
> (203/276)[6]

Habermas's accusation of there being a normative deficit in Horkheimer and Adorno's approach is prima facie more plausible in the realm of morality. In favor of such a reading, he quotes the authors' claim, at the end of the second excursus, that reason cannot furnish "a fundamental argument against murder" (93/142). For Habermas's reading to have any bite, to show that Horkheimer and Adorno's position leads to moral skepticism, it must be assumed that, in order to be cognitively orienting, moral thinking must be rationally grounded. This means not just that reasons play a role in grounding; rather, the ground itself must be a reason or rational procedure. Habermas holds such a view: for a norm to count as morally valid, it must be rationally acceptable to all those affected by the implementation of the norm. Horkheimer and Adorno, by contrast, consider human reason, unless supported by other faculties or capacities, to be too compromised to be able to deliver moral insight. Reason may support agents in thinking morally – for example in analyzing and interpreting complex social phenomena and in paying sufficient attention to abstract notions of fairness, justice, equity, etc. But their view is that moral thought has its ground in a form of embodied, predominantly though not exclusively, pre-conceptual acknowledgment of the Other.

DE contains no "positive" ethical theorizing of this sort. Its contribution to ethics is restricted to "negativity," i.e., to the critique of rationalist theories of moral value, in particular theories of a Kantian, universalist bent. Such theories, they argue, not only are incapable of generating a coherent account of morality but, when internalized and acted upon, may in fact be detrimental to an individual's ability to be motivated by moral concerns. The more positive account, which Adorno develops to some extent in *Minima Moralia* and *Negative Dialectics*, relies on the concept of mimesis – is Habermas's *bête noir*. Mimesis in its moral application consists in a bodily feeling of identification and protection, packaged together. In modernity both the identificatory and the protective elements have been marginalized. Nonetheless, the mimetic ability carries normative, indeed, moral implications. Recognition of the Other requires one to offer them support. Here is Adorno in his 1965 lectures on metaphysics:

> If I say to you that the true basis of morality is to be found in bodily feeling, in identification with unbearable pain, I am showing you from a different side something which I earlier tried to indicate in a far more

abstract form. It is that morality, that which can be called moral, i.e., the demand for right living [*die Forderung nach dem richtigen Leben*], lives on in openly materialist motifs; that precisely the metaphysical principle of such a "Thou shalt" – and this "Thou shalt" – is indeed a metaphysical principle that points beyond mere facticity – can find its justification only in the recourse to material reality, to corporeal, physical reality, and not to its opposite pole, pure thought.[7]

As many commentators have pointed out, neither Horkheimer nor Adorno develops the account of moral responsiveness into a full *theory* – that is, a set of theoretical statements that are inferentially structured, conceptually regimented, distinguished systematically and comprehensively from competing views, and furnished with responses to objections. While heroic efforts to provide such a theoretical account have been made, it is more in the nature of works like *DE* and *Minima Moralia* to exhibit with all exigency intact philosophical "reports" of their experience that bear on others who suffer similarly.[8] Like Wittgenstein's "remarks" in the *Philosophical Investigations*, they are performative, i.e., they confront the reader not with argument but with a different vision of what is taking place in order to invite her to recognize in herself the same dispositions and responses.[9]

Theories of morality are external to moral agency and, for that reason, weak vehicles for change. One doesn't have to be Aristotle, Montesquieu, or Hegel to hold that ethical theories are by their very nature retrospective. They display argumentative connection and put into systematic form precepts that already have been circulating within the culture more broadly. The arguments are there not so much to convince those unfamiliar with the perspective from which the theory is issued as to concentrate commitments that are already there. It is always open to one, after all, to challenge a premise of an ethical argument in order to challenge its conclusions. In principle such challenges are never-ending; there is always an equivocation one can force. The point is that bodies of argument are almost never game-changers. They purport to dictate duties, instead of adjusting their mode of presentation to deliver moral change. They close down the space of possibility, are "traditional" in Horkheimer's original sense, and, as such, they cannot be "critical" and, to put the point as Horkheimer and Adorno might be glad to do, eminently exemplify a form of identity thinking. Accordingly, rather than theorizing, moral philosophy should bring into view what it is for someone to respond to someone in particular.[10] We ought to acknowledge our commitments not as impersonal regularities but, instead, as first-person capacities to respond adequately to the particular Other *qua* particular Other.

As the frequent references to "bourgeois coldness" in *DE* indicate, it is perfectly possible to be alienated from this source of moral responsiveness and obligation. At least in some contexts, given certain conditions (e.g., war, surgical operating theaters, or, for that matter, abattoirs), some people are not going to feel the requisite identification with suffering. Or, in a case such as torture, they may identify suffering for what it is, as unjust, and refuse to act morally in response to it. However, the counterexamples – for Adorno, most conspicuously, the inhumanity of Auschwitz – do not "falsify" the moral import of the observations. All that they show is that moral life can present us with forms of unresponsiveness, i.e., blindness or blankness. Those who display such features need to be addressed, corrected, or resisted. Principles, however well justified, are not likely to do this job, requiring as they do some antecedent shared grounds from which to operate.

Habermas would not recognize the deontic element in Adorno's observations on moral experience and suffering. He would object that just pointing out that, *qua* natural beings, we *happen* to respond in certain ways to suffering cannot establish that we have a *duty* to help others. For him, Horkheimer and Adorno turn moral obligation into something arbitrary, a matter of blind luck. You have to be a certain kind of person in a certain kind of situation and with certain other conditions met for the moral impulse to be active, let alone decisive. Even then, the response would be purely empirical, just a contingent fact about you.

In response, Horkheimer and Adorno might distinguish between the merely causal order and the normative order to which they appeal. In their view, both orders belong to a comprehensive view of what counts as nature. Surely, a Kantian such as Habermas would distinguish between, on the one hand, the order of causality, or what one might think of as the order of disenchanted nature and, on the other, the order of rational freedom in which agents are able to see themselves as acting on self-imposed, rationally justified norms. Yet, seeking to problematize that Kantian construal of the nature/normativity dualism (while also viewing it as the inevitable result of modern identity thinking), Horkheimer and Adorno call on their readers to consider *a form of naturalism that allows for normativity*. They are moral realists of a non-Platonic sort, or perhaps non-essentializing virtue ethicists, or neo-Schopenhauerian care ethicists. It is difficult to pigeonhole their views using the standard groupings. In any case, the ethical response counts as natural in the sense that creatures such as we tend to find suffering unwanted or unacceptable; thus, just as someone who ate with relish a rotten apple would seem strange or "off," so callousness or coldness seems "inadequate" or "incorrect" as forms of response to suffering. A "competent" human responds differently. It is in this respect a part of what one might think of as human nature (as we recognize it).

The ethical response is not "natural," however, if by that one means "common" or "commonsensical." Horkheimer and Adorno think of their ethical fragments as not only materialistic in orientation, requiring a serious consideration of the expressive nature of human embodiment, but also as metaphysical. The attention they pay to singularity, to the status of the Other *qua* Other, seems often at odds with our actual normative practices, which in modernity have become associated more or less exclusively with coordinating, identifying, and instrumentalizing. Fragile though it is, ethical experience *transcends* that immanence. From this perspective Kant-style moral thinking – including Habermas's discourse ethics, which favors abstraction over embodied responsiveness as the source of moral authority – continues to play by the rules of what has become of modernity. It is moral thinking for hard times, when nature appears wholly disenchanted and reason has been so rationalized that it is no longer able to countenance the vulnerability of the Other as the main source of moral authority.

Second-generation Critical Theory, as it is represented by Habermas and his followers, stands as a genuine break with its first-generation predecessor. Its emphasis on discursive rationality, formal pragmatics, and neo-Kantian normativism sets it apart. However, neither the interpretation nor the critique of *DE* that one finds in Habermas's writings is entirely compelling. In hindsight, considering the legacy of first-generation Critical Theory not only in Germany but in Europe and the United States more generally, one might question the assumption of linear development that informs the talk of "generations" of Critical Theory.

READING *DIALECTIC OF ENLIGHTENMENT* IN A CHANGING CONTEXT

Although the authors of *DE* aimed to provide a panoramic view of the process of rationalization characteristic of Western history, this is a book whose contemporary implications were unmistakable. Horkheimer and Adorno criticized commodification and the fate of culture in highly commercial societies; they deplored the loss of autonomy in highly organized societies of both capitalist and communist kinds; and they offered a complex view of antisemitism. Following in the footsteps of Weber's conceptualization of the "steel-hard carapace" of modernity, *DE* represents a rebuke of all procedures whereby individuals are treated simply as numbers in some larger undertaking. The publication of this book coincided not only with the satanic culmination of fascism in Auschwitz, and with the West's realization of the evils of Stalinism, but also with a growing appreciation in the social sciences that the individual is imperiled in mass society.

After half a century of neoliberal initiatives, followed by market-driven hyper-individualization and a concomitant weakening of the welfare-state in the United States and in many European countries, the image of society – familiar from Chaplin's *Modern Times* – as a thoroughly integrated machine that leaves no aspect of human life untouched can today seem timebound, a relic of an age when large-scale industrialism and armies of workers performing mindless tasks along conveyor belts still dominated capitalism and when blueblood politicians like the Roosevelts and Rockefellers still believed in the elitist power of bureaucracy to implement progressive social change. Neoliberal policies aim at increasing competition and strengthening private initiative and, to those ends, transfer risk from groups to individuals. In a stated effort to make citizens less dependent on social welfare, downsized government and deregulated financial institutions have been the new wave. Unlike the emphasis on production in modern industrial societies, the late-modern risk-society in which we find ourselves places a premium on consumption, not class, as the mark of one's social position.

It cannot be denied that the capitalist society which forms the backdrop for *DE* must be distinguished from the kind of capitalism that one sees today. The famous concept of the "totally administered society" (*totalverwaltete Gesellschaft*) with which Horkheimer and Adorno confronted their own period – a dispensation in which any burgeoning symptoms of economic crisis would be quickly eliminated by governmental intervention – seems like an anachronism during the age of boom-and-bust cycles, deregulation, and fluctuating labor markets composed of short-term positions and gig-workers. In what Zygmunt Bauman calls the "liquid" society of today, the freedom denied to Horkheimer and Adorno's subjects can seem no longer pertinent.[11] Rather than being constrained by class, cultural tradition, and long-term expectations both at work and in the home, one is now expected to continually reflect on one's relationships, gender, education, job, short-term interests, financial dispositions, instantaneous culture, etc. Flexibility is the norm and the expectation. In a society that no longer recognizes any binding past, everything becomes a matter of individual choice in the great Here and Now.

What Isaiah Berlin categorized as "negative liberty," the absence of external obstruction to personal action, has been the mantra of neo-liberalism.[12] However, Horkheimer and Adorno would have viewed today's realization of the right to be let alone as a pseudo-freedom. The modernity of short-termism and constant demand for reinvention, especially predominant in the United Kingdom and United States, weakens workers' bargaining power and makes them apt to conform to employer expectations.[13] Moreover, the frequently observed need to "sell" oneself, exacerbated by the internet and social media, involves not only an intensified level of commodification of the self but requires one to internalize as binding a whole range of obstructions that would count as external for Berlin. Horkheimer and Adorno's remarks on the fate of names eerily anticipate the kind of corporate setting in which so many of today's workers find themselves. As opposed to "the family name which, instead of being a trademark, individualized its bearers by relating them to their prehistory" (134/193), names are now stylized into advertising brands or standardized collectively so as to allow for smooth interaction in the office space. Reduced to the bare sign itself, which can easily be exchanged, meaning disappears.

Even if one allows that the present state of modernity invites the analysis Horkheimer and Adorno provide of conformism and commodification, one might insist that the self of this new dispensation has changed. Drawing on Freud's reflections on the superego and its oppressive role in the Victorian psyche, Horkheimer and Adorno see the modern self as highly disciplined and even authoritarian, ready to submit to outside constraints – in a word, hyper-neurotic. Many cultural theorists and therapists have argued, however, that the self of late capitalism tends to display traits more easily associated with narcissism than with the ascesis associated with Freud's neurotic subjects.[14] While the self as *DE* understands it would regress by seeking substitutes for the father-imago in authoritarian leaders, today's narcissistic self-regresses to the psychosexual level of comprehensive self-love, largely uninterrupted by the formation of the superego with its culturally mediated demands for self-control.

The shift from an ethics of production to an ethics of consumption that accompanies the emergence of narcissism as a dominant psychological form is arguably anticipated in Horkheimer and Adorno's reflections specifically on the culture industry. While conceptions of discipline and authoritarianism play important roles in *DE*, they seem only to a limited degree applicable to the culture industry. Culture consumers do internalize external imperatives, but this is coupled with the drive to seek easy enjoyment and on-hand social recognition. With new technologies of transmission and communication the significance of the culture industry has never been greater, and much of what Horkheimer and Adorno say about commodification, standardization, and identification seems fully applicable to them.

There are, however, complications. Take the internet. Horkheimer and Adorno largely assume that mass media involve one-way communication. Popular culture gets transmitted from a corporate source to its recipients; there is no reciprocity. As such, the content can quite readily take the form of propaganda. The internet may appear much more dialogical. Not only was it conceived, at least "on paper," to enhance dialogue and the exchange of information, but the ability to participate both as sender and receiver may suggest that it is more democratic than radio and television ever were.

Internet users *may* take part in political, cultural, and scientific debates. They *may* access an enormous amount of information. However, the internet can also isolate, falsify, and pacify. Indeed, due in part to the prevalence of smartphones, users have at their perpetual disposal a colossal amount of cheap entertainment in the form of film and music, the aesthetic reception of which is quite compromised. The way in which this content is received as well as the content itself (e.g., "fake news") calls precisely for the kind of analysis that Horkheimer and Adorno provide. Superficial plurality does not rule out commodification, standardization, and identification – the key features of the culture industry. In fact, it rules them in.

Celebrating surface over depth, illusion over truth, and representation over reality, much of the postmodern discourse of the 1980s and 1990s cultivated an affirmative stance toward cultural commodification. The old quest for authenticity and objectivity which had animated so many of the crucial Western aspirations in the post-Enlightenment era could finally be dismissed. To the postmodern imagination only culture existed – an infinitely malleable system of signs, the reference of which was safe to ignore. All that mattered was how signs could be manipulated so as to generate as much excitement and "joy" (recall the slightly naughty *jouissance*) as possible.

It is possible to argue just here that Horkheimer and Adorno continue to be relevant. As we have seen, dialectics reveals potentially fatal tensions and contradictions at the heart of what otherwise appears to be perfectly functional and rational. "The sense of something grim and impending within the polluted sunshine of the shopping mall," as Frederic Jameson puts it in his commentary on *DE*, captures the idea that drives the dialectic of enlightenment, i.e., that of the reversibility of progress, how the principles governing our sense of progress and liberation harbor a potential for regression. It is striking that the celebratory discourse of postmodernism ended rather abruptly in the first decade of the new millennium, its burst bubble leaving undisturbed suppressed Others, who navigate the artifice of Jameson's shopping mall, namely nature.

DIALECTIC OF ENLIGHTENMENT AND ECOLOGY

For all its talk of nature and accounting for it in its own terms *DE* is not usually considered a foundational work of ecological philosophy.[15] Despite the overwhelming threat of climate change and species extinction, it seems an expression mainly of Weberian despair over the social consequences of one-sided rationalization. Thinkers and activists in various green movements have for decades been searching for a form of philosophy able to address the ecological crisis. Figures from the European tradition such as Spinoza, Schelling, Bergson, and Heidegger have been invoked, as have been the American Transcendentalists, in particular Thoreau. Today, a substantive and growing body of work discusses questions related to anthropocentrism, intrinsic natural value, nature as a self-regulating system, the ethics of eating and farming, and predations of industry. How might Horkheimer and Adorno add anything to this discourse? Is there a latent ecological awareness in *DE*?

If *DE* is understood as an extension of Marxism, the answer is going to have to be negative. The Marxist tradition has always related value exclusively to human labor and, while commodified labor under capitalism is theorized as alienated in that tradition, the overcoming of alienated labor would not entail restricting the use of nature for human purposes. Marx rarely challenged the techno-industrial interpretation of natural items in terms of their potential to be treated as resources. The more industry the better, for revolution as well for any communist society that results from such a revolution.

Horkheimer and Adorno forego the restrictive use of the term "domination" common to much orthodox Marxism. On Horkheimer and Adorno's account, the pressing and relevant application of *Herrschaft* takes place as *Naturherrschaft*. A critique of the domination of nature seems inevitably and ultimately to engage with industrial civilization and (in this case) its commodification and instrumentalization of nature. It is hard not to hear a lament over the policies and practices behind environmental destruction in key formulations, such as the following:

> The technical process, to which the subject has been reified after the eradication of that process from consciousness, is as free from the ambiguous meanings of mythical thought as from meaning altogether, since reason itself has become merely an aid to the all-encompassing economic apparatus. Reason serves as a universal tool for the fabrication of all other tools, rigidly purpose-directed and as calamitous as the precisely calculated operations of material production, the results of which for human beings escape all calculation.
>
> (23/53)

Some interesting conclusions can be drawn from an application of what one might call the *Herrschaft* theorem to the environmental crisis. One is that understanding nature to be essentially a resource for material production, while intimately related to capitalist commodification and industrial management, has a long history. The anthropocentrism involved in the domination of nature coincides with nothing less than the history of civilization. One may of course weigh the destructive implications of industrialism quite differently from those of farming and the domestication of animals. The point is that the process of enlightenment is ambivalent: what counts as progress contains regressive elements that lock humans into cycles in which the heedless control of nature reinforces the natural foundation of their own being. To put the point in its ironic fullness: Our deficient understanding of ourselves as natural beings causes us to treat nature at large as unnatural.

A second conclusion one may draw is that any genuine form of critique of anthropocentric exploitation of nature must be *radical*. Since instrumental reason defines both civilization and our sense of self, it is not something from which we can simply walk away and be done with. Horkheimer and Adorno's view does not seem to welcome an incremental approach to the problem, and that of course poses a major challenge for environmentalism: The present magnitude of the crisis warrants policies of comprehensive social, economic, and cultural change. Given the complexities involved in any wholesale transformation of the system of production, however, it seems unavoidable that certain types of change must take place gradually.

The critique of incessant commodification, of industrial exploitation of nature, and of the anthropocentric bent of human history as such, may seem to align Horkheimer and Adorno with various representatives and schools of deep ecology. Human beings, deep ecologists maintain, are parts of nature at large, on which they depend for their very existence. Nor is the human species a privileged part of nature, *prima inter pares*. It is not some final "purpose" of the universe. To destroy nature is to destroy ourselves.

Assigning the label "deep ecologists" to Horkheimer and Adorno is, however, problematic. One crucial difference relates to how each theorizes the part/whole relation. Deep ecologists assign primacy, both ethically and ontologically, to nature as a whole *over its individual parts*. The parts are what they are insofar as they belong to the whole, and the whole is not reducible to the sum of its parts; thus, protection must first and foremost extend to all of nature considered as a whole. Nature is *Gaia*, all organisms and the inorganic environments in which they live, and that is what ultimately matters.[16] While Horkheimer and Adorno freely apply totalizing figures and occasionally seem to follow Hegel and Lukács in conceiving of societies as organic totalities, their strategic and metaphysical nominalism – the belief that only particulars are fully real – prevents them from following deep ecologists in the veneration of nature as a whole whose totality has primacy over its parts. From Spinoza to Schelling and Heidegger and his deep ecologist adherents, that *hen kai pan* was construed as opposed to the Enlightenment, contrary to scientific rationalism. Nature displays a oneness and unity that is in principle inaccessible to science. Horkheimer and Adorno would be concerned that suffering, the vulnerability of the individual, becomes epiphenomenal if one indulges too much in the imagery of Gaia. Behind the deep ecologists' awe of nature lurks the grandiosity of the sublime, tokening power and domination in the overriding of individuality. In other words, there are possible authoritarian implications.

Another significant difference between the *DE* and deep ecological thinking relates to the question of humanism and conceptions of the human subject. Deep ecology is marked by a pervasive skepticism of, and even hostility to, modern philosophies of the subject – attributions of freedom, a privileged form of moral dignity, a nonnatural status able to explain moral accountability, and the ascription of rights exclusively to the human subject *qua* subject. The deep ecologist considers human beings to be fundamentally on par with other animals; we have no special standing. In its most radical forms deep ecology attacks humanism head-on. Horkheimer and Adorno are also delivering a critique of the subject and, like this strand of ecological thinking, they see the conception of the sovereign subject central to Western science, morality, and law as grounded in power (viz. self-preservation) and hence, when viewed sideways-on, continuous with nature. However, as dialectical thinkers, they do not flatly reject the conception of the subject characteristic of Western humanism, nor do they outright dismiss the Enlightenment and modernity. As we have seen, they argue instead that "freedom in society is inseparable from enlightenment thinking" (xvi/18); their project is to rescue enlightenment thinking from its self-destruction.

How might criticizing but not completely rejecting the key elements of humanism offer a standpoint from which to embrace green alternatives to the current techno-capitalist ravaging of nature? One approach would simply be to appeal to self-preservation and argue that, rightly interpreted, what it dictates is that humans should preserve and protect whatever it may be that makes them thrive. Not to secure one's own fundamental conditions of existence seems irrational not only from a dialectical but also from a strictly instrumental point of view, and making sure that the oceans are not overfished, that deforestation is reversed or at least kept within reasonable limits, and that our energy supplies are renewable and minimally polluting, etc. expresses such a commitment. Since it appeals to self-interest, this argument seems not only compelling on strictly intellectual grounds but likely to exercise a strong motivational pull: if our survival is at stake, we will do what is necessary – won't we? Indeed, much public debate about, say, greenhouse gas emissions and climate change takes precisely this form.

While this strategy – which basically holds that the problem with instrumental reason is that we do not have enough of it, or that we need to re-interpret what it demands – finds plenty of proponents today, it would, at least if pursued as the *only* strategy, not be what Horkheimer and Adorno favor. Instrumental reason for them is a one-sided, across-the-board application of self-preservation to the world; accordingly, it provides no context from which to advocate for nature's intrinsic value. No one would deny that green solutions are very often going to be technical; yet, an environmentalism exclusively grounded in instrumentalism would be self-defeating. It would leave intrinsic value out in the cold and, in so doing, have no principled way to distinguish between acts of destruction and acts of protection.

How, then, from the conceptual resources contained in this book, might a non-instrumentalist ecological awareness be articulated? *DE* is shot through with despair. A good deal of that anguish has to do with what Horkheimer and Adorno take to be the self-vitiating, yet self-perpetuating nature of instrumental rationalization. Total despair would be inconsistent, however, with the interest in emancipation that runs through all the writings coming out of the Frankfurt School. Surely, its negativism – the refusal to seek out and identify existing practices on which to base one's ethical views – precludes any straightforward recourse to "sanctuaries," i.e., natural areas or entities which, given how we relate to them, may serve as exemplary of how nature should be treated. In *Minima Moralia*, Adorno sometimes writes as though the expressive relations internal to the bourgeois family can offer sanctuary from the chill of capitalist exchange relations. Similarly, in *Aesthetic Theory* he tries to rehabilitate the category of natural beauty, arguing that it expresses the non-identical in an age of total administration and control. Yet he never claims that a genuine alternative to rationalization can be found. He is in Weber's camp there.

To believe that one can simply step away from rationalization is to try to live an illusion. It is escapist and, moreover, is just the sort of illusion rationalization wishes to generate for its own self-preservation. It is an integral part of rationalization to encourage people to believe that things are less bad than they really are. Consider this example. The British naturalist and TV-personality Richard Attenborough increasingly has been presented with the criticism that, while enchanting, his many film productions that surround him with pristine nature, replete with thriving exotic animals, distract attention away from ecological destruction. Attenborough showed nature as though nothing bad had ever been done to it, as if it were a perpetual Garden of Eden. He took the point and has recently included scenes of environmental degradation in his nature films. By contrast, one might think that Horkheimer and Adorno's incessant negativism would indicate that ecological awareness can only be inculcated by being exposed to the worst: images of Chernobyl, colossal oil spills in the Gulf of Mexico, deforestation in Brazil, and the scrap yards in China. And, to be sure, Horkheimer and Adorno would not have shied away from negativity on these fronts.

In one of the postscript sketches, "Man and Beast," the relevant term is "concern" (*Sorge*) – "to show concern for animals" (211/286). In Western civilization, they argue, such concern has been the prerogative of women insofar as they are those within the world of reason's mastery who have been deemed closest to nature. "She became an embodiment of biological function, an image of nature, in the suppression of which this civilization's claim to glory lay" (206/280).[17] The main point of the entry, however, is that concern for animals is "a betrayal of progress" (211/286); such concern counteracts the demands of rationalizing reason. To care for animals is ultimately an act of remembrance, in which the disfigured object of instrumentalization starts to matter again. Horkheimer and Adorno are keen to emphasize that the remembrance – which they also think of as a form of "peace" (*Frieden*) – does not restore nature. All it does is to bring the world of animals to our attention as something worth protecting. It is a subtle point. They claim that what we are then dealing with is a productive illusion (*Schein*), rather than a fact. Unlike mere illusions, which have no cognitive value, the remembrance of nature refers us to reality, i.e., to animal life as representative of life itself. In non-human animals we see a reflection of ourselves from across the divide of culture.

The ethics of remembrance hinges on our ability to be affected – and thereby to acknowledge – the Other and its relationship to us. In his *The Denial of Nature* the philosopher and ecologist Arne Johan Vetlesen reports an encounter he had with an eagle on one of his hikes in the Norwegian wilderness.[18] The bird appeared suddenly before him and looked not only at him but straight into his eyes. It *regarded* him; it had authority. It demanded, as it were, respect. Any attempt to objectify it would violate the bird's being what it is (who it is?). The remembrance in this case would involve recognizing both the animal's independence as the being it is and its relation to the human world in those terms. In other words, the human world would have to make a place within it for the eagle world. By being open to the experience of its otherness, Vetlesen felt forced by the bird to take up a concerned position vis-à-vis it: let it be what it is – a wild animal with intrinsic value (or at least value not reducible to exchange-value). That would count as an act of ethical resistance to the imperatives of rationality.

In a joint interview with Horkheimer and Adorno from 1956, Adorno remarks that "Philosophy exists in order to redeem what you see in the look of an animal" (*Die Philosophie ist eigentlich dazu da, das einzulösen, was im Blick eines Tieres liegt*) (Horkheimer and Adorno 2011: 71; Horkheimer 1985a: 19.58). To become mindful of what we as members of an industrial civilization do to animals, and to nature more generally, requires an act of recognizing what we know yet cannot bring to full awareness. We must confront ourselves. That is a prerequisite for action in this sphere.

We may think of this as being brought to employ sensitivities that make up a certain moral worldview, however threatened or marginalized. And even though Adorno refers to a feeling, these sensitivities are not independent of language. Having a practical orientation to the world, expressed in particular judgments and responses, is part of what it is to have a language; however, it is also what makes up our practical identity. It is about who you are as a practical agent – an identity that is forever to be articulated, negotiated, and expressed. Inviting us to obtain a point of view internal to the practices that sustain such a worldview, Horkheimer and Adorno seek to resist both abstraction and return words to the ordinary contexts in which they make full sense.

Horkheimer and Adorno's call to remembrance of repressed and forgotten nature is reminiscent of the novelist J. M. Coetzee's character Elizabeth Costello, a writer and professor who urges a lecture audience to acknowledge how animals are treated in slaughterhouses.[19] Animals are alive to the world just as we are. Why, then, is it so difficult for us to feel for their experience, to have sympathy for the fullness of animal being? Why are we able to look the other way while knowing the extent of the suffering that takes place? We know that something is wrong; yet we do nothing to prevent it. Why is that? Costello herself has no answer. She agonizes over the silence at a crime that, in her view, is comparable to the Holocaust. Horkheimer and Adorno would pause at that comparison, but they would see the silence as very long-standing, rooted as it is in the history of civilization itself. The responsiveness that Vetlesen and Costello find lacking has been marginalized across the board and for a great deal of time.

Regaining the responsiveness would require refashioning ourselves, and that means radically rethinking culture. A major part of that process would consist in having the courage to face up to our wrongdoing and the damage it has wrought. Costello does so – but finds that she cannot come to terms with her fellow human beings. They have become strangers to her, just as she is now a stranger to them. The extent to which environmentalists should be frank about the degree of damage inflicted by humans on nature has been subject to debate. Too much forthrightness, it is sometimes claimed, may have the effect of stifling action: people no longer see the point of doing anything. By contrast, the authors of *DE* would insist that, however disarming it might be, only the abject truth will serve.

FURTHER READING

For accounts of the postwar development of Critical Theory, see Hohendahl 1991 and Später 2024. Pollock 1963/1956 is an in-depth consideration of the social and economic significance of mass automation in the United States from a Critical Theory perspective. Habermas 2023 is an attempt to understand digital media from the vantage point of his theory of communicative action.

NOTES

1. Wiggershaus 1995: 538.
2. Habermas 1984: 1.387: "The two attitudes of mind are representation and action. The subject relates to objects either to represent them as they are or to produce them as they should be. These two functions of mind are intertwined: knowledge of states of affairs is structurally related to the possibility of intervention in the world as the totality of states of affairs; and successful action requires in turn knowledge of the causal nexus in which it intervenes." For Horkheimer and Adorno, Habermas continues, "the attributes of mind – knowing, acting for an end – are transformed into functions of the self-maintenance of subjects that, like bodies and organisms, pursue a single 'abstract' end: to secure their continued (and contingent) existence. [...] Objectivating thought and purposive-rational action serve to reproduce a 'life' that is characterized by the knowing and acting subject's devotion to a blind, self-directed, intransitive self-preservation as his only 'end.'" It is worth noticing that Habermas's language is wavering somewhat between the normative ("secure," "serve," "devotion," "pursuing an end," "producing objects as they should be") and the descriptive (with knowledge and action being "functions") registers.
3. Habermas 1993a: 119.
4. Habermas 1984: 1.385.
5. Adorno 1983: 230/1970: 5.231.
6. Admittedly, the quote seems to allow that there are two senses of "truth" – the first being non-epistemic or semantic (holding that there are truths regardless of epistemic contact), the second being epistemic, involving the idea that truth (or at least the experience of it) involves commitment to a proposition. While the tension between these two accounts is undeniable, it may ultimately be the concept of experience that for Horkheimer and Adorno is decisive. They may grant that non-epistemic truths exist. However, the emphatic, philosophical truths that matter in their work can only be ascertained via experience. The question, then, which remains central especially in Adorno's writings, is what experience really amounts to. At the very least, it requires some form of active involvement with dialectical opposites such that the particular appears as what it truly is. Rather than a mere correspondence between truth-bearer and fact, there is a Platonic element to this account: truth is what occurs when an item is presented in such a way as to reveal its true nature. Since Adorno rejects the notion of eternal, ahistorical truth, a presentation of this kind must itself be historical.
7. Adorno 2000: 116–17/1996ff.: IV.14.182–3.

8 For two examples, see Bernstein 2001 and Freyenhagen 2013. The term "exhibition" (*Darstellung*) has a technical use in early German Idealism. It refers to a philosophical theory that does not merely advance ordered propositions but instantiates the impulse that brought them into being. This is one of the aspects of Idealism that was of continuing importance for Marx.

9 Bernstein 2001: 301 rightly points to Wittgenstein's *Philosophical Investigations* § 284, about the wriggling fly: "Look at a stone and imagine it having sensations. – One says to oneself: How could one so much as get the idea of ascribing a sensation to a thing? One might as well ascribe it to a number! – And now look at a wriggling fly and at once these difficulties vanish and pain seems able to get a foothold here, where before everything was, so to speak, too smooth for it." While not ethical in its intent, the entry serves as a reminder of how we apply mental concepts. We do so in response to living bodies.

10 As Heidegger and others have emphasized, the meaning of the Greek verb *theōreō* is "look at, behold." Only with Plato does one get a specification of *theōria* to "contemplative structure."

11 Bauman 2005: 1–2.

12 Berlin 1969. He is of course writing prior to the more recent trend in hyper-individualization. His favored conception of liberalism is more "classical."

13 Bauman 2005; see also Sennett 1998.

14 Lasch 1979 is often viewed as having initiated the critical discourse of pathological narcissism under late-capitalist conditions.

15 For a noteworthy exception, see Cook 2011.

16 Lovelock 1982 is the founding text of Gaia theory. Compare Devall and Sessions 2007, 7: "Deep ecology is emerging as a way of developing a new balance and harmony between individuals, communities and all of Nature." Presumably, extraterrestrial nature is also included under the general heading "nature." It will not be too long before mining on the Moon or colonization of it or Mars will be under consideration. Moreover, what counts of being "of the Earth" is vague, e.g., are objects like orbiting satellites and various sorts of "space junk" included?

17 As we saw, Horkheimer and Adorno write that women and Jews are alike in their relation to nature and prejudice based on that relation. See 87–88/117–19.

18 Vetlesen 2015: 204:

> Have you ever experienced being actively looked at by an animal, say, an eagle or a heron? I have. […] That look fixed me in a manner as elusive as it was commanding. Its intelligence captivating, irrefutable, making mockery of Cartesian doubt. It forced me to ask myself what I looked like from that point of view, a view I had no chance to check, as I might have had were the onlooker another human being. Nonetheless, being the object of a look from a bird who, in looking at me, clearly was not an object but fully a subject did more to repudiate Descartes's view that "animals have no souls, no thoughts or experiences, and are in fact automata" than do dozens of books of philosophy (citation omitted).

19 Coetzee 1999.

CONCLUDING REMARKS

DE is a signal work in twentieth-century European philosophy, but unusual in presentation. It is neither a treatise, like Heidegger's *Being and Time*, nor as historically focused and detailed as Foucault's *Discipline and Punish*. It is more like an extended testimony, the intended audience of which is comprised of philosophical intimates. Even its 1947 general publication retains an insular character. To read it gainfully one had to be an insider, someone for whom the book would put ideas that were current into a striking, new form.

One might think to conclude a discussion of *DE* by asking and trying to answer the question: what doctrinal and methodological impact might the book have on social theory today? That's certainly a reasonable undertaking, but it is not perhaps the most telling way to assess *DE*'s timeliness. We pose a different question, which is harder to answer: what would it take nowadays for such a book to so much as gain a proper audience? Return to Adorno's framing metaphor of *DE* being a message in a bottle. Who is there on the beach to pick up that bottle, open it, read the message, write up one's own thoughts in response, place the old and new message back in the bottle, and set it to sea again? These questions are pointed because, if Horkheimer and Adorno are right, there is no guarantee that such a book might be written today or that it could find its intended audience.

Any critical theorist will stress that *DE* is a child of its time, written in exile during the Second World War. The cultural differences between the place of exile and the place exiled from could not have been starker: Southern California, all but inundated in Hollywood movies and an intellectual thinktank from the defunct Weimar Republic. From that fraught and fragile vantage point, Horkheimer and Adorno were concerned to point out hidden complexities in what were for them socially emergent phenomena: the marriage of authoritarianism to capitalism, the reduction of qualitative in favor of quantitative experience, great expansions in mass media, the Shoah. These were in their view all strongly interrelated. They did not think of course that they emerged out of nowhere. The main thrust of the book is that such phenomena are due to subtle developments born out of latent and overlooked historical sources. But that development does, for its contingent comingling, make up a world. And, in order to be intellectually alive to that world, one had to pierce appearances to understand it for what it actually was, in terms of where it actually came from. A mere glance at the concerns listed above sparks the question: are we not now just further down that same road? With this thought a more pressing concern arises: are we so far down it that there is no turning back, so far down the road that a book like *DE* is no longer timely?

Consider this canary in a coal mine: the humble T-shirt. On any casual walk down a city street, visit to a suburban park, or hike on a woodsy trail, you will encounter people wearing T-shirts. Even were you an anthropologist stationed in deepest Amazonia, you would find the people there wearing similar shirts. T-shirts often, even usually, display logos or brand names. These might reflect the corporation that makes the garment, but often enough one finds insignia of sports teams, travel destinations, universities, political causes, or music groups. People wear T-shirts for cover, comfort, and style, but also to show affiliation with the brand names or logos printed on them.

What is it to feel that *a brand* is expressive of an aspect of one? What bit of subjectivity are you "rocking" when you choose today to wear your Che Guevara T-shirt? Che was a socialist revolutionary, leading actions in Cuba, the Congo, and Bolivia. What is an image of his face doing on a piece of leisurewear in the first place? And, by the way, that representation of him is a stock image, trademarked, as is the shirt. To be precise, the image is a replica on cloth of a famous photograph taken by Alberto Korda in 1960 that has come to have the title *Guerrillero Heroico*. An image of the "guerilla hero" has become a commodity, one that is expressive of some aspect of the image with which you identify and through which you project that identification to the public. There is an old adage, venerable enough for Erasmus to quote it: "clothes make the man" (*vestis virum facit*).[1] That thought has not "dated out."

But what are these T-shirts *really*? Where do they come from, and under what conditions are they made? Some generalities will suffice. The answer is that it depends on what you mean by "made." Most T-shirts are the result of several steps. The cotton for yours may have been grown in India, milled in Pakistan, and sewn in El Salvador. That is because outsourcing production of, say, US goods is cheaper than making them in the United States. The labor is cheaper, the raw stock is cheaper, environmental and labor laws are lax, etc. (Few are fair trade, and you might even question how fair is fair trade anyhow.) The environmental cost of a single purchase of the T-shirt is difficult to calculate precisely, but it is certainly there: farming, milling, dying, and manufacturing the cotton are not impact-neutral.

Let's linger with the thought. Maybe you bought that T-shirt online. Perhaps you searched for it specifically or happened to run across it in an ad while viewing something else. Maybe you saw posts about it on your social media or were put in mind of it by an influencer. The point is that to order the shirt online is to indirectly support the oligarchs who own the internet: its design, its maintenance, what gets sold and told on it, everything about it. And that in no way completes their interest in you. Your purchase is tracked by cookies, an algorithm about your likely preferences is generated, and the next time you go online, suggestions will be

CONCLUDING REMARKS 229

posted to you about other garments, political causes, in short, other identity "markers." Every time you visit a site, it is out there. You have no privacy; all you have is a novel sort of anonymity. You are in a faceless crowd but, precisely as *faceless*, you are incessantly addressed.

It can get more pronounced and darker. As this book is submitted to the press, a billionaire demagogue with a background in commercial real estate and showbusiness has just won the US presidential election by a significant margin of electoral votes. This will be his second term in office, and his agenda could not be more obvious: root out political enemies, conduct mass deportations, regulate speech and research at universities, ignore judicial rulings, populate agencies with lackies, and use military force against residents and citizens alike. Perhaps he is not, clinically speaking, a fascist. That would require a stable ideology, whereas Donald Trump seems always driven by self-interest, wherever it may lie. But the program and procedures that he intends to institute are oligarchic and populist in the extreme. They appeal to business people who crave no limits and to a segment of US society that feels betrayed by liberal, intellectual elites and scapegoats immigrants and people of color. Leadership is to be tested by their defeat, and the measures to be taken are not subject to democratic decision. For, this is an emergency, which greatly broadens executive prerogatives to do "what is necessary." Most striking, perhaps, is that this president displays no care for truth. In its place is reactivity without responsiveness, in other words, self-preservation operating under no restriction as to means. The very concept of the rule of law is in jeopardy and, with it, democracy.

Democracy has turned on itself. The new regime has grown out of the form of rationality constitutive of neoliberalism, which has exploited the opportunities on offer in liberalism to turn politics into spectacle, capitalize on the grievances of underprivileged groups, and cart out the myth of the entrepreneur-leader. Marx famously remarked that world-historical facts recur, appearing first as tragedy, then as farce. Is this parody of Mussolini our own creation? Horkheimer and Adorno strongly suggest: Yes, he is.

El sueño de la razón produce monstruos – "the sleep of reason produces monsters," Francisco Goya called his 1799 print that depicts how reason, if it is not vigilant, can be overtaken by folly, ignorance, and corruption. It sums up with eerie precision what our authors set out to do in *DE*. Could a latter-day version of it be written and read for all it is worth under such conditions? Can we see through a T-shirt's mundanity? Can we see in Trump a creature born of the culture industry? Can we see them both as parts of a single totality? *DE* may help one detect such things. But it is one thing to recognize a thing that needs changing and another to prescribe specific change. *DE* does none of the latter; it only "constantly denies."[2] That is strategy, not shirking. *DE* is intent on leaving space open for new forms of social imagination. Is it possible or permissible to indulge such philosophical discretion today?

NOTES

1 Erasmus 1982: 34.204–05 [*Adages* III.i.60], citing Quintilian, *Institutio Oratoria* VII.i.20 as the source.
2 *Faust* I.1340.

BIBLIOGRAPHY

Adorno
2025. *Fighting Antisemitism Today*, trans. W. Hoban. London: Polity.
2009. *In Search of Wagner*, trans. R. Livingstone. New York: Verso.
2006. *Current of Music*, ed. R. Hullot-Kentor. Frankfurt/M: Suhrkamp.
2000. *Metaphysics: Concepts and Problems*, trans. E. Jephcott. Stanford: Stanford University Press.
1998. *Critical Models: Interventions and Catchwords*, trans. H. Pickford. New York: Columbia University Press.
1997. *Aesthetic Theory*, trans. R. Hullot-Kentor. Minneapolis: University of Minnesota Press.
1996ff. *Nachgelassene Schriften*, ed. R. Tiedemann. Frankfurt/M: Suhrkamp.
1996. "Chaplin Times Two," trans J. McKay, *Yale Journal of Criticism* 9.1: 57–61.
1983. *Against Epistemology: A Metacritique*, trans. W. Domingo. Cambridge, MA: MIT Press.
1982. *Prisms*, trans. S. W. Nicholsen and S. Weber. Cambridge, MA: MIT Press.
1978. *Minima Moralia*, trans. E. Jephcott. London: Verso.
1970. *Gesammelte Schriften*, ed. R. Tiedemann. Frankfurt/M: Suhrkamp.
1954. "How to Look at Television," *The Quarterly of Film, Radio and Television* 8: 213–35.
Adorno and Hanns Eisler
2007. *Composing for the Films*. London: Continuum.
Adorno and Max Horkheimer
2011. *Towards a New Manifesto*, trans. R. Livingstone. London and New York: Verso.
2002. *Dialectic of Enlightenment: Philosophical Fragments*, trans. E. Jephcott. Stanford: Stanford University Press.

Adorno et al.
1978. *Der Positivismusstreit in der deutschen Soziologie*. 6th ed. Darmstadt: Luchterhand.
1950. *The Authoritarian Personality*. New York: Norton.

Fromm
1976. *Escape from Freedom*. New York: Harper and Row.

Habermas
2024. *A New Structural Transformation of the Public Sphere and Deliberative Politics*, trans. C. Cronin. Cambridge: Polity.
2023. *Also a History of Philosophy*, trans. C. Cronin. Cambridge: Polity.
1993a. *The Philosophical Discourse of Modernity: Twelve Lectures*, trans. F. Lawrence. Cambridge, MA: MIT Press.
1993b. *Postmetaphysical Thinking: Philosophical Essays*, trans. W. M. Hohengarten. Cambridge, MA.: MIT Press.
1984. *The Theory of Communicative Action*, trans. T. McCarthy. London: Heinemann.

Horkheimer
1995. *Critical Theory: Selected Essays*, trans. M. J. O'Connell et al. New York: Continuum.
1993. *Between Philosophy and Social Science: Selected Early Writings*, trans. G. F. Hunter, M. S. Kramer, and J. Torpey. Cambridge, MA: MIT Press.
1985a. *Gesammelte Schriften*, ed. S. Schmidt and G. Schmid Noerr. Frankfurt/M: Fischer.
1985b. *Zur Kritik der instrumentellen Vernunft*. Frankfurt/M: Fischer.
1978. *Dawn & Decline: Notes 1926–31 and 1950–69*, trans. M. Shaw. New York: Continuum.
1977. *Kritische Theorie. Studienausgabe*, ed. A. Schmidt. Frankfurt/M: Fischer.
1974a. *Critique of Instrumental Reason: Lectures and Essays Since the End of World War II*, trans. M. O'Connell et al. New York: Continuum.
1974b. *Eclipse of Reason*. New York: Continuum.
1974c. *Notizen 1950–1969 und Dämmerung*, ed. W. Brede. Frankfurt/M: Fischer.
1946. "Sociological Background of the Psychoanalytic Approach," in *Anti-Semitism: A Social Disease*, ed. E. Simmel. New York: Int'l University Press, 1–10.
1945. "Response to Survey," in *The Classification of Jewish Immigrants and Its Implications: A Survey of Opinion*, ed. N. Goldberg, J. Lestchinsky, and M. Weinreich. New York: Yiddish Scientific Institute–YIVO, 64–6 [no. 117].

Löwenthal and Guterman
1949. *Prophets of Deceit: A Study of the Techniques of the American Agitator*. New York: Harper.

Marcuse
1964. *One-Dimensional Man*. Boston: Beacon.

Neumann
1944. *Behemoth: The Structure and Practice of National Socialism 1933–1944*, 2d rev. ed. Oxford: Oxford University Press.

Neumann and Kirchheimer

1996. *The Rule of Law Under Siege: Selected Essays of Franz L. Neumann and Otto Kirchheimer*, ed. W. Scheuerman. Berkeley: University of California Press.

Pollock

1957. *Automation: A Study of its Economic and Social Consequences*, trans. W. O. Henderson and W. H. Chaloner. New York: Praeger.

1963. *Automation. Materialen zur Beurteilung ihrer ökonomischen und sozialen Folgen*, 2d ed. Frankfurt/M: Europäische Verlagsanstalt.

1982. "State Capitalism: Its Possibilities and Limitations," in *The Essential Frankfurt School Reader*, ed. A. Arato and E. Gebhardt. New York: Continuum, 71–94.

OTHER PRIMARY SOURCES

Alter, Robert. 2004. *The Five Books of Moses: A Translation and Commentary*. New York: Norton.

Althusser, Louis. 2006. *For Marx*, trans. B. Brewster. London: Verso.

Aristotle. 1965. *De arte poetica*, ed. R. Kassel. Oxford: OCT.

Augustine. 2009. *Confessions*, trans. H. Chadwick. Oxford: Oxford University Press.

Bachelard, Gaston. 2000. *La formation de l'esprit scientifique*. Paris: Vrin.

Bachofen, Johann Jakob. 1967. *Myth, Religion, and Mother*, trans. R. Mannheim. Princeton: Princeton University Press.

Barthes, Roland. 1976. *Sade, Fourier, Loyola*, trans. R. Miller. New York: Farrar, Straus, Giroux.

Barthes, Roland. 1975. *The Pleasure of the Text*, trans. R. Miller. New York: Farrar, Straus, Giroux.

Bataille, Georges. 2004. *On Nietzsche*, trans. B. Boone. New York: Continuum.

Bataille, Georges. 1985. *Visions of Excess: Selected Writings, 1927–1939*, ed. and trans. A. Stoekl. Minneapolis: University of Minnesota Press.

Baudelaire, Charles. 1962. *Le Peintre de la vie modern*, in *Curiosités esthétiques, L'art romantique, et autres œuvres critiques*, rev. ed., ed. H. Lemaitre. Paris: Garnier, 453–502.

Bauman, Zygmunt. 2005. *Liquid Life*. Oxford: Polity.

Bauman, Zygmunt. 1989. *Modernity and the Holocaust*. Oxford: Polity.

Becker, Gary. 1975. *Human Capital*, 2d ed. New York: Columbia University Press.

Benjamin, Walter. 2019. *Origin of the German Trauerspiel*, trans. H. Eiland. Cambridge, MA: Harvard University Press.

Benjamin, Walter. 2004ff. *Selected Writings*, ed. H. Eiland and M. Jennings. Cambridge: Harvard University Press.

Benjamin, Walter. 1968. *Illuminations*, trans. H. Zohn, ed. H. Arendt. New York: Schocken.

Bergson, Henri. 1912. *Laughter: An Essay on the Meaning of the Comic*, trans. C. Brereton. New York: MacMillan.

Berlin, Isaiah. 1978. *Karl Marx*, 4th ed. Oxford: Oxford University Press.

Berlin, Isaiah. 1969. *Four Essays on Liberty*. Oxford: Oxford University Press.

Bloch, Ernst. 2000. *The Spirit of Utopia*, trans. A. Nassar. Palo Alto: Stanford University Press.

Blumenberg, Hans. 1988. *Work on Myth*, trans. R. Wallace. Cambridge, MA: MIT Press.

Boileau, Nicolas. 1966. *Œuvres complètes,* ed. F. Escal. Paris: Pléiade.

Buffon (Leclerc, George-Louis). 1844. *Œuvres complètes*. Paris: Duménil.

Certeau, Michel de. 1988. *The Writing of History*, trans. T. Conley. New York: Columbia University Press.

Coetzee, J. M. 1999. *The Lives of Animals*. Princeton: Princeton University Press.

Coffa, J. Alberto. 1991. *The Semantic Tradition from Carnap to Kant: To the Vienna Station*. Cambridge: Cambridge University Press.

Dahms, Hans-Joachim. 1998. *Positivismusstreit. Die Auseinandersetzung der Frankfurter Schule mit dem logischen Positivismus, dem amerikanischen Pragmatismus und dem kritischen Rationalismus*. Frankfurt/M: Suhrkamp.

Daston, Lorraine. 1988. *Classical Probability in the Enlightenment*. Princeton: Princeton University Press.

Davidson, Donald. 1984. *Essays on Truth and Interpretation*. Oxford: Clarendon Press.

Devall, Bill, and Sessions, George. 2007. *Deep Ecology: Living as if Nature Mattered*. Salt Lake City: Gibs Smith.

Dilthey, Wilhem. 1993. *Der Aufbau der geschichtlichen Welt in den Geisteswissenschaften*, ed. M. Riedel. Frankfurt/M: Suhrkamp.

Dilthey, Wilhem. 1991. *Introduction to the Human Sciences*. Vol. 1 of *Selected Writings*, ed. R. Makreel. Princeton: Princeton University Press.

Erasmus, Desiderius. 1982. *Collected Works*, trans. M. M. Phillips, ed. R. A. B Mynors. Toronto: University of Toronto Press.

Ferry, Luc. 1995. *The New Ecological Order*, trans. C. Volk. Chicago: University of Chicago Press.

Feyerabend, Paul. 1975. *Against Method: Outline of an Anarchistic Theory of Knowledge*. London: New Left.

Foucault, Michel. 2010. *Birth of Biopolitics: Lectures at the Collège de France 1978–1979*, trans. G. Burchell, ed. A. Davidson. London: Picador.

Foucault, Michel. 2009. *Security, Territory, Population: Lectures at the Collège de France 1977–1978*, trans. G. Burchell, ed. A. Davidson. London: Picador.

Foucault, Michel. 2003. *'Society Must Be Defended'*, trans D. Macey, ed. A. Davidson. New York: Picador.

Freud, Sigmund. 1989. *Civilization and Its Discontents*, trans. J. Strachey. New York: Norton.

Freud, Sigmund. 1953ff. *The Standard Edition of the Complete Psychological Works*, ed. J. Strachey. London: Hogarth.

Gadamer, Hans-Georg. 1975. *Truth and Method*. 2d rev. ed., trans. J. Weinsheimer and D. Marshall. London: Sheed & Ward.

Goethe, J. W. 1999. *Werke. Hamburger Ausgabe*, 10th ed., ed. E. Trunz. München: Beck.

Graeber, David. 2012. *Debt: The First 5,000 Years*. New York: Melville House.

Hacking, Ian. 1990. *The Taming of Chance*. Cambridge: Cambridge University Press.

Hacking, Ian. 1983. *Representing and Intervening*. Cambridge: Cambridge University Press.

Hacking, Ian. 1975. *The Emergence of Probability*. Cambridge: Cambridge University Press.

Halbertal, Moishe, *and* Margalit, Avishai. 1998. *Idolatry*, trans. N. Goldblum. Cambridge, MA: Harvard University Press.

Halliwell, Stephen. 2002. *The Aesthetics of Mimesis: Ancient Texts and Modern Problems*. Princeton: Princeton University Press.

Hamann, J. G. 2007. *Writings on Philosophy and Language*, trans. and ed. K. Haynes. Cambridge: Cambridge University Press.

Hanson, Norwood. 1958. *Patterns of Discovery: An Inquiry into the Conceptual Foundations of Science*. Cambridge: Cambridge University Press.

Hegel, G. W. F. 2019. *The Phenomenology of Spirit*, trans. and ed. T. Pinkard. Cambridge: Cambridge University Press.

Hegel, G. W. F. 1991. *Elements of the Philosophy of Right*, trans. H. B. Nisbet, ed. A. Wood. Cambridge: Cambridge University Press.

Hegel, G. W. F. 1988a. *The Difference Between Fichte's and Schelling's System of Philosophy*, trans. and ed. W. Cerf and H. S. Harris. Albany: SUNY Press.

Hegel, G. W. F. 1988b. *Faith and Knowledge*, trans. and ed. W. Cerf and H. S. Harris. Albany: SUNY Press.

Hegel, G. W. F. 1975. *Lectures on the Philosophy of World History. Introduction: Reason in History*, trans. H. B. Nisbet, ed. D. Forbes, Cambridge: Cambridge University Press.

Heidegger, Martin. 2002. *Off the Beaten Track*, trans. J. Young and K. Haynes. Cambridge: Cambridge University Press.

Heidegger, Martin 1962. *Being and Time*, trans. and ed. J. Macquarrie and E. Robinson. New York: Harper and Row.

Herder, J. G. 2002. *Philosophical Writings*, trans. and ed. M. Forster. Cambridge: Cambridge University Press.

Homer. 1996. *The Odyssey*, trans. R. Fagles. London: Penguin.

Homer. 1962. *Opera*, vols. III and IV, ed. T. Allen. Oxford: OCT.

Homer. 1912. *Odyssee*, trans. J. H. Voß. Berlin: Deutsche Bibliotek.

Honneth, Axel. 2008. *Reification*. Oxford: Oxford University Press.

Jacobi, F. H. 2004. *Werke. Gesamtausgabe*, ed. K. Hammacher and W. Jaeschke. Hamburg: Meiner.

Jaspers, Karl. 1953. *The Origin and Goal of History*, trans. M. Bullock. New Haven: Yale University Press.

Kant, Immanuel. 2017. *The Metaphysics of Morals*, rev. ed., trans. M. Gregor, ed. L. Denis. Cambridge: Cambridge University Press.

Kant, Immanuel. 2012. *Groundwork of the Metaphysic of Morals*, rev. ed., trans. and ed. M. Gregor and J. Timmerman. Cambridge: Cambridge University Press.

Kant, Immanuel. 2005. *Political Writings*, trans. H. B. Nisbet, ed. H. S. Reiss. Cambridge: Cambridge University Press.

Kant, Immanuel. 2000. *Critique of the Power of Judgment*, trans. P. Guyer and E. Matthews, ed. P. Guyer. Cambridge: Cambridge University Press.

Kant, Immanuel. 1998. *Critique of Pure Reason*, trans. and ed. P. Guyer and A. Wood. Cambridge: Cambridge University Press.

Kant, Immanuel. 1996. *Practical Philosophy*, trans. M. Gregor, ed. M. Gregor and A. Wood. Cambridge: Cambridge University Press.

Kant, Immanuel. 1902ff. *Gesammelte Schriften*, Königlich Preußischen Akademie der Wissenschaften. Berlin (all reputable English translations of Kant give the pages to this edition marginally for ease of reference, with the exception of the *Critique of Pure Reason*, to which we have, per usual scholarly practice, cited to the first and second editions of the original publications, 1781 and 1787 respectively, in A/B format).

Kierkegaard, Søren. 2009. *Two Ages*, trans. and ed. H. Hong and E. Hong. Princeton: Princeton University Press.

Köhnke, Klaus Christian. 1986. *Entstehung und Aufstieg des Neukantianismus. Die deutsche Universitätsphilosophie zwischen Idealismus und Positivismus.* Frankfurt/M: Suhrkamp.

Korsch, Karl. 2013. *Marxism and Philosophy*, trans. F. Halliday. London: Verso.

Kracauer, Siegfried. 2002. *Jacques Offenbach and the Paris of His Time*, trans. G. David and E. Mosbacher, ed. G. Koch. Princeton: Princeton University Press.

Kracauer, Siegfried. 1995. *The Mass Ornament*, trans. T. Levin. Cambridge, MA: Harvard University Press.

Kuhn, Thomas. 1962. *The Structure of Scientific Revolutions*. Chicago: University of Chicago Press.

Lacan, Jacques. 2007. *Écrits,* trans. B. Fink. New York: Norton.

Lasch, Christopher. 1979. *The Culture of Narcissism: American Life in An Age of Diminishing Expectations*. New York: Norton.

Lenin, V. I. 1970. *Imperialism: The Highest Stage of Capitalism*. New York: International Publ.

Lenin, V. I. 1964. *Collected Works*, ed. Marx-Lenin Institute. Moscow: Progress.

Lovelock, James. 1982. *Gaia: A New Look at Life on Earth*. Oxford: Oxford University Press.

Lukács, Georg. 2021. *The Destruction of Reason*, trans. P. Palmer. London: Verso.

Lukács, Georg. 1974. *Theory of the Novel*, trans. A. Bostock. Cambridge, MA: MIT Press.

Lukács, Georg. 1972. *History and Class Consciousness*, trans. R. Livingstone. Cambridge, MA: MIT Press.

Marx, Karl. 1993. *Capital*, ed. D. Fernbach. New York: Penguin.

Marx, Karl. 1967. *Marx-Engels Werke*. Berlin: Dietz.

Mead, George Herbert. 1967. *Mind, Self, and Society*, ed. C. Morris. Chicago: University of Chicago Press.

Nietzsche, Friedrich. 2007. *On the Genealogy of Morality*, trans. C. Diethe, ed. K. Ansell-Pierson. New York: Cambridge University Press.

Nietzsche, Friedrich. 2001. *The Gay Science*, trans. J. Nauckhoff, ed. B. Williams. New York: Cambridge University Press.

Nietzsche, Friedrich. 1999. *The Birth of Tragedy*, trans. R. Speirs, ed. R. Geuss. New York: Cambridge University Press.

Nietzsche, Friedrich. 1992. *Ecce Homo*, trans. R. Hollingdale, ed. M. Tanner. New York: Penguin.

Novalis (Hardenberg, Friedrich). 1997. *Philosophical Writings*, trans. M. Stoljar. Albany: SUNY Press.

Penrose, Roger. 2004. *The Road to Reality: A Complete Guide to the Laws of the Universe*. New York: Vintage.

Pinker, Steven. 2019. *Enlightenment Now: The Case for Reason, Science, Humanism, and Progress*. New York: Penguin.

Plekhanov, G. I. 1976. "Fundamental Problems of Marxism," in *Selected Philosophical Works*. Moscow: Progress, 3.117–83.

Quine, W. V. O. 1953. *From a Logical Point of View*. Cambridge, MA: Harvard University Press.

Reich, Wilhelm. 1980. *The Mass Psychology of Fascism*. New York: Farrar, Straus, Giroux.

Reichenbach, Heinrich. 1951. *The Rise of Scientific Philosophy*. Berkeley: University of California Press.

Rickert, Hans. 1986a. *Kulturwissenschaften und Naturwissenschaften*, 7th ed., ed. F. Vollhardt. Stuttgart: Reclam.

Rickert, Hans. 1986b. *The Limits of Concept Formation in Natural Science*, ed. and trans. G Oakes. Cambridge: Cambridge University Press.

Rorty, Richard. 1979. *Philosophy and the Mirror of Nature*. Princeton: Princeton University Press.

Sade, Donatien Alphonse François, Marquis de. 1969. *Juliette*, trans. S. A. Wainhouse. New York: Grove Press.

Sade, Donatien Alphonse François, Marquis de. 1966a. *120 Days of Sodom*, trans. R. Seaver and A. Wainhouse. New York: Grove Press.

Sade, Donatien Alphonse François, Marquis de. 1966b. *The Complete Justine, Philosophy in the Bedroom, and Other Essays*, trans. R. Seaver and A. Wainhouse. New York: Grove Press.

Schelling, F. W. J. 1993. *System of Transcendental Idealism (1800)*, trans. P. Heath. Cambridge: Cambridge University Press.

Schelling, F. W. J. 1989. *Ideas for a Philosophy of Nature*, trans. E. Harris and P. Heath, ed. R. Stern. Cambridge: Cambridge University Press.

Schiller, Friedrich. 1983. *On the Aesthetic Education of Man*, trans. and ed. E. Wilkinson and L. A. Willoughby. Oxford: Oxford University Press (with facing German text).

Schlegel, Friedrich. 1991. *Philosophical Fragments*, trans. P. Firchow. Minneapolis: University of Minnesota Press.

Schopenhauer, Arthur. 1966. *The World as Will and Representation*, trans. E. F. J. Payne. New York: Dover.

Sellars, Wilfrid. 1997. *Empiricism and the Philosophy of Mind*, ed. R. Brandom. Cambridge, MA: Harvard University Press.

Sennett, Richard. 1998. *The Corrosion of Character: The Personal Consequences of Work in the New Capitalism*. London: Norton.

Sohn-Rethel, Alfred. 2020. *Intellectual and Manual Labor*, trans. M. Sohn-Rethel. Leiden: Brill.

Sombart, Werner. 1987. *Der moderne Kapitalismus*. München: DTV.

Stendhal (Beyle, Pierre). 1975. *Love*, trans. G. Sale and S. Sale. New York: Penguin.

Veblen, Thorstein. 2007. *The Theory of the Leisure Class*, ed. M. Banta. Oxford: Oxford University Press.

Vetlesen, Arne Johan. 2015. *The Denial of Nature: Environmental Philosophy in the Era of Global Capitalism*. London: Routledge.

Weber, Max. 2004. *The Vocation Lectures*, trans. R. Livingstone, ed. D. Owen and T. Strong. Indianapolis: Hackett.

Weber, Max. 1956. *Protestant Ethic and the Spirit of Christianity*, trans. and ed. T. Parsons. New York: Scribner's.

Windelband, Wilhelm. 1919. *Präludien*, 6th ed. Tübingen, Mohr.

SECONDARY SOURCES

Abromeit, John. 2011. *Max Horkheimer and the Foundations of the Frankfurt School*. New York: Cambridge University Press.

Ahrensdorf, Peter. 2022. *Homer and the Tradition of Political Philosophy: Encounters with Plato, Machiavelli, and Nietzsche*. Cambridge: Cambridge University Press.

Allen, Amy. 2020. *Critique on the Couch: Why Critical Theory Needs Psychoanalysis*. New York: Columbia University Press.

Allen, W. S. 1968. *Vox Graeca*. Cambridge: Cambridge University Press.

Avineri, Shlomo. 1968. *The Social and Political thought of Karl Marx*. Cambridge: Cambridge University Press.

Backhuys, Thomas. 2017. "Dialektik der Aufklärung und Odyssee. Bemerkungen zu einer Fehlzitat," *Rheinische Museum für Philologie* 160: 223–34.

Baeza, Natalia. 2020. "Adorno's Wicked Queen of Snow White: Paranoia, Fascism, and the Fate of Modernity," *European Journal of Psychoanalysis*, online.

Bahr, Ehrhard. 2007. *Weimar on the Pacific: German Exile Culture in Los Angeles and the Crisis of Modernism*. Berkeley: University of California Press.

Beiser, Frederick. 2005. *Hegel*. London: Routledge.

Bendix, Reinhard. 1977. *Max Weber: An Intellectual Portrait*, rev. ed. Berkeley: University of California Press.

Benhabib, Seyla, Bonß, Wolfgang, and McCole, John, eds. 1993. *On Max Horkheimer: New Perspectives*. Cambridge, MA: MIT Press.

Benhabib, Seyla. 1986. *Critique, Norm, and Utopia: A Study of the Foundations of Critical Theory*. New York: Columbia University Press.

Bernstein, J. M. 2001. *Adorno: Disenchantment and Ethics*. Cambridge: Cambridge University Press.

Bernstein, J. M. 1992. *The Fate of Art: Aesthetic Alienation from Kant to Derrida and Adorno*. State Park, PA: Penn State Press.

Bernstein, J. M. 1984. *The Philosophy of the Novel: Lukács, Marxism and the Dialectics of Form*. Minneapolis: University of Minnesota Press.

Bleicher, Thomas. 1971. *Homer in der deutschen Literatur vom Frühhumanismus bis zur Aufklärung (1450–1740). Zur Rezeption der Antike und zur Poetologie der Neuzeit*. Stuttgart: Metzler.

Buck-Morss, Susan. 1991. *The Dialectics of Seeing: Walter Benjamin and the Arcades Project*. Cambridge, MA: MIT Press.

Buck-Morss, Susan. 1977. *The Origin of Negative Dialectics*. New York: Free Press.

Claussen, Detlev. 2010. *Theodor W. Adorno: One Last Genius*, trans. R. Livingstone. Cambridge, MA: Harvard Belknap.

Claussen, Detlev. 1987. *Grenzen der Aufklärung. Die gesellschaftliche Genese des modernen Antisemitismus*. Frankfurt: Fischer.

Cook, Deborah. 2011. *Adorno on Nature*. New York: Routledge.

Deleuze, Gilles. 1984. *Kant's Critical Philosophy: the Doctrine of the Faculties*, trans. H. Tomlinson and B. Habberjam. Minneapolis: University of Minnesota Press.

Diner, Dan, ed. 1988. *Zivilisationsbruch. Denken nach Auschwitz*. Frankfurt/M: Fischer.

Elster, Jon. 1985. *Making Sense of Marx*. Cambridge: Cambridge University Press.

Finley, M. I. 1979. *The World of Odysseus*, 2d rev. ed. New York: Penguin.

Fleming, Katie. 2012. "Odysseus and Enlightenment: Horkheimer and Adorno's *Dialektik der Aufklärung*," *International Journal of the Classical Tradition* 19: 107–28.

Frank, Manfred. 1988. *Gott im Exil. Vorlesungen über die neue Mythologie, II. Teil*. Frankfurt/M: Suhrkamp.

Freyenhagen, Fabian. 2013. *Adorno's Practical Philosophy: Living Less Wrongly*. Cambridge: Cambridge University Press.

Friedrich, Otto. 1986. *City of Nets: A Portrait of Hollywood in the 1940s*. New York: Harper and Row.

Früchtl, Josef. 1986. *Mimesis. Konstellation eines Zentralbegriffs bei Adorno*. Würzberg: Königshaus + Neumann.

Gauchet, Marcel. 1997. *The Disenchantment of the World: A Political History of Religion*, trans. O. Burge. Princeton: Princeton University Press.

Geuss, Raymond. 1981. *The Idea of a Critical Theory*. Cambridge: Cambridge University Press.

Giddens, Anthony. 1971. *Capitalism and Modern Social Theory*. Cambridge: Cambridge University Press.

Goldmann, Lucien. 1977. *Lukács and Heidegger*, trans. W. Boelhower. London: Routledge.

Halliwell, Stephen. 2002. *The Aesthetics of Mimesis: Ancient Texts and Modern Problems*. Princeton: Princeton University Press.

Hammer, Espen. 2015. *Adorno's Modernism: Art, Experience, and Catastrophe*. Cambridge: Cambridge University Press.

Hammer, Espen. 2006. *Adorno and the Political*. New York: Routledge.

Haines, Simon. 2005. *Poetry and Philosophy from Homer to Rousseau: Romantic Souls, Realist Lives*. New York: Palgrave Macmillan.

Hansen, Miriam. 2012. *Cinema and Experience*. Berkeley: University of California Press.

Held, David. 1980. *Introduction to Critical Theory: Horkheimer to Habermas*. Berkeley: University of California Press.

Heller, Ágnes, ed. 1983. *Lukács Reappraised*. New York: Columbia University Press.

Hohendahl, Peter Uwe. 1991. *Reappraisals: Shifting Alignments in Postwar Critical Theory*. Ithaca, NY: Cornell University Press.

Hulatt, Owen. 2016. *Adorno's Theory of Philosophical and Aesthetic Truth*. New York: Columbia University Press.

Immanen, Mikko. 2025. *Adorno's Gamble: Harnessing German Ideology*. Ithaca, NY: Cornell University Press.

Jacobs, Jack. 2015. *The Frankfurt School, Jewish Lives, and Antisemitism*. Cambridge: Cambridge University Press.

Jameson, Fredric. 1990. *Late Marxism: Adorno, or the Persistence of the Dialectic*. London: Verso.

Jameson, Fredric. 1972. *The Prison-House of Language: A Critical Account of Structuralism and Russian Formalism*. Princeton: Princeton University Press.

Jay, Martin. 1980. "The Jews and the Frankfurt School: Critical Theory's Analysis of Anti-Semitism," *New German Critique* 19: 139–40.

Jay, Martin. 1973. *The Dialectical Imagination: A History of the Frankfurt School and the Institute of Social Research, 1923–1950*. New York: Little, Brown.

Kaufmann, Walter. 2013. *Nietzsche: Philosopher, Psychologist, Antichrist*, 5th ed. Princeton: Princeton University Press.

Koch, Gertrud. 2000. *Siegfried Kracauer*, trans. J. Gaines. Princeton: Princeton University Press.

Kojève, Alexandre. 1980. *Introduction to the Reading of Hegel*, trans. J. Nichols, ed. A. Bloom. Ithaca, NY: Cornell University Press, 1980.

Lawrence Rose, Paul. 1992. *Revolutionary Antisemitism in Germany from Kant to Weimar*. Princeton: Princeton University Press.

Lear, Jonathan. 2005. *Freud*. London: Routledge.

Leslie, Esther. 2002. *Hollywood Flatlands: Animation, Critical Theory and the Avant-Garde*. London: Verso.

Löwy, Michael. 1979. *Georg Lukács: From Romanticism to Bolshevism*, trans. P. Camiller. London: Verso.

Marchand, Suzanne. 2003. *Down from Olympus: Archeology and Philhellenism in Germany, 1750–1970*. Princeton: Princeton University Press.

Menke, Christoph. 1998. *The Sovereignty of Art*, trans. N. Solomon. Cambridge, MA: MIT Press.

Mészáros, István, ed. 1971. *Aspects of History and Class Consciousness*. London: Routledge.

Morgan, Daniel, and Peter E. Gordon, eds. 2007. *The Cambridge Companion to Modern Jewish Philosophy*. Cambridge: Cambridge University Press.

Müller-Doohm, Stefan. 2009. *Adorno: A Biography*, trans. R. Livingstone. Cambridge: Polity.

Namli, Elena, Svenungsson, Jayne, and Vincent, Aalana, eds. 2014. *Jewish Thought, Utopia, and Revolution*. Amsterdam: Rodolpi.

Nehamas, Alexander. 1985. *Nietzsche: Life as Literature*. Cambridge, MA: Harvard University Press.

O'Connor, Brian. 2012. *Adorno*. London: Routledge.

O'Connor, Brian. 2005. *Adorno's Negative Dialectic: Philosophy and the Possibility of Critical Rationality*. Cambridge, MA: MIT.

Paddison, Max. 1998. *Adorno's Aesthetics of Music*. Cambridge: Cambridge University Press.

Parkinson, G. H. R. 1977. *Georg Lukács*. London: Routledge.

Parkinson, G. H. R., ed. 1970. *Georg Lukács: The Man, His Work, and His Ideas*. London: Weidenfeld & Nicholson.

Pensky, Max. 2001. *Melancholy Dialectic: Walter Benjamin and the Play of Mourning*, rev. ed. Amherst: University of Massachusetts Press.

Pinkard, Terry. 1994. *Hegel's Phenomenology: The Sociality of Reason*. New York: Cambridge University Press.

Pinker, Steven. 2019. *Enlightenment Now: The Case for Reason, Science, Humanism, and Progress*. New York: Penguin Books.

Pippin. Robert B. 1989. *Hegel's Idealism: The Satisfactions of Self-Consciousness*. New York: Cambridge University Press.

Porter, James. 2010. "Odysseus and the Wandering Jew: The Dialectic of Jewish Enlightenment in Horkheimer and Adorno," *Cultural Critique* 74: 200–13.

Postone, Moishe. 1980. "Anti-Semitism and National Socialism: Notes on the German Reaction to the Holocaust," *New German Critique* 19: 97–115.

Pulzer, Peter. 1988. *The Rise of Political Anti-Semitism in Germany and Austria*, rev. ed. Cambridge, MA: Harvard University Press.

Rabinbach, Anson. 2000. "Why Were the Jews Sacrificed? The Place of Anti-Semitism in *Dialectic of Enlightenment*," *New German Critique* 81: 49–64.

Rabinbach, Anson. 1997. *In the Shadow of Catastrophe: German Intellectuals between Apocalypse and Enlightenment*. Berkeley: University of California Press.

Rensmann, Lars. 2017. *The Politics of Unreason: the Frankfurt School and the Origins of Modern Antisemitism*. Albany: SUNY Press.

Robinson, J. Bradford. 1994. "The Jazz Essays of Theodor Adorno: Some Thoughts on Jazz Reception in Weimar Germany," *Popular Music* 13.1: 1–25.

Ross, Stephen. 2017. *Hitler in Los Angeles*. New York: Bloomsbury.

Rush, Fred. 2016. *Irony and Idealism*. Oxford: Oxford University Press.

Rush, Fred, ed. 2004. *The Cambridge Companion to Critical Theory*. Cambridge: Cambridge University Press.

Saunders, Thomas. 1996. *Hollywood in Berlin: American Cinema and Weimar Germany*. Berkeley: University of California Press.

Schacht, Richard. 1983. *Nietzsche*. London: Routledge.

Scheuerman, William. 1994. *Between the Norm and the Exception: The Frankfurt School and the Rule of Law*. Cambridge, MA: MIT Press.

Schmidt, James. 2016. "'Racket', 'Monopoly', and the *Dialectic of Enlightenment*," *Persistent Enlightenment*, online: persistentenlightenment.com

Schwartz, Frederic. 2005. *Blind Spots: Critical Theory and the History of Art in Twentieth-Century Germany*. New Haven: Yale University Press.

Später, Jörg. 2024. *Adornos Erben. Eine Geschichte aus der Bundesrepublik*. Berlin: Suhrkamp.

Stern, Alexander. 2019. *The Fall of Language: Benjamin and Wittgenstein on Meaning*. Cambridge, MA: Harvard University Press.

Stoetzler, Marcel, ed. 2023. *Critical Theory and the Critique of Antisemitism*. London: Bloomsbury.

Taylor, Charles. 1975. *Hegel*. New York: Cambridge University Press.

Theunissen, Michael. 1969. *Gesellschaft und Geschichte. Zur Kritik der kritischen Theorie*. Berlin: de Gruyter.

Thyen, Anke. 1989. *Negative Dialektik und Erfahrung. Zur Rationalität des Nichtidentischen bei Adorno*. Frankfurt/M: Suhrkamp.

Vermeule, Emily. 1972. *Greece in the Bronze Age*, rev. ed. Chicago: University of Chicago Press.

Weber Nicholsen, Shierry. 1997. *Exact Imagination, Late Work*. Cambridge, MA: MIT Press.

Wellmer, Albrecht. 2000. "The Death of the Sirens and the Origin of the Work of Art," *New German Critique* 81: 5–19.

Whitebook, Joel. 1995. *Perversion and Utopia: A Study in Psychoanalysis and Critical Theory*. Cambridge, MA: MIT Press.

Wiggershaus, Rolf. 1995. *The Frankfurt School: Its History, Theories, and Political Significance*, trans. M. Robertson. Cambridge, MA: MIT Press.

Wollheim, Richard. 1971. *Freud*. London: Fontana.

Wood, Allen. 1981. *Karl Marx*. London: Routledge.

INDEX

Adorno, Theodor: *Aesthetic Theory* 6, 49, 58, 88, 201, 208, 220; *Against Epistemology* 205; *The Authoritarian Personality* 7, 132, 165, 214; *Composing for the Films* 132; *Essay on Wagner* 131; on mass art 71, 131–33; on mimesis 33, 58, 63; *Minima Moralia* 3, 6, 73, 131, 132, 157, 208, 209, 220; on musical regression 131; on negative dialectic 201, 208; *Negative Dialectics* 6, 9, 48, 52, 58, 62, 66, 87, 208; *Philosophy of New Music* 132; on radio 7, 131, 139, 141, 152, 156; on television 139, 152

aesthetics 15, 29, 39, 50, 83, 88, 135, 138–39, 142, 144–45, 150–51, 185, 208, 215; *see also* Adorno, Theodor, *Aesthetic Theory*; art

alienation 12–15, 18–19, 25, 27, 29–30, 38, 47, 58, 67, 84, 97, 122, 169–73, 179; and capitalism 17, 27, 38, 144, 157; in Hegel 14, 18, 27, 84; in Marx 12, 17, 27; and reification 27–29, 38; as self-alienation 48, 71, 84, 90, 97, 100

amusement 133, 143–44; and fun 133, 143–47, 150; *see also* culture industry

animals 61, 87, 88, 217–23; non-human 73, 221–23

antisemitism 4, 7, 14, 23, 25, 39, 79, 127, 138, 164–93, 200, 212; and authoritarianism 7, 165, 166; and bureaucracy 69; and capitalism 166, 179, 182–83, 190; and fascism 69, 165–166, 168, 170, 181, 183–87, 190–94; and Hollywood 131, 165; liberal 180–83, 190; nationalist (*völkische*) 180–81; and National Socialism 167, 170, 178, 183; paranoid structure of 165, 175, 183–85, 193–94; religious origins of 177; and the *Shoah* 170, 178, 227; in the United States 165

apperception, synthetic unity of 109, 114–15

Aristotle 53, 63, 78, 209

Arnheim, Rudolf 135

art 15, 21, 31, 39, 71, 83, 110, 120, 135–38, 141, 144, 147–51, 157–58,

208, 214–15, 218; autonomy of 144, 150; avant-garde 156–157; cartoons and comics 132, 145–46; commodification of 137–39, 142, 150–51; high versus low 144; mass art 71, 132–39, 141, 144–45, 150; *see also* aesthetics; culture industry; film; mimesis
Attenborough, Richard 221
aura 54, 136–37, 148; *see also* Benjamin, Walter
authoritarianism 7, 69, 132, 165–68, 190, 214, 227; *see also* fascism; totalitarianism
autonomy 13, 46, 51–52, 89, 91, 106, 143; *see also* freedom

Bachofen, Johann Jakob 126–27
Bacon, Francis 63, 80
Baeumler, Alfred 127
Balázs, Béla 135, 145
Baudelaire, Charles 120, 132
Bauman, Zygmunt 213
beauty 50, 59, 81, 83, 88, 140, 148–49, 155
Benhabib, Seyla 199
Benjamin, Walter 4, 6, 14, 31–36, 53–58, 79–80, 135, 153–54; "Art in the Age of Mechanical Reproducibility" 136; on constellations 6, 33–35, 80; on mechanical reproducibility 136, 140; on mimesis 33, 58, 110; on names 35, 55, 96, 153–54; *Origin of the German Trauerspiel* 79
Bergson, Henri 120, 216
Berlin, Isaiah 213
The Birth of Tragedy 80, 127
Blumenberg, Hans 55, 97
Boileau, Nicolas 139–40
Borchardt, Rudolf 81
bourgeoisie 44–45
Brecht, Bertolt 130, 137
Buffon, Georges-Louis Leclerc de 139

bureaucracy 69, 165, 213; *see also* Weber, Max
Burckhardt, Jacob 78

Calvinism 27
capitalism 6, 8, 17–18, 26–28, 38, 68–71, 131–32, 138–39, 144, 148, 157, 166–68, 179, 182–83, 190, 192, 212–15, 227, 229; and antisemitism 166, 179, 182–83, 190; late capitalism 24, 69, 71, 136, 157, 214, 226; monopoly capitalism 6, 166–168; relation to fascism 166–168, 190
Cassirer, Ernst 64
Chaplin, Charlie 131, 145, 212
chance 133, 147–50
Christianity 13, 119, 124, 176–77, 181–82; *see also* sacrifice
class 8, 22–23, 56, 83, 123, 164; conflict 19, 83; society 123
Coetzee, J. M. 223
Cohen, Hermann 64
comedy 144–46
commodification 28, 32, 69, 70, 130–63, 179, 214–15, 228–29; of art 137–39, 142, 150–51; of language 152–56; *see also* culture industry; reification
commodity 12, 27, 28, 32, 70, 136–39, 142, 143, 157–58, 214, 218, 228; fetishism 2, 12, 28, 131
concepts 11, 16–18, 20–21, 25, 27, 31–36, 48, 56–62, 106, 109–13, 121, 154, 175, 185, 211; and abstraction 47, 57, 60–63, 117, 172, 179; and enlightenment 56–62; and language 56–62; *see also* identity thinking
conformism 138, 141, 157, 214–15
conscience 82, 86, 95, 177
constellations 6, 31, 33–35, 80
consumerism 150, 157, 166, 183, 214–15
Cornelius, Hans 5–6

crime 126, 145, 150
culture 1, 2, 6–7, 15, 23–25, 28–29, 36, 39, 44, 55, 62, 69, 72–73, 78, 90, 127, 131–33, 138, 144, 147, 150–51, 157–60, 176, 178, 200, 212–16, 227, 229; mass culture 71, 132–39, 141, 144–45, 150; *see also* culture industry
culture industry 4, 71, 80, 83, 110, 130–63, 214–215, 227, 229–230; and advertising 71, 133, 152, 155–56, 159; and chance 133, 147–49; and comedy 144–46; and fun 133, 143–47; and language 133, 152–56; and style 133, 139–143; and tragedy 133, 149–50
Curtiz, Michael 130

Dadaism 33, 120, 145
debt and guilt 82, 179
deep ecology 219–21
democracy 69, 123, 167–68, 190, 229; liberal 69, 167
Descartes, René 106, 114
Dewey, John 51, 218
dialectical materialism 68
dialectic(s) 14, 17, 20, 22, 31, 39, 47–48, 53, 77, 81, 83, 99, 157, 186–87, 202, 204–06, 208, 211; of enlightenment and myth 19, 48, 53, 77, 80, 81, 83, 99, 169; in Hegel 14, 17, 20, 39, 47–48, 186–87; *see also* negative dialectic
Dieterle, William 130
Dietrich, Marlene 130
Dilthey, Wilhelm 120
disenchantment 25–26, 57, 62, 97, 125, 202
Disney, Walt 131, 134
domination 6, 38, 49–50, 56–57, 60–63, 68, 81–82, 84, 97, 202, 218–21; of nature 49, 63, 68, 218–21
Donen, Stanley 155

ecology 216–24; as deep ecology 219–21
economics 6, 24, 39, 69, 132, 138, 164, 166–67, 179, 182–83, 190
ego 24, 50, 85–86, 113, 214
Eisenstein, Sergei 135
Eleatics 53
Eliot, T. S. 71
emancipation 1, 15, 49; *see also* freedom; liberation
enchantment 26, 50, 54, 89, 97, 126, 180, 220
enlightenment 1, 2, 12–13, 19–20, 22, 25, 44, 76–77, 81, 83, 89, 94, 99, 104–07, 111, 115–16, 118–19, 122, 124, 126, 135, 144, 169–70, 172, 175, 177, 180, 184, 187, 192–93, 202–08, 210–22; as domination 49, 57, 60, 63, 68, 82, 218; and the Enlightenment (historical period) 12, 44–46, 54, 104–05, 107, 116, 124, 201; and Kant 46, 51, 64, 104–19; and Mosaic law 171–72; and myth 1, 19, 48, 53–57, 67, 77, 81, 99, 169, 170; and Sade 104, 118–22, 126; as self-preservation 51, 67–68, 85, 177, 202, 219; reversion to mythology 1, 48, 53–54, 62, 67, 99, 187
entertainment 133, 141, 144, 146, 148, 159, 160, 215; *see also* culture industry
entrepreneur 121, 123, 175, 229
epistemology 108, 114, 184
Erasmus, Desiderius 228, 230
essentialism 91, 173
ethics 13, 15, 21, 26, 47, 50, 78, 84, 104, 116, 117, 125, 209–11, 221; *see also* morality
Euripides 97
exchange 27–28, 60, 70, 82, 90, 100, 175, 179, 182
explanation 25, 37, 38, 49, 51, 55, 64–66, 72, 164, 166, 173, 188, 210–11, 216–22

expression 28–29, 46, 50, 55, 62–63, 68, 71, 96, 110, 152–56, 172, 176, 186, 204, 209–22

fascism 7, 22, 25, 39, 69, 71, 81, 123–24, 131, 156, 164–68, 180–81, 183–87, 190–93, 201, 203–05, 212–13, 227, 229; and antisemitism 69, 165–66, 168, 170, 181, 183–87, 190–94; and capitalism 166–68, 190; and the F-scale 165; *see also* authoritarianism; National Socialism; totalitarianism
fate 20, 53, 55, 67, 78, 83, 97, 99
fear 1, 48–50, 55, 82, 86, 94, 97, 119, 145, 156, 181, 202, 207, 219
Fenichel, Otto 24
fetishism 2, 12, 28, 131; false 174–75, 185; *see also* Freud, Sigmund
Feuchtwanger, Lion 7, 130
Fichte, J. G. 13, 91
film 71, 130, 132–37, 141–42, 145, 148, 150, 152, 155–56, 215; *see also* culture industry
fixation 22, 183
Forst, Rainer 212
Foucault, Michel 159, 226
freedom 11–14, 17–18, 22, 24, 45–49, 51–53, 68, 71, 81–83, 96, 98, 108, 126, 151, 167, 182, 191, 212, 214, 217, 220–21; *see also* autonomy; liberation
Freud, Sigmund 1, 4, 14, 18, 22–24, 50, 84–86, 114, 173–74, 183–84, 186, 205, 214; *Civilization and Its Discontents* 24, 84, 86; on fixation 183; *The Future of an Illusion* 23; on introjection 24, 85; on paranoia 165, 175, 183–85, 193–94; on projection 23, 165, 173–75, 183–85, 187, 193–94; on repression 24, 57, 82, 86, 89, 175; structural theory of the unconscious 23, 85; on sublimation 24, 86; *Totem and Taboo* 23, 173–74
Fromm, Erich 6, 22, 24, 127, 200

Gadamer, Hans-Georg 79
Gaia theory 220
Gauchet, Marcel 98
genealogy 21–22, 57, 81, 170, 172, 177, 181; *see also* Nietzsche, Friedrich
genericity 32, 61, 70, 110, 138, 140, 143–44, 154, 156
George, Stefan 78
German Idealism 3–5, 11, 13–14, 25, 52
Goethe, J. W. 46, 78–79
Goya, Francisco 229–30
guilt 21, 57, 68, 82, 86, 95, 173, 177, 188; *see also* Nietzsche, Friedrich; sacrifice
Guterman, Norbert 165

Habermas, Jürgen 2, 8, 39, 40, 46, 61, 72, 85, 87, 200–12; *The Philosophical Discourse of Modernity* 203; *The Theory of Communicative Action* 201, 202
Hamann, J. G. 13, 153
happiness 50, 53, 59, 82, 84, 86–89, 91, 140, 175, 214
Hegel, G. W. F. 1, 4, 14, 16–18, 20, 27, 30–31, 39, 46–48, 53, 64, 68, 78, 80, 84, 91, 98, 117, 150, 176, 185–87, 201, 205, 208, 211; on alienation 14, 18, 27, 84; on dialectic 14, 17, 20, 39, 47–48, 186–87; on master and slave 84, 185–86; *Phenomenology of Spirit* 14, 46, 84, 98, 185; on reconciliation 19, 48, 84, 175
Heidegger, Martin 2, 66, 71, 156, 216, 218, 226
Heine, Heinrich 178
Heraclitus 53
Herder, J. G. 13, 150, 153
Hesiod 53
Hill, Geoffrey 154
Hitchcock, Alfred 156

Hitler, Adolf 7, 145, 191
Hobbes, Thomas 182
Hölderlin, Friedrich 13
Holocaust *see* Shoah
Hollywood 7, 113, 130–31, 135, 145, 159, 165
Homer 19, 29, 53, 77–80, 95, 100; *Iliad* 78, 98; *Odyssey* 4, 19, 50, 77–100, 170
Honneth, Axel 199
Horkheimer, Max: on antisemitism 165, 189–94; *Dämmerung* 3; on traditional versus critical theory 36–39
humanism 220
Humboldt, Wilhelm von 153
Husserl, Edmund 66

iconoclasm 172
Idealism 11, 13–15, 25, 52, 107, 109, 118, 154; *see also* German Idealism; transcendental idealism
identity thinking 52, 61–62, 69, 158, 211
ideology 6, 38, 46, 72, 81, 138, 144, 167–68, 190, 214–15
illusion 23–24, 50, 52, 80, 87–88, 210, 222
imagination 14, 31, 52, 71, 95, 110, 112–13, 144, 147, 151, 185, 230
inclination 106, 116–17
individualism 45, 71, 127, 150, 214
individuality 13, 19, 22, 71, 81, 95, 115, 122, 126, 140, 142, 150, 152, 183, 205, 214
individuation 19, 175
industrialism 144, 157, 213
information 138, 152–56, 215
inhibition 23–24
Institute for Social Research 1, 6, 16, 132
instrumentalization 4, 28, 56–57, 62, 68, 97, 107, 118, 120, 147, 218–22

intellectuals 3, 7, 8, 78, 131, 157, 160, 200–25
internet 136, 147, 152, 159
intuition 64, 106, 108–13, 143
irrationalism 3, 120, 204

Jaeggi, Rahel 212
Jameson, Fredric 61, 218
Jaspers, Karl 98
Jews 5, 127, 138, 164–65, 169–93, 205, 212, 227; *see also* antisemitism; Judaism
Jobs, Steve 123
Judaism 164, 172, 176–77, 188
judgment 5, 13, 26, 46, 60, 64, 71, 78, 99, 108–10, 112, 117, 139, 149–230
Jung, Carl 23

Kafka, Franz 4
Kant, Immanuel 3–5, 11, 13, 15, 21, 25–26, 36, 46–47, 51, 64–65, 71, 80, 82–83, 91, 104–19, 122, 124–27, 135, 139, 143, 150, 175, 184–85, 203, 205–06, 208, 211; *Critique of the Power of Judgment* 65, 150; *Critique of Pure Reason* 4, 64, 105; *Groundwork of the Metaphysic of Morals* 117; on moral judgment 26, 116–18; and Nietzsche 122–26; and Sade 104, 118–22, 124–25; on schematism 64, 109–13, 117, 143; on subsumption 64, 106, 109, 185; "What Is Enlightenment?" 46, 105
Kantianism 64, 107, 117, 125, 201, 203, 212; *see also* neo-Kantianism
Kaufmann, Walter 123
Keaton, Buster 145
Kierkegaard, Søren 6, 56, 147, 178
Kirchheimer, Otto 6, 200
Klages, Ludwig 61, 127
Korda, Alberto 228
Korngold, Erich 130
Kracauer, Siegfried 6, 65, 132, 135, 150
Krenek, Ernst 130
Kripke, Saul 35

La Mettrie, Julien Offray de 119
language 13, 31, 35, 56–62, 95–96, 112, 127, 133, 152–56, 171–72, 204–05, 212; commodification of 152–56
Lang, Fritz 130
Lasch, Christopher 214
law 6, 17, 21, 26, 31–32, 36–37, 51, 63–64, 82, 86, 89, 92, 106, 108, 116–17, 120, 126, 164, 169, 171–72, 176–78, 181–82, 188, 191, 193, 229; Mosaic 171–72; natural 38, 64, 119; rule of 191, 229
Leibniz, G. W. F. 30, 46, 106
Lenya, Lotte 137
Lessing, G. E. 46
liberalism 69, 144, 165, 181–84, 190, 214, 229
liberation 2, 12, 45, 49, 51–53, 57, 217; *see also* emancipation; freedom
lifeworld (*Lebenswelt*) 66, 203, 204
Locke, John 182
logic 17, 36, 51, 60, 68–70, 108, 111, 153, 202, 204, 211–12
Lorre, Peter 130
love 23–24, 86–87, 91, 100, 126, 184, 214
Lovelock, James 220
Löwenthal, Leo 6, 165, 200
Lubitsch, Ernst 130, 142
Lukács, Georg 4, 14, 18, 25, 27–30, 69–70, 131, 145, 157, 201, 218; on reification 27–29, 69–70, 139; *Theory of the Novel* 29; on totality 18, 29–30, 38–39, 107, 182, 202

magic 56, 59, 88–89, 176
mana 54, 58–59
Mann, Heinrich 130
Mann, Thomas 7, 130
Marburg School 64, 184
Marcuse, Herbert 6, 49, 97, 200
market 28, 70, 138, 142, 148, 151, 160, 182, 203, 213–15
marriage 70, 90–92

Marx, Karl 2, 4–5, 12, 14–19, 24, 27–29, 39, 56, 87, 95, 123, 132, 138, 164, 167–68, 178, 201–02, 216, 229; on alienation 12, 17, 27; on commodity as fetish 2, 12, 28; and the "Jewish Question" 178; Marxism 5, 6, 16, 24, 25, 71, 123, 132, 166–68, 201; on reification 27–29
mass art *see* culture industry
mass culture *see* culture industry
master and slave 84, 185–186; *see also* Hegel, G. W. F.
materialism 6, 11, 39, 106–07, 119–20, 132, 200–02; dialectical 68; eliminative 119
mathematics 31, 63–65
Mauthner, Fritz 153
meaning 11–12, 17, 21, 28, 30–31, 35, 48, 55, 61, 65, 67, 72, 80, 137, 153–54, 156, 187, 202–25
mechanical reproducibility 36, 136, 140, 148; *see also* Benjamin, Walter
melodrama 30, 150
Menke, Christoph 199
metaphysics 19, 20, 26, 35, 50, 63, 65, 115
Mill, John Stuart 182
mimesis 33, 58–59, 63, 88, 110, 170–72, 175, 208–21, 218, 221–22; *see also* Benjamin, Walter
modernity 1, 2, 12, 15, 25, 26, 28, 32, 35, 44, 52, 57, 66, 68–69, 71, 77, 81, 115, 118, 120, 154, 159, 172, 177, 178, 184, 212–216, 226–227
monotheism 98, 171
Montale, Eugenio 39
Montesquieu, Charles de Secondat 209
morality 21, 26, 63, 81, 116–117, 120, 209–210; *see also* ethics
Moses 171–72, 176
Mother-Right 126–27
Murnau, F. W. 130
Mussolini, Benito 190, 229
myth 1, 4, 19, 20, 35, 44, 48, 52–57, 62, 67, 72, 77–78, 80–81, 83–84,

INDEX 249

88–92, 94–100, 104, 120, 126–27, 148, 169–71, 180, 202–03, 218, 229; and Bachofen 126–27; and enlightenment 1, 19, 48, 53–57, 67, 77, 81, 99, 169–70; and the Odyssey 77–100; as repetition 55, 67, 89, 100; and sacrifice 56, 84, 90, 170–72

naming 31, 35, 55, 59, 92–94, 96, 153–154; *see also* Benjamin, Walter
narcissism 214
National Socialism 123, 127, 167–68, 170, 178, 183, 190–191; *see also* fascism
Natorp, Paul 64
naturalism 51, 123, 218, 221
nature 2, 15, 19, 20, 23–26, 33–36, 38, 48–60, 63–68, 82, 84–86, 88–89, 94, 96–97, 99, 106–11, 115–16, 119–20, 122, 125–28, 135, 145, 169–73, 175–77, 180–81, 184–88, 202, 204–12, 216–24; domination of 49, 63, 68, 218–21; internal *vs.* external 49–50; and mimesis 33, 58, 110, 170–71, 208–11, 218, 221–22; return to 50, 67, 89, 122, 126, 180–81
negation 35, 128, 186–187
negative dialectic 6, 48, 52, 58, 62, 66, 73, 87, 208; *see also* Adorno, Theodor, *Negative Dialectics*
neo-Kantianism 5, 64, 184
neoliberalism 2, 28, 212–15, 229
Neumann, Franz 6, 24, 166–68, 200; *Behemoth* 167
Newton, Isaac 6
Nietzsche, Friedrich 1–2, 4, 6, 14–15, 19–22, 49, 51, 53, 57, 72, 78, 80–82, 84, 91, 104, 107, 118, 122–27, 150, 184, 203, 207, 216, 218; on genealogy 21, 57, 81; and Kant 122–26; on pity 119, 124–25; and Sade 122–26; on suffering 20; on the Übermensch 122, 126
nominalism 33, 93, 220
normativity 16–17, 30, 47, 72, 86, 117, 139, 146, 203–25
Novalis (Friedrich von Hardenberg) 13, 128

Ophüls, Max 130
Oppenheimer, J. Robert 191
Other, the 49, 59, 92, 172, 175, 179, 184, 186, 204, 208, 211, 222

paranoia 23, 165, 175, 183–85, 193–94; *see also* Freud, Sigmund; projection
Pasolini, Pier Paolo 124
Penrose, Roger 65–66
perception 38, 58, 61, 64–65, 88, 106, 109, 113, 174–75, 185
phenomenology 30, 47, 66–67, 84, 98, 185
philosophy of language 153, 205, 212
photography 15, 132, 136–37
Pinker, Steven 44
pity 119, 124–25
Plato 53, 62–63, 78, 153
pleasure 85, 90, 120–22, 133
Pollock, Friedrich 6, 24, 166–68, 200
positivism 6, 37, 39, 72
poststructuralism 157, 215
power 6, 24, 32, 34, 38, 49, 53–55, 59–60, 62–63, 67, 69–72, 81–82, 89, 93–96, 98–99, 108, 110, 125, 127, 145, 148, 154, 168, 171–72, 176–77, 184, 186–87, 191, 193, 203–25
pragmatism 201
prejudice 7, 46, 132, 165, 173, 185, 190, 192, 214
probability 23, 147, 148, 159
progress 2, 12, 14, 44, 45, 53, 67, 68, 86, 200, 215, 217, 222
projection 23, 54, 127, 165, 173–75, 178, 183–85, 187, 193–94, 205; false 174–75, 185; *see also* Freud, Sigmund

propaganda 134, 167, 215
Protestantism 26, 27, 177
Proust, Marcel 88
psychoanalysis 5, 6, 18, 22–24, 173, 183; *see also* Freud, Sigmund

race 2, 44, 69, 123, 127, 180–81, 183, 190–92, 214; anti-race 170, 180
rationalization 2, 25–27, 37, 53, 57, 62, 67–68, 92, 202, 218; *see also* instrumental reason; Weber, Max
Realism 65–66, 209–11
reason 1–2, 12, 14, 20, 26, 31, 36, 45–48, 51–52, 68, 72, 82, 99, 104–06, 108, 110–11, 116–18, 120, 177, 187, 193, 201–25, 229–30; communicative 201–02, 204, 212; instrumental 2, 68–69, 202–04, 217–20; pure versus impure 116–17; and systematicity 106, 108, 110–11, 116–28
recognition 14, 23–24, 59, 86, 90, 185–86
reconciliation 19, 48, 84, 88, 175
Reich, Wilhelm 24
reification 27–30, 37, 56, 69, 73, 139, 157, 182; *see also* commodification; Lukács, Georg
rejection 3, 22, 44, 49, 53, 91, 95, 107, 124, 125, 201–25
religion 23, 25–26, 35, 47, 54, 56, 87, 118, 124, 136, 176, 177, 180–81, 188
remembrance 50, 95, 222
renunciation 81–84, 89, 93, 188
repetition 55–56, 67, 83, 89, 94, 100, 111, 115, 171
representation 19, 31, 35, 51, 59, 64, 111–12, 135, 149, 153–54, 171–72
repression 24, 50, 57, 68, 82, 86, 89, 127, 175, 183; *see also* Freud, Sigmund
resistance 24, 71, 73, 86, 90, 96, 150, 186, 188, 201, 208, 210, 212, 214–25
Riefenstahl, Leni 131, 134, 193
Rimbaud, Arthur 120
Romanticism 14, 78, 120, 180

Rousseau, Jean-Jacques 12, 153
Ryle, Gilbert 7

sacrifice 56, 59, 84, 90, 93, 95–96, 99, 170–72, 176–77, 179, 188; introversion of 85–86
Sade, Marquis de 3, 80, 104, 118–22, 124–26, 184; *120 Days of Sodom* 121–23; *Juliette* 105, 119–22, 126, 184; *Justine* 121; *Philosophy in the Bedroom* 121
Scheler, Max 6
Schelling, F. W. J. 13, 78, 216, 218
schematism 64, 109–13, 117, 143; *see also* Kant, Immanuel
Schiller, Friedrich 13, 78
Schlegel, Friedrich 13–14, 34, 79, 153
Schoenberg, Arnold 7, 130
Schopenhauer, Arthur 5, 11, 15, 20, 50, 110, 175
science 4, 15, 25, 31, 37, 38, 44–45, 54, 62–67, 70, 72, 121, 160, 167, 184, 216–25
self-preservation 51, 67–68, 85, 90, 115, 176, 177, 202, 207, 219, 229
Sellars, Wilfrid 52
semblance (*Schein*) 50, 221
sexuality 89–90, 95, 120–22, 126, 128, 184
Shakespeare, William 150, 178–79
Shoah 170, 178, 227
singularity 31, 34–36, 58, 96
Sisyphus 100
slavery 45
socialism 7, 16, 132, 167–68
sociology 3, 6, 37, 39, 138, 200–12, 213–30
Sophocles 21, 98
Spengler, Oswald 2, 20, 61, 71
Spinoza, Baruch 4, 218
spirit (*Geist*) 46, 53–54, 176, 186
standardization 137–38, 200, 214–15
stoicism 124
Stravinsky, Igor 79
style 123, 133, 139–43, 150, 227

subjectivity 4–5, 49, 51, 64, 84–85, 98, 100, 115, 146, 158, 198, 204–05, 228
sublimation 24, 85
suffering 19–20, 49, 56, 87, 125, 149, 150, 210–11, 218, 223
superego 24, 85–86, 214
surrealism 33, 120, 145
synthesis 109–112, 114

technology 4, 15, 37, 49, 63, 67–68, 136, 138, 152, 154, 160
Thoreau, Henry David 216
time 15, 26, 55–56, 88, 111–12, 117, 172, 212
totalitarianism 69, 166–68, 203–04; *see also* authoritarianism, fascism
totality 18, 27, 29–30, 38–39, 47, 72, 80, 115, 182, 230
tragedy 30, 149–50, 229; *see also The Birth of Tragedy*, culture industry and tragedy
transcendental idealism 64, 104, 107, 109, 111

the unconscious 18–24, 59, 67, 113, 115, 143, 151, 165, 172, 183–85, 206

utopian thinking 3, 24, 50, 87, 92, 115, 203

Vetlesen, Arne Johan 222–23
Vienna Circle 39, 72
Visconti, Luchino 123

Wagner, Richard 131, 145, 181
Weber, Max 1, 4, 14, 25–27, 57, 68–69, 80, 97, 125, 202, 212, 216, 220
Welles, Orson 141–42
Wellmer, Albrecht 61, 199
Wilder, Billy 130
Wittgenstein, Ludwig 61, 209
women 23, 90–92, 95, 126–28, 174, 221

Xenophanes 53

Zola, Émile 95

For Product Safety Concerns and Information please contact our EU representative GPSR@taylorandfrancis.com
Taylor & Francis Verlag GmbH, Kaufingerstraße 24, 80331 München, Germany

www.ingramcontent.com/pod-product-compliance
Lightning Source LLC
Chambersburg PA
CBHW070314240426
43661CB00057B/2640